"A tour de force Planet X - 2012 page turner. Required reading for those who get it and want to live through it."—*Echan Deravy, Solar Code*

"Written in an easy-to-read style that honors the 2012 predictions of the Maya."—*Maya Anthropologist George Erikson, author of Atlantis in America: Navigators of the Ancient World*

"Chilling insights into how the world's power elites are preparing for 2012. Truth that's hard to handle."—*Philip Gardiner, Secret Societies, Gnosis, The Shining Ones*

"Delivers practical, life-sparing concepts that make sense."—*Frank Joseph, There Are No Coincidences, Survivors of Atlantis, Discovering the Mysteries of Ancient America*

"Required reading for those who are beyond the Planet X debate and now want to do something about it."—*Greg Jenner, Planet X and The Kolbrin Bible Connection*

"Be prepared, be very prepared: you need this book for 2012!"—*Andy Lloyd, The Dark Star*

"Excellent analysis of the looming 2012 solar threat, and how Western governments are responding to it."—*Patrick Geryl, How To Survive 2012, The World Cataclysm in 2012, The Orion Prophecy*

Planet X Forecast and 2012 Survival Guide

"Chance favors the prepared mind."—Louis Pasteur

Planet X Forecast and 2012 Survival Guide

Jacco van der Worp, MSc
Marshall Masters
Janice Manning

Your Own World Books
Silver Springs, NV

planetxforecast.com
yowbooks.com
yowusa.com

Copyright

No part of this book may be reproduced or transmitted in any form or by any means, graphic, electronic, or mechanical, including photocopying, recording, taping, or by any information storage retrieval system, without the written permission of the publisher.

Planet X Forecast and 2012 Survival Guide
Jacco van der Worp, MSc
Marshall Masters
Janice Manning

Second Edition – November 2007
©2007 Your Own World, Inc.
All Rights Reserved
planetxforecast.com
yowusa.com

Trade Paperback
ISBN-10: 1-59772-075-5
ISBN-13: 978-1-59772-075-5

YOUR OWN WORLD BOOKS
an imprint of Your Own World, Inc.
Silver Springs, NV USA
yowbooks.com
SAN: 256-1646

Notices

Every effort has been made to make this book as complete and as accurate as possible and no warranty or fitness is implied. All of the information provided in this book is provided on an "as is" basis. The authors and the publisher shall not be liable or responsible to any person or entity with respect to any loss or damages arising from the information contained herein.

Trademarks

All terms mentioned in this book that are known to be trademarks or service marking have been capitalized. Your Own World, Inc. cannot attest to the accuracy of this information and the use of any term in this book should not be regarded as affecting the validity of any trademark or service mark.

Table of Contents

Illustration Index

Acknowledgments

This book is a culmination of 7 years of study into global warming, space threats, ancient history and prophecy. The authors are grateful to all those who have supported the yowusa.com web site through article contributions and subscriptions. Special thanks to:

- **Echan Deravy** for his help in developing the book concept.
- **Jeff Bryant** for contributing the background art for the book front cover.
- **Mic Royal** for contributing the photo used on the print book back cover.
- **Greg Jenner** for his brilliant analysis of *The Kolbrin Bible*.
- **Walter Phelps** for his extraordinary support and encouragement.

This book deals with a very difficult topic, and the authors especially appreciate their friends and families for nurturing them through the process. Additionally, a special group of people inspired the authors.

In May 2007, the authors reached a content depth decision point. Were there enough readers interested in taking action on the threat? It was not only important to test a willingness to take action, but more importantly, their willingness to take action based on a gut instinct decision. After 7 years of study, the authors have identified a person's ability to trust his or her gut instinct as the most important 2012 survival trait of all.

To test for this trait, we composed and published a simple 4-paragraph pre-sale advertisement for this book on yowusa.com for a limited premier edition. The advertisement offered the book, sight-unseen and described it in a sketchy manner, to screen out conservative mainstream buyers. The goal was to attract those possessing the most important 2012 survival trait of all. The ability to take independent action. The response was substantial and gratifying.

Consequently, those who purchased the limited premier edition proved that the number of independent thinkers doing their own Planet X research is growing. Not only do they now 'get it' — they want to get through it. This encouraged the authors to add deeper levels of content to the book.

The following limited premier edition patrons have allowed the authors to publicly thank them: *Kurt Mrowicki, Duncan "Supra" Murray, Nicolaas Joubert, Rene Aries, Rev. William G. Gallagher (retired), W.C. Brainerd, Walter Winslow Phelps, Kevin Costa, James McCullough and Marilynn Haun.*

Introduction

Planet X is a generic term used to describe a large and yet unknown object in our solar system. Known as Nibiru to the ancient Sumerians, it is many times the size of the Earth and has a long period orbit of approximately 3600 years. The date of 2012 generally identifies a period of cataclysmic events predicted by the ancient Mayans.

What is Planet X? It could be a comet, rogue planet, or as this book maintains, a dying brown dwarf companion to Sol. In the years to come, its elliptical orbit will bring it into the core of our system, where it will enrage our Sun. Once that happens, Earth's greatest pains will come; the moment fate puts us in the cross hairs of a perfect solar storm.

Whatever this massive perturber proves itself to be, the search for Planet X essentially dates back to the discovery of Uranus in 1781. Described in numerous ancient texts and folklore of indigenous peoples all around the world, the predictions of its return are numerous.

The scientific harbinger data of this impending flyby are also being reported at an ever-increasing pace and can no longer be ignored. This is why many who have investigated the matter on their own now believe the time has come to take action. In essence, they already 'get it', and now they're feeling the need to get through it!

The purpose of this book is to help those who now agree that time is of the essence. It does this by offering a practical 2012 tool kit of how-to survival knowledge for those who'll be left to fend for themselves.

Regardless of whether you can afford to build a bunker or can barely afford a shovel, the information in this book is designed to be equally useful. This is because the key to surviving 2012 is more about what's in your head than what's in your wallet.

There are no guarantees. The best you can do is to enhance your odds of survival, which does not necessarily mean building a better bunker. Rather, as Louis Pasteur so aptly explained, "Chance favors the prepared mind."

Pasteur's message for 2012 is clear. The better prepared you are, both mentally and emotionally, the more likely you'll be to recognize and capitalize upon survival opportunities in a timely and useful manner.

Therefore, the first step towards bettering your odds is to hardwire your mind for survival. No rocket science is required — just a little time. The process is simple, and this book will show you how easy it is to get started. The sooner you begin, the better your odds of survival will be.

Also, ignore the fear mongers, when they say that the tribulations of 2012 will cause humankind to revert to some kind of barbaric, pseudo-cinematic state. The opposite will happen.

When future historians look back on 2012, what they see will be less about catastrophe and more about human evolution. Case in point is the Black Death (or Black Plague) pandemic of the 14th century. It serves as a perfect 2012 historical precedent.

Historical Precedent for 2012 Evolution

In the context of a post-historic world, the global pains of 2012 will be far greater than those of the Black Death. This 14th century pandemic swept through Europe and claimed upwards of two thirds of the population, according to some estimates.

This sudden and massive depopulation not only caused immense terror and suffering, but it also triggered an evolutionary event.

The Black Death broke the Church's thousand-year suppression of secular philosophy and science. This sowed the seeds of enlightenment for the coming Renaissance through two major depopulation consequences: independent thought and automation.

- **Short Term Consequence:** Many survivors became less inclined to toe the Papal line. They began to think more independently, because the Church proved to be wholly impotent before this mysterious natural catastrophe. Disillusioned, they began looking elsewhere for answers. One early benefit of this trend towards independent thought was the emergence of medical science.

- **Long Term Consequence:** The economic impacts of a greatly reduced work force were hard felt. Hence, the development of automation to replace what had previously been an abundant pool of cheap labor. An excellent example of a Black Plague-stimulated technology development event was the invention of the Gutenberg Press in the mid 15th century.

We will likely suffer a 2012 cataclysm far worse than the 14th Century Black Death. However, there is a more urgent point to keep in mind. Those who endure 2012 with dignity will live to help plant the seeds of a future evolutionary event. One in which humanity will emerge from it all, like the butterfly from the chrysalis, as a far more spiritual and compassionate race.

With a future this ennobling and hopeful, this matter becomes quite simple. How do we get from here to there, and with whom? The answer to those questions begins with the threat, itself.

Planet X Threat

The greatest threat we face is not Planet X itself, although it will pelt the Earth with horrific meteorite storms and impact events. Rather, it will be the catastrophic interactions between it and our Sun.

Suffice it to say we are not threatened by one single object or thing in 2012. Nor will we experience a single day of cataclysm, in a Biblical sense. What can we expect? A slow motion train wreck for the world, as we know it, and on a global scale.

As it has in the past, the Planet X flyby will trigger a convergence of multiple man-made and natural catastrophic events, which will occur over a period of years. Once the nightmare is over, the survivors will emerge to create humanity's next golden Renaissance.

In the meantime, when will this cosmic train wreck begin? It already has.

The Planet X Panic

The current global warming debate has achieved one notable result. Paralysis. As the old saying goes, seeing is one thing, and believing is another. When our attention is being deflected away from what really matters, what are we to believe? Or do we even care?

This seems to be more the case for global warming, because for as long as conjecture can be used to deflect attention away from this serious (and expensive) threat, that is exactly what most people will do. Be deflected — and happily so.

The reason why this global warming deflection works as well as it does can be attributed to an inconvenient omission. The closing distance between Planet X and our Sun is the primary causality for global warming on Earth.

The same holds true for Mars and Pluto, which are also evidencing clear signs of global warming. Therefore, many of the global warming issues are indeed cyclic because Planet X flybys are cyclical in nature.

Man-made pollution is very real, but it only aggravates the core problem. Nonetheless, it remains a grave concern. This is because we're pushing the resiliency of our biosphere ever closer, towards the tipping point of catastrophic failure.

All the data is there, but what's missing? The context of an inconvenient omission.

Without the proper context, Earth change concerns are unlikely to serve as mainstream proof for Planet X. Furthermore, corporate news media outlets will equivocate about the presence of this threat for as long as possible. Their aim will be to prevent a public panic. After all, that would stop most people from showing up for work and paying taxes.

Therefore, the debate will ramble on until something greater throttles it. That will be Planet X as it approaches the core of our solar system. A large ball of dust and debris will precede it, much like a royal procession. In time, it will encroach upon the space surrounding Earth, and this is when the mainstream will really start to 'get it.'

At first, we'll begin to see communication outages, as Planet X takes the joy out of channel surfing. Cable television networks will be especially vulnerable, because they depend upon communication satellites in geosynchronous orbit.

Distance is a difference between these cable television satellites and the Global Positioning System (GPS) satellites used by the navigation systems used in military vehicles, airliners and automobiles.

A geosynchronous orbit (GEO) allows a satellite to match the Earth's own 24-hour day. Consequently, it is always pointed at the same spot on Earth. This is called a footprint, and what makes it work is the fact that the satellite is parked in space at a distance of 22,369 miles (36,000 km) from the Earth.

On the other hand, a satellite in a low Earth orbit (LEO) is going to be somewhere between 124 to 1,243 miles (193 to 2,000 km) above the surface of the Earth. To help put this in perspective, the LEO of the International Space Station (ISS) is 207 miles (333.3 km) above the Earth.

So then, how does this play out?

As dust and debris from Planet X begins to impact the GEO satellites used by the cable television networks, this is when we'll start to see entire blocks of channels going off the air as satellite transponders become damaged and fail.

Initially, these interruptions will be manageable, as these GEO satellites typically handle scores of channels. Switching affected broadcasts to other transponders on the satellite will quickly restore programming. However, over time, increasing impact damage will leave increasing numbers of GEO communication satellites impaired or useless.

What viewers will see as we approach 2012 will be more interruptions and progressively fewer channels. During this time, the cable television networks will scramble to switch over to underground and sub-sea fiber optic communication networks. However, they'll have to compete for fewer and fewer resources, so there will be no easy panacea there.

Eventually, we'll return to the 1970's era of cable television with somewhere between 20 to 40 channels of programming. Even with all this, many will continue to let Planet X debunkers deflect their concerns.

When will the mainstream finally ring the alarm bell? Odds are, that will happen when the ball of dust and debris surrounding Planet X finally reaches low Earth orbit. This is when NASA will likely be forced to abort a manned LEO mission.

Worse yet, astronauts aboard the International Space Station (ISS) could suddenly be forced to abandon ship and return to Earth in an emergency evacuation craft. If ground controllers cannot maintain the station's orbit, the ISS will fall back to Earth in an uncontrolled, fiery descent. This is when the Planet X bells will ring for sure.

Save Yourself — Not the World

The mainstream will eventually wake up, but regrettably, it will be too late by then. By that time, Earth will have crossed the threshold into the worst period of the Planet X flyby. Like a woman going into labor, the bad news will begin to arrive at an ever-quickening pace and at ever-increasing severity.

At this point, the noble urge to save everyone will be naïve and futile. If you are prepared, stay focused on your own immediate zone of survival. As brutal as this may sound, save yourself and those you can.

Attempting to save those overwhelmed by a rapid succession of catastrophic events will be as dangerous as trying to save someone who is drowning. Get close to them when they're thrashing about, and they'll beat you senseless. Then, they'll drag you down with them.

For those who chose deflection over preparation, this will be their time to "cross that bridge when they come to it." Before they get there, you will be on the far side and well on your way to a safe haven. Maybe they'll survive, and you will not. Who knows? Nonetheless, how do you wish to decide the matter?

That is why this book is not about judging or being judged. It is about choice. You choose to prepare — or not. Either way, there are no guarantees. That being said, Louis Pasteur's advice is worth repeating. "Chance favors the prepared mind."

Chance and the Prepared Mind

Before the December 7, 1941 attack on Pearl Harbor, Americanintelligence experts desperately struggled with a cryptic jigsaw puzzle. They knew Japan would launch the attack and why, but they could not lock down the critical how, where and when pieces of the puzzle. Consequently, they failed to prepare in time, and the result was a humiliating defeat in Hawaii and America's subsequent entry into WWII.

The odd thing is that it did not have to happen that way. In 1924, General Billy Mitchell warned the American Navy well in advance. An ardent advocate of air power, he foresaw Japan's expansionist goals in the Pacific. He delivered a 323-page report to the Navy that accurately predicted the attack on Pearl Harbor.

Mitchell was a man to be taken seriously. He was a leading aviation visionary in his day, and the B-25 Mitchell bomber of WWII was named after him. This very bomber was used in the Doolittle Tokyo raid that rattled Japan's imperialistic hubris in 1942.

In his 1924 report, Mitchell predicted the Japanese would attack on Pearl Harbor at 7:30 AM on December 7, 1941. The actual attack started at 7:55 AM that day. He also predicted an aerial attack on Clark Field in the Philippines at 10:40 AM that same day. They actually started at 12:35 PM that day.

Had the Navy read Mitchell's report in 1924, America would have seen an entirely different outcome. Instead, the Navy chose to mock and ridicule his report and thereby seal the fate of many unknowing sailors and soldiers — all with a simple act of arrogant deflection.

In the spirit of General Mitchell's 1924 report, this book offers a pragmatic vision of what is to come in 2012. Based upon years of continuous research and the publication of numerous articles, books and audio courses on the topic, it offers a distillation of this data in a straightforward manner. The hope is that you will vet it and then decide for yourself.

Were General Mitchell alive today, he would likely say that the arrogant manner in which he was mocked in 1924 is not what hurt him most. Rather, it was the needless American deaths that occurred on December 7, 1941 as a direct consequence of it. Ergo, the point of this book is not to be right. It is to save life! Do with it as you will.

Marshall's Motto

**Destiny finds those who listen,
and fate finds the rest.**

**So learn what you can learn,
do what you can do,
and never give up hope!**

Part 1 – Understanding the Threat

"Obscured by the Sun
Apocalyptic clash
Cities fall in ruin
Why must we die?

Obliteration of mankind
Under a pale grey sky
we shall arise..."

—*Sepultura, Arise (1991)*

Many have intuited the threat of Planet X and 2012 for decades, and recent scientific observations are now adding new dimensions to our deepest fears. Understanding the true nature of this threat is essential to human survival, both on a personal level, and as a species.

1

Harbinger Signs
of Planet X

An interesting aspect of Planet X is that most of us find ourselves becoming immersed in this topic by coincidence. One day, something odd catches our eye and piques our curiosity. Then as we begin to scratch this nebulous itch, the blinders come off, and we begin to see the harbinger signs of Planet X's approach.

We see our Sun, planets and moons affected by its approach as comets break up in mysterious ways. Taken all together, these observations show us signs of something big in our Solar system.

NASA Press Release 1992

"Unexplained deviations in the orbits of Uranus and Neptune point to a large outer solar system body of 4 to 8 Earth masses, on a highly tilted orbit, beyond 7 billion miles from the Sun."

Eventually, the facts pile up upon our thoughts, and then the blinders come off. It is as though we're standing in a dark theater as the lighting technician switches on every bank of lights in the house. In the glaring light, we ask ourselves a very sane question: "Am I seeing what I'm seeing, or am I nuts?"

This chapter answers that question in two ways. First, to tell you you're not nuts! Regrettably, this confirmation will not make Planet X and the havoc it will wreak upon us fade away, but it will help you to better cope with it.

The second goal is to help you explain to those close to you, with a simple, cocktail napkin presentation approach. If you feel the urge to announce this threat to anyone who'll hold still long enough to hear you out, resist this urge. Planet X is a topic that each person must come to in their own way, and evangelizing it will only result in you being mocked like Noah in the Biblical account of the deluge.

Think about it. How many had the foresight to ask, "Noah, what's available in the way of cabins above the waterline?" Instead, they mocked and humiliated him, and we know how that worked out. Ergo, be your own personal Noah, and focus on saving those you can.

If someone asks you about Planet X, and their interest is serious, give them a cocktail napkin presentation like the one shown in this chapter. If they demand hard evidence, refer them to "Appendix A — Harbinger Technical Analysis" at the back of this book, and end your presentation right there. When they're ready to open their mind, they'll come back, and they'll want to hear what you have to say. When they do, start your presentation with a historical view of the scientific process of discovery that led to our present day understanding of Planet X.

Planet X Defined

The term Planet X is a generic term used by astronomers to denote an, as yet undiscovered planet. When discussing Planet X with others, you may encounter the common misperception that Planet X is a newly discovered dwarf planet called Eris (formerly Xena).

This is a red herring, because Eris is not Planet X. The confusion is the result of coincidence. Pluto and Eris lack the mass to be Planet X. In fact, both are smaller than our own moon and are classified as dwarf planets.

On the other hand, when someone asks "is Planet X the same as Nibiru?" answer with a resounding "Bingo! Give the man a cigar."

In fact, the Planet X discussed in this book is well documented in ancient folklore and wisdom texts from all around the globe, and it is known by many different names.

According to noted author and researcher Zecharia Sitchin, the ancient Sumerians called it Nibiru. Likewise, *The Kolbrin Bible* offers extensive historical accounts regarding previous flybys of Planet X, and its books were authored by the Egyptians after the Exodus and by the Celts after the death of Jesus.

According to this secular anthology, the Egyptians called Planet X the Destroyer, as do corroborating passages in the Holy Bible. The Druid ancestors of the Celts called it the Frightener.

Nonetheless, until this elusive perturber is officially sighted, its moniker shall remain the generic term of Planet X — the undiscovered planet. A modern term that can trace its roots back to the discovery of Uranus in 1781.

Search for the Perturbers

Today's present search for Planet X actually began in the blossoming age of science, as astronomers and mathematicians discovered the planets Uranus and Neptune through a process of intellect and observation. The starting point of this process was the observed perturbations in the planet Saturn.

The term "perturbation" is used in astronomy to describe how the orbit of one object, such as a planet, can be altered as the result of a gravitational interaction with one or more other bodies. In a human sense, one could say that belly dancers entertain us by perturbing their hips. (It's those little wiggles that catch our eye.)

For millennia, the beautiful ringed planet of Saturn was the furthest planet we could see with the naked eye, but after the Dutch began constructing and using powerful telescopes in the 17th century, things changed.

In short order, early astronomers observed perturbations in the orbit of Saturn and this led William Herschel, a German-born British astronomer to discover the planet Uranus in 1781. At which point, "the Planet X game was afoot," to paraphrase the character, Sherlock Holmes.

With many curious eyes now turned towards Uranus, perturbations were also observed in the orbit of this newly discovered planet. This led 19th century British mathematician and astronomer John Couch Adams to predict the existence and position of this completely new perturber, solely through the use of mathematics. This in turn led to the discovery of Neptune in 1846 by German astronomer Johann Galle. An amazing feat!

Further observations showed that, just as with Saturn and Uranus, the orbit of Neptune was also perturbed. This led French mathematician Urbain Le Verrier to announce that there was yet another perturber beyond Neptune. In essence, this is when the modern quest for Planet X, as we think of it, first came to be. Yet, unlike previous discoveries, this one has been more problematic.

Tombaugh's False-Positive Discovery

In the early 20th century, Percival Lowell founded the Lowell Observatory in Flagstaff, Arizona and began searching the night skies to find Neptune's perturber, as predicted by Urbain Le Verrier in 1846.

Lowell's own searches for Planet X failed, but 14 years after his death, his assistant Clyde Tombaugh discovered Pluto in 1930.

Pluto immediately earned two honors. It was classified as a planet, even though Earth's own moon is half again as large as Pluto, and it was hailed as Neptune's perturber. For a brief moment in time, Tombaugh was the discoverer of the elusive Planet X. Then, mathematicians began running the numbers.

Once the numbers were crunched, Pluto proved to be too small to account for the perturbations in the orbit of Neptune. So much for Planet X status. Worse yet, Pluto was recently demoted from "planet" to "dwarf planet," which only goes to prove that fame is equally as fleeting in astronomy as it is in Hollywood.

This brings us back to the search for Urbain Le Verrier's Planet X, which first began in 1846, because to this day, there has not been a satisfactory explanation that counters Le Verrier's theory.

The "Official" Discovery of Planet X

Many Planet X researchers believe that Planet X was unofficially imaged for the first time in 1983 by NASA's Infrared Astronomical Satellite (IRAS). This belief was further deepened in April 2006, when yowusa.com was the first to publish an article about the South Pole Telescope (SPT), which is located at the Amundsen-Scott South Pole Station in Antarctica.

A highly sophisticated infrared observatory, the SPT became operational in early 2007. It is the perfect instrument, at the perfect place and at the perfect time to observe Planet X, and it could likely be tracking Planet X even as this book goes to press.

Until the US government stands up and announces that Planet X "R" US, this perturber shall "officially" remain in the dark. However, if you're starting an office pool, a likely candidate to deliver the "official" sighting announcement will be Project Wormwood at the Learmonth Solar Observatory. Specializing in the study of Planetary threats and space debris, it is located on the North West Cape of Western Australia.

Until Project Wormwood or someone else gets the "official" credit for sighting Planet X, does this mean we need to believe in the existence of this object as a matter of faith? Heavens, no!

Planet X Is Perturbing Our Entire Solar System

As previously mentioned, it was the perturbations in the orbit of Saturn that led to the discovery of Uranus. Likewise, perturbations in the orbit of Uranus led to the discovery of Neptune. The point here is that we find objects in our solar system much like hunters who find their game by following tracks and other signs.

When we apply the same proven method of discovery to Planet X, we see the tracks of a whole herd of harbinger signs, all across our solar system. Here is what they look like:

- **Sun:** More activity since 1940 than in previous 1150 years. The next solar cycle (#24) will be the most violent on record and will peak in 2012.

- **Mercury:** Violently active because of its proximity to the Sun, scientists were recently surprised by the discovery of polar ice and a stronger than expected magnetic field.

- **Venus:** Subtle changes are almost lost in the mayhem of its atmosphere, but a recent 2500% increase in the planet's auroral brightness was observed, along with substantial global atmospheric changes.

- **Earth:** The debate over "global warming" is over, and we're now experiencing more severe weather than ever before.

- **Mars:** There was never a "global warming" debate with regards to Mars. It just happened, along with huge storms and the disappearance of polar icecaps.

- **Jupiter:** An increase of over 200% in the brightness of surrounding plasma clouds, and significant heating have recently been observed on its moons.

- **Saturn:** The planet's equatorial jet stream has slowed dramatically in less than 20 years, plus there is now a large surge of gamma rays (in the X-ray frequencies), which are emanating from near the equator. Like Jupiter, Saturn's auroral activity in the gamma ray region has brightened dramatically.

- **Uranus:** Significant changes have been observed in Uranus's clouds. They are more numerous, active and brighter. This cannot be explained in terms of the planet's inherent ability to create these kinds of clouds.

- **Neptune:** In 1846, Le Verrier said that Planet X was Neptune's perturber, and he was right on the money — Neptune is the smoking gun! Since 1996, a 40% increase in atmospheric brightness has been observed, along with a highly agitated storm system. Neptune does not possess the natural ability to create these kinds of anomalies. Likewise, it is too far away from the Sun for it to be perturbed by increased solar activity. Therefore, this energy can only be coming from an unseen perturber.

- **Pluto:** After reaching the closest point in its orbit to the Sun in 1989, the planet began evidencing "global warming" similar to that of Earth and Mars, and it cannot be explained as seasonal weather. The atmospheric pressure rose by over 300%, while the average surface temperature rose 3.6 degrees Fahrenheit (2 degrees Celsius) as it traveled away from the Sun.

This of course begs the question, "where do they look for Planet X?" Time to find a pen and some cocktail napkins, as you'll need to cover a few of the basic astronomical concepts relevant to Planet X.

The following illustrations will give you a cocktail napkin explanation for those with little or no understanding of astronomy. Again. Do not volunteer this information. Wait to be asked.

Basic Concepts

Our Solar System

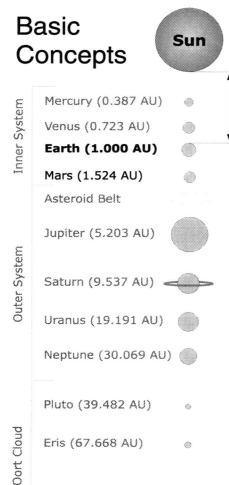

ASTRONOMICAL UNIT (AU): The average distance between the Earth and the Sun. Approx. 93 million miles (150 million kilometers.)

INNER SYSTEM: Often called the core of the system, it is home to four planets of dense, rocky composition. Earth is the 3rd rock from the Sun. The asteroid belt between Mars and Jupiter is a boundary between the inner and outer systems

OUTER SYSTEM: Also called the mid-system, this is where the big gas giants live. They, along with their planet-sized moons comprise 99% of all the matter that orbits our Sun.

Jupiter sweeps up most of the asteroids and comets that would otherwise impact the Earth. Were it a little larger, it would have enough mass to become a brown dwarf like Planet X.

OORT CLOUD: There are two main areas. The Inner Oort Cloud (Kuiper Belt) and the Outer Oort Cloud. Within these massive regions are smaller areas, such as the Kuiper Gap and the Scattered Disk.

BROWN DWARF: Our Sun has a smaller twin. A type of unborn sun called a brown dwarf. Scientists have recently discovered that Brown Dwarfs are the most common type of star in our universe. Planet X is mostly likely a Brown Dwarf in an unstable orbit.

Illustration 1: Cocktail Napkin #1 — Our Solar System

Basic Concepts

The Ecliptic

NORMAL ORBITS AROUND THE ECLIPTIC: Imagine yourself at the center of the sun. Then, shoot a laser beam out from the center of the sun in every direction — through its equator — then through the planets of our solar system — and out into deep space. At the far end of the beam are the twelve signs of the zodiac. In between, we see the planets in our solar system. They orbit East to West or West to East around the Sun, very near or directly on the plane of our imaginary laser beams.

KOZAI MECHANISM: Used by astronomers to describe the way large objects behave when they orbit about each other. In the illustration above, the planets are orbiting on or near the ecliptic. This is a celestial happy spot, because they follow nice predictable orbits.

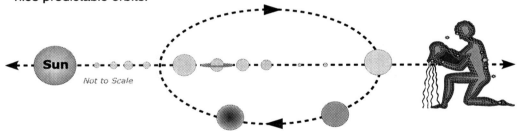

PERPENDICULAR ORBITS: Unlike our planets, objects with perpendicular orbits follow a North to South or South to North path that takes them way below and way above the ecliptic. The Kozai Mechanism tells us that these objects will have erratic orbits that can throw them out into deep space or cause them to crash into the Sun.

Comet Hale-Bopp is a good example. In 1997, it passed close enough to Jupiter to cause it's 4,200 year orbit to suddenly shrink to just 2,380 years. It could very well be that Planet X is a brown dwarf that was once in a stable orbit along the ecliptic. Then, something caused it to enter into a sharply perpendicular orbit that is now degrading.

Illustration 2: Cocktail Napkin #2 — The Ecliptic

Basic Concepts

Elliptical Orbits

PERIHELION and APHELION: Planets do not orbit the Sun in perfectly circular orbits. This is why the Astronomical Unit (AU) represents the average distance between the Earth and the Sun. Earth also has two other distances: perihelion and aphelion.

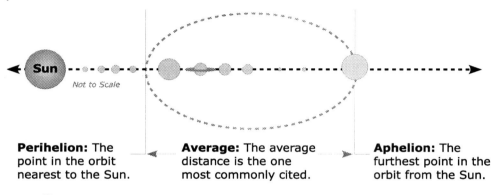

Perihelion: The point in the orbit nearest to the Sun.

Average: The average distance is the one most commonly cited.

Aphelion: The furthest point in the orbit from the Sun.

Planet	Perihelion	Average	Aphelion
Mercury	0.307	0.387	0.467
Venus	0.718	0.723	0.728
Earth	0.983	1.000	1.017
Mars	1.381	1.524	1.666
Jupiter	4.952	5.203	5.455
Saturn	9.021	9.537	10.054
Uranus	18.286	19.191	20.096
Neptune	29.811	30.069	30.327
Pluto	29.658	39.482	49.305
Eris	37.770	67.668	97.560
Planet X	2.850	237.500	475.000

Elliptical Orbits: Earth's orbit is not a perfect circle, so it is described as being somewhat elliptical, whereas the orbit of Planet X is highly elliptical (comet-like). At aphelion, it visits a distant region of our solar system where no spacecraft have ever traveled. At perihelion, it passes through the asteroid belt between Mars and Jupiter.

Illustration 3: Cocktail Napkin #3 — Elliptical Orbits

Basic Concepts

Solar Interaction

PLANET X ORBITAL PARAMETERS: Planet X has an inclined orbit that lies in a plane that is almost perpendicular to the ecliptic. At aphelion (237.5 AU), it is well below the plane of the ecliptic. However, as it enters the inner solar system, it will cross the plane of the ecliptic shortly before it reaches perihelion (2.85 AU), where its most violent interactions with the Sun will occur.

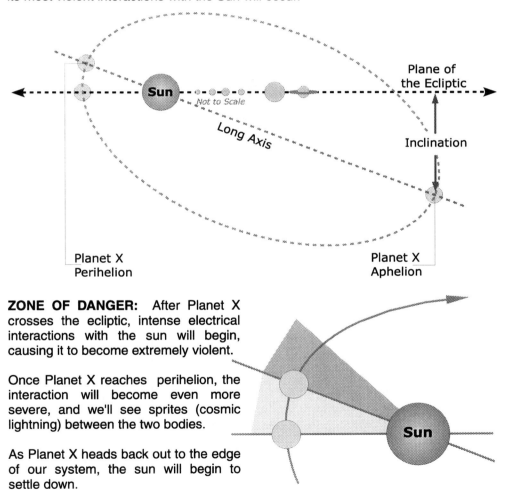

ZONE OF DANGER: After Planet X crosses the ecliptic, intense electrical interactions with the sun will begin, causing it to become extremely violent.

Once Planet X reaches perihelion, the interaction will become even more severe, and we'll see sprites (cosmic lightning) between the two bodies.

As Planet X heads back out to the edge of our system, the sun will begin to settle down.

Illustration 4: Cocktail Napkin #4 — Solar Interaction

2

Planet X Forecast
Through 2014

Planet X is approaching the inner Solar system for a near future flyby. We know this not by direct observation at this time, but by the manner in which this object is interacting with familiar objects in our solar system, such as the Sun and planets. This forecast combines these observed interactions with historical accounts of previous flybys and statistically relevant paranormal experience trends.

It must be strongly emphasized that, although interactions between Planet X and the various bodies within our system are clearly visible, this object will not be visible to amateur astronomers in the Southern hemisphere range until 2009 or even possibly 2010. Therefore, this forecast is simply nothing more than that – a forecast.

This chapter focuses on the 9-slide color PDF presentation that was first made available at yowusa.com in January 2007. The free version of this presentation can be downloaded from this site.

In subsequent editions of this work, we will update this forecast to reflect new data as it becomes available. In the meantime, our present forecast is based on a data snapshot of our present research, beginning in late 2001 and lasting through June 2007. We've used this data to construct an orbit that satisfies as much of the evidence as possible, based on the following assumptions:

Value	Assumption	Comments
Orbit	Eccentric Elliptical	An elliptical orbit is oval as opposed to being circular. When it is eccentric, it is dramatically lopsided like the orbit of Pluto.
Period	Approximately 3,660 Years	The time it takes for Planet X to complete one full orbit from perihelion to aphelion and back to perihelion again. Perihelion is the point in Planet X's orbit, at which it is closest to the Sun. Aphelion is the point in Planet X's orbit, at which it is furthest away from the Sun.
Perihelion	2.85 AU	An astronomical unit "AU" is the distance between the Earth and the Sun, which is about 93 million miles (150 million kilometers.) Given that Mars is 1.52 AU from the Sun, the point in Planet X's orbit, at which it comes closest to our Sun lies well between the orbits of Mars and Jupiter, at a distance of some 265 million miles from the Sun.
Aphelion	472 AU	To help put 472 AU in context, Pluto's aphelion is 39.5 AU. That means that Planet X travels to the outer edge of our solar system to a point that is nearly as far as 12 Pluto distances from the Sun. This means that Planet X spends a lot of its time in what's called the Kuiper Gap, which is in the mid-Kuiper Belt region beyond the orbit of Pluto.
Inclination to the Ecliptic	Nearly Perpendicular	To imagine the ecliptic, visualize a flat disc emanating from the center of the Sun out to the 12 constellations of the Zodiac. The planets in our solar system orbit the Sun within a few degrees of the ecliptic, in an East to West or West to East fashion. When an object is in an orbit perpendicular to the ecliptic, it circles the Sun from North to South or South to North. In this case, Planet X is nearly perpendicular and is currently approaching perihelion from the South. Approximately 90% of all observed objects are in the 12 constellations of the Zodiac. Planet X is well below that, which is one reason why it has not been officially sighted yet.
Infrared Observation	Now visible to infrared space telescopes and Southern observatories.	Several Planet X researchers believe that in 1983, the Infrared Astronomical Satellite (IRAS) space telescope spotted a planet bigger than Jupiter in the constellation of Sagittarius with a temperature of 240 Kelvin. In April 2006, yowusa.com broke a story on the South Pole Telescope. This large infrared telescope became operational at the South Pole in early 2007. It is the perfect instrument, at the perfect place and at the perfect time to observe the approach of Planet X and monitor it continuously.

Value	Assumption	Comments
Amateur Telescope Observation	Mid-2009	Observation will depend on location, time and atmospheric conditions. Amateurs in the Southern Hemisphere will most likely be able to view Planet X using backyard telescopes and high-powered binoculars.
Naked Eye Observation	Mid-2009	It will be clearly visible at night as a bright, reddish object to those living in the Southern Hemisphere.
2nd Sun	2012	Planet X will appear as a second sun in the sky.

For those wishing to further analyze this projection using an astronomy computer program, the following orbital parameters were used to generate this forecast:

Parameter	Value
Mean distance (a)	237.50 AU
Eccentricity	0.988
Inclination	85.00 degrees
Ascending node	200.00 degrees
Argument of pericentre	12.00 degrees
Mean anomaly	358.71 degrees
Epoch	2451545 (Julian day)

These parameters can also be used to track the object back to 1983, when it was first "unofficially" spotted by the Infrared Astronomical Satellite (IRAS) at a distance of 51 AU away from Earth, with an orbit that puts it at 37 degrees below the ecliptic.

Keep in mind that IRAS surveyed the skies in 1983; Planet X was still 1.3 times further away than Pluto, which is a difficult distance for visible light telescopes. It would be a slow mover at that distance, easily mistaken for a star much further away. However it would have been well within the capabilities of IRAS, which at that time represented the state of the art for space-based infrared telescopes.

For more detailed technical information, see "Appendix C — Forecast Addendum."

Forecast for April 15, 2007

The 3,660-year orbital path of Planet X is represented by a sharp ellipse that enters from the lower right hand side and curves through the center of the illustration, before exiting at the upper right hand side. In this illustration, Planet X is approaching the inner Solar system from below the ecliptic, just inside the orbit of Saturn at about 15 AU from the Sun.

Solar System

The approach of Planet X is perturbing the Sun and most of the major bodies in the solar system. Planets are evidencing increased levels of atmospheric activity, due to changes in their electrical fields. These changes will further exacerbate, as the Sun begins to enter solar cycle 24, which is due to peak in 2011 or 2012.

NASA is forecasting solar cycle 24 to be one of the worst in the last 400 years. This forecast is very conservative.

Earth

We will also see more perturbations for Earth, as increasing solar activity is transferring more energy to the interior of all affected planets. This transfer will result in increased earthquake activity, which began increasing in 2004. As we approach 2012, the frequency of severe earthquakes will trend sharply upwards.

Likewise, global warming will continue to accelerate, causing severe droughts in some locations. In May 2007, the Chinese government announced that a persistent drought in the country has dried up hundreds of small reservoirs. The drought caused drinking water shortages for 4.81 million people and 4.84 million livestock.

South Pole Telescope

The South Pole Telescope became operational in February of 2007. Academics will use it for two months out of the year. Although Planet X is still invisible to the naked eye, it is clearly visible in the infrared wavelength range of this telescope, which is perfectly situated to monitor Planet X's approach for several years.

By continuously observing Planet X for erratic behaviors or changes in its orbit, scientists will be better able to determine how it will interact with our Sun during the 2012 flyby.

April 15, 2007 — Distance from Sun 15 AU

Planet X incoming from below the ecliptic. Ideal position for start of continuous observation by the South Pole Telescope (SPT).

Solar Cycle 24
- *Early Signs Aug-2006*
- *Four X-Class Flares Dec-2006*
- *SPT Operational January 2007*
- *Highest Activity in 400 Years*

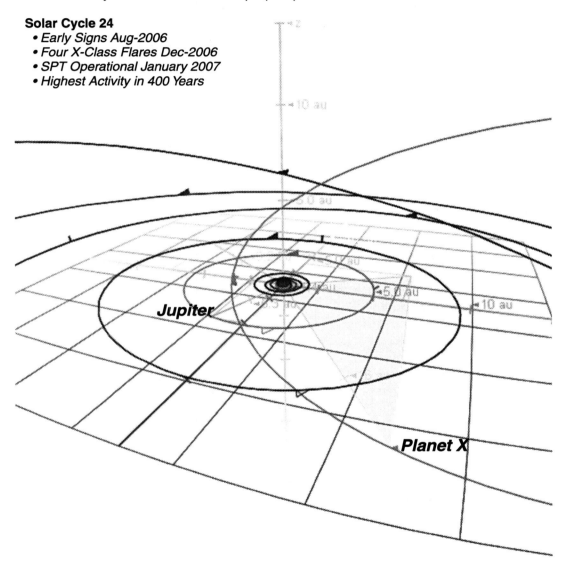

Illustration 5: Planet X Forecast for April 15, 2007

Forecast for May 15, 2009

On May 15, 2009, Planet X will be 11 AU from the Sun, almost directly beneath the asteroid belt in between Mars and Jupiter. At this point, amateur astronomers in the Southern Hemisphere will see it as a dark red spot, using popular consumer telescopes or even powerful binoculars. Those living in the tropical zone above the equator might also observe it.

Solar System

By 2009, the Sun will be well into solar cycle 24, so the perturbations caused by the approach of Planet X on the planets and the Sun will be even greater. Early signs of flooding might even begin to appear towards the end of 2009 on the Planet Mars, as increased solar radiation permeates the planet's frozen surface, thereby melting its vast underground caches of frozen water.

Earth

The average magnitude of earthquakes will continue to increase, and hurricanes and tornadoes will be far more powerful. Weather patterns will be more extreme all around the world. More prolonged drought and periods of severe rainfall will no longer be the exception — they will be the rule. Consequently, global weather patterns will reverse themselves, and where there was rain, there will be drought, and vice-versa.

Space-based Solar Observatories

The growing number of active sunspots will produce increasingly powerful solar flares. By 2009, they could begin to wreak havoc with our communication networks and power grids, as the interaction between our Sun and Planet X begins to grow sharply. Unless we're prepared for them, solar storms could lay waste to the modern technologies that shape our lives.

This is why the industrialized nations of the world will have a fleet of 6 solar observatories in orbit around our Sun by late 2008. It will include the ESA: SOHO and Proba-2, JAXA: Solar-B, and NASA: Stereo Twin Satellites and the Solar Dynamics Observatory. Together, they form a vital early warning network to help protect us from impending solar storms.

May 15, 2009 — Distance from Sun 11 AU

Below the asteroid belt, the object becomes bright enough for amateurs in the Southern hemisphere to see. Viewing requires high-powered binoculars or small telescope.

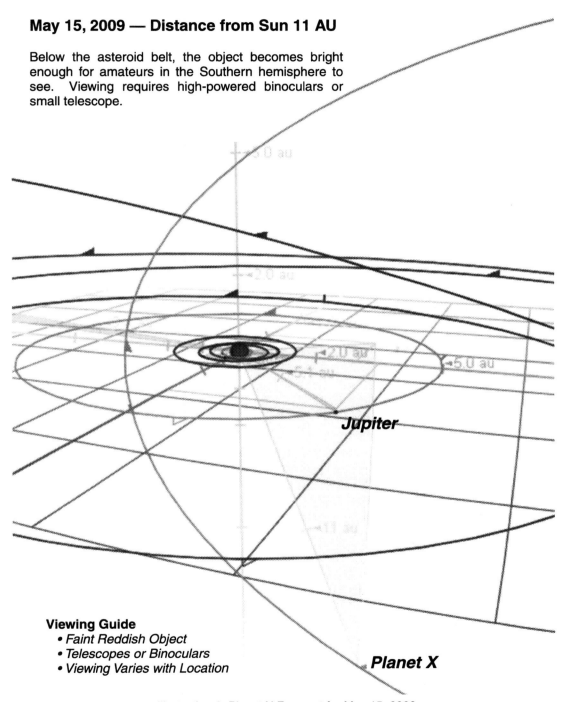

Viewing Guide
- *Faint Reddish Object*
- *Telescopes or Binoculars*
- *Viewing Varies with Location*

Planet X

Jupiter

Illustration 6: Planet X Forecast for May 15, 2009

Forecast for May 15, 2011

On May 15, 2011, Planet X will be almost directly below the Sun at a distance of 6.4 AU from the Sun. During this part of its orbit, Planet X will be moving through a denser part of the solar magnetic field. This will cause a significantly stronger interaction between Planet X and the Sun. As a result, Planet X will start to brighten faster.

Those living in the Southern Hemisphere will be able to see Planet X with the naked eye. During dusk or dawn it will appear as a pale red dot. Once the Sun slips just below the horizon, Planet X will become increasingly brighter with a more intense, reddish color. At this time, it will be equal in brightness to Venus or possibly brighter.

Solar System

Between May 21, 2011 and December 21, 2012, the approach of Planet X will cause the Sun to begin sending out powerful eruptions in all directions. During this period, we will begin to lose orbiting solar observatories to these eruptions. No doubt, plans are already underway to build replacements, so they can be ready for launch during this time.

Luckily for Earth, most of these violent solar eruptions will be aimed in the direction of Planet X due to the electrical interaction between the two bodies. However, given the numerous sunspots NASA has predicted for next solar maximum, which peaks in 2012, Earth will be in the cross hairs for a freakish, perfect solar storm. This storm could erupt with a magnitude of violence that is far off the end of the present scale.

Earth

The weather on Earth by mid-2011 will be more violent than any weather ever seen in recorded history. Earthquakes will continue to break records, and we will see a steady increase in volcanism. The resulting cataclysms will destabilize social structures, as governments struggle to prevent ethnic and economic disputes from flaring into bloody regional wars.

According to the ancient historical accounts of the last Planet X flyby in *The Kolbrin Bible,* the last flyby was so terrifying that men became impotent and women barren. Similar social ills will begin to surface in 2011, as a sense of global panic begins to set in.

Communication Satellites

Solar flares will cripple most of our communication satellites, paralyzing various communications systems. The use of underground and undersea fiber optic cables will be greatly expanded. The days of cellular phones and cable television will begin to draw to an end, but dial-up Internet speeds will still be available. Broadband access will likely be restricted for use by governments, hospitals and designated business concerns only.

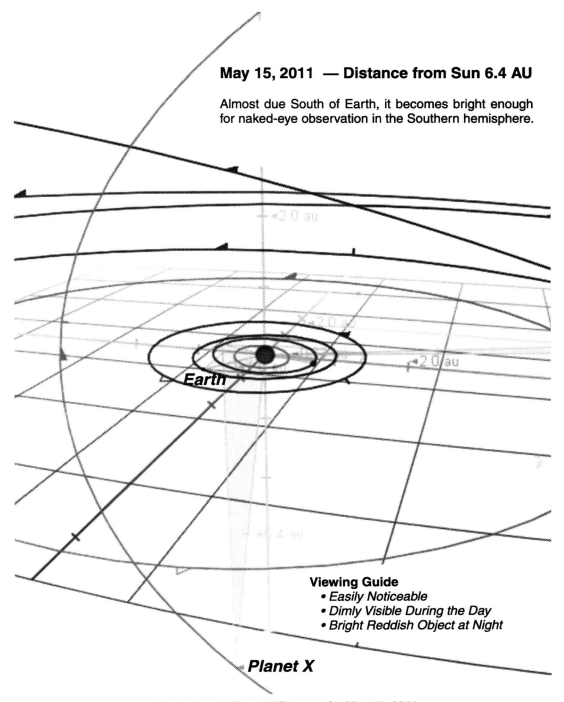

May 15, 2011 — Distance from Sun 6.4 AU

Almost due South of Earth, it becomes bright enough for naked-eye observation in the Southern hemisphere.

Viewing Guide
- *Easily Noticeable*
- *Dimly Visible During the Day*
- *Bright Reddish Object at Night*

Planet X

Illustration 7: Planet X Forecast for May 15, 2011

Forecast for December 21, 2012

According to Mayan researchers, there are two key harbinger dates for the future: one spiritual, the other astronomical. October 10, 2011 is the spiritual date when humanity begins its next evolutionary cycle, but December 21, 2012 is the date that is tinged with dread. Coinciding with the Winter Solstice in 2012, this ominous date is based on the calculations of the Mayan Calendar, as represented in the Dresden Codex. This will be a time when our Sun passes through the densest plane of the galaxy, fraught with unseen dangers.

Solar System

On this date, Planet X crosses through the ecliptic plane and begins its most electrically active state as it races towards perihelion on February 14, 2013. That is the point where it comes closest to the Sun. Initially, it will be brighter than a full Moon at night and possibly visible during the day. As it nears perihelion, it will swell in appearance and will likely rival the Sun or the Moon in size.

At this time, we will also witness 'sprites' jumping between the Sun and Planet X. Simply put, sprites are electrical discharges, and they will appear as tentacles of cosmic lightning, emanating from Planet X towards the Sun. By this time, most of our solar observatories and communication satellites will have been reduced to toasted bits of space debris.

Earth

Planet X will be attended by a swarm of preceding and following objects, many of which can cause catastrophic impact events and deadly meteorite showers. The last flyby of Planet X was during the Exodus, and according to the Hebrew account in the Torah (Old Testament), the 7th plague of Exodus was 'Barad' (hail mixed with fire). *The Kolbrin Bible*, the Egyptian account of the event, corroborates this plague as meteorite storms. However, this is not the worst of it.

Yellowstone Supervolcano Eruption

There will be a steep increase in the kinds of earthquakes that caused the Indian Ocean tsunami in December 2004. During this time, all eyes will be turned towards Yellowstone National Park in Wyoming. The greatest supervolcano in the USA (if not the world), Yellowstone is long overdue for another eruption and has been evidencing growing volcanism since 2003. Highly susceptible to the growing solar violence caused by Planet X, it could very well erupt at this time, destroying America's bread basket and triggering a mini-ice age in the process.

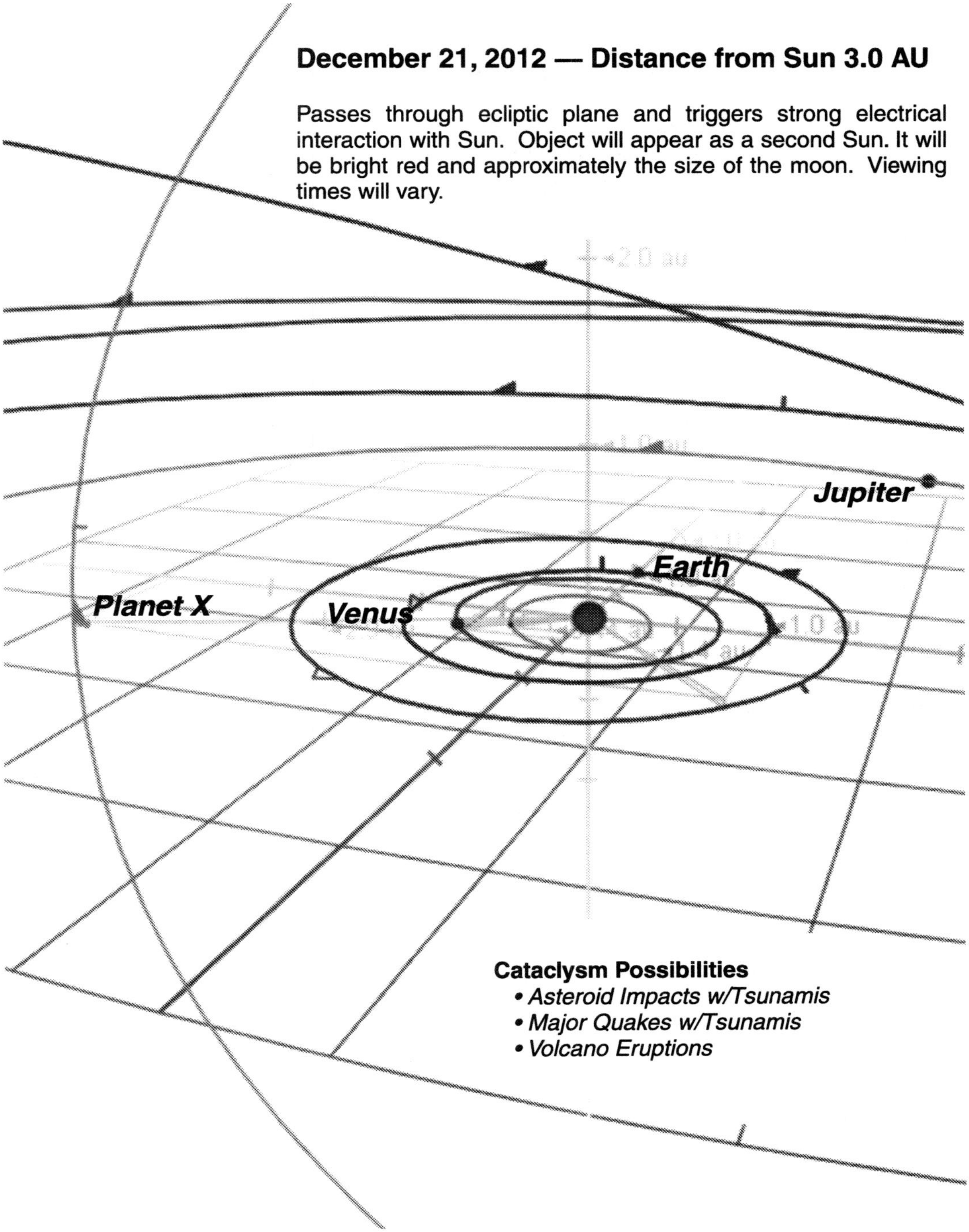

December 21, 2012 — Distance from Sun 3.0 AU

Passes through ecliptic plane and triggers strong electrical interaction with Sun. Object will appear as a second Sun. It will be bright red and approximately the size of the moon. Viewing times will vary.

Jupiter

Earth

Planet X

Venus

Cataclysm Possibilities
- *Asteroid Impacts w/Tsunamis*
- *Major Quakes w/Tsunamis*
- *Volcano Eruptions*

Illustration 8: Planet X Forecast for December 21, 2012

Forecast for February 14, 2013

The doomsday for humanity in this forecast is February 14, 2013 — not December 21, 2012. On this day, Planet X reaches perihelion (its closest point to the Sun), and the electrical interaction between the two will soar to the maximum levels. Unfortunately, Earth's orbit will put us between Planet X and the Sun as these two astronomical behemoths duke it out with unimaginable electrical blows.

Solar System

As Earth approaches a position between Planet X and the Sun, a serious risk emerges that we will be struck by electrical discharges between the two giants. This would cause extremely violent electrical atmospheric effects on Earth, because solar super storms would unleash terrible CME eruptions. We would literally see fire raining down from the sky, as plasma forms in the atmosphere with strange, glowing colors.

Earth

It is difficult to predict an extent of the possible effect Planet X will have on Earth during this time, but we can expect a period of cataclysms of Biblical proportions that will be unlike anything seen in modern history.

- Natural cataclysms, such as supervolcano eruptions, magnitude 9+ earthquakes along major fault lines and tsunamis will occur globally at a breathtaking pace.

- Global weather patterns will become violent as summer and winter merge into a single season. Major coastal cities will be ground to pieces under angry seas.

- Part of our atmosphere could become ionized and become poisonous to breathe. Entire regions of the planet could become poisonous to all forms of life.

- Earth's power grids, transportation systems and communication networks will already have been destroyed or become paralyzed. Only hardened government, corporate and military systems will survive.

Those who remain on the surface at this time will be exposed to lethal electrical charges and poisonous gases caused by the electrical interactions between our Sun and Planet X. Those who take shelter underground will be somewhat protected from these threats, and from the effects of secondary radiation, as well.

Feb 14, 2013 — Distance from Sun 2.85 AU

Planet X passes through perihelion, and maximum electrical interaction with Sun begins. This is the most catastrophic period for Earth and peaks when Earth moves between Planet X and the Sun.

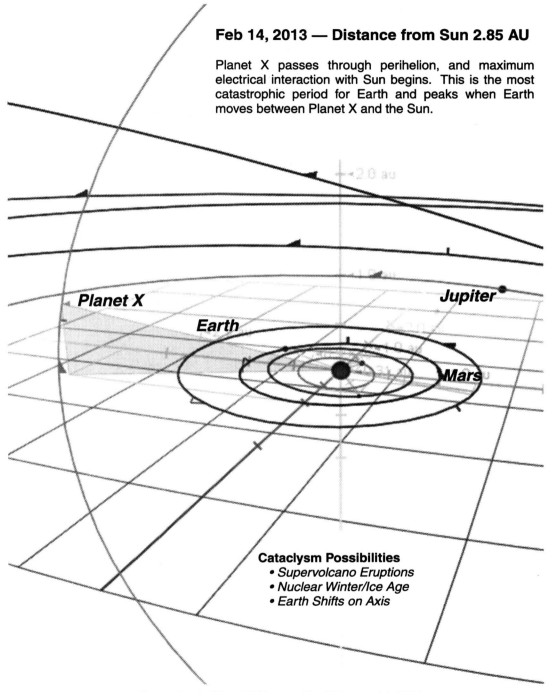

Cataclysm Possibilities
- *Supervolcano Eruptions*
- *Nuclear Winter/Ice Age*
- *Earth Shifts on Axis*

Illustration 9: Planet X Forecast for February 14, 2013

Forecast for July 14, 2013

The interaction between the Sun and Planet X will finally begin to diminish, as Planet X begins to transit out of our solar system on July 14, 2013, and it will look like a huge, red comet as it recedes from the Sun. This will mark the beginning of a bittersweet time for fly-by survivors, as Earth's oceans, lands and atmosphere slowly begin to settle back down into more "normal" levels of activity. However, this period will also be plagued with the deadly aftereffects of the Planet X flyby.

- The atmosphere will be darkened in part by dust and smoke from volcanic activity, resulting in a Nuclear Winter scenario. Global warming gases created through man-made pollution will help mitigate the severity and duration of this cooling trend. If we're lucky, our auto tail pipe and smoke stack emissions may yet prove useful.

- Much of the planet's drinking water resources and arable lands will be polluted. Many will continue to die from thirst, hunger and disease.

- All above ground infrastructure, such as highway overpasses and bridges, will be in a state of collapse, and most buildings and homes will be destroyed or unsafe.

- Military short wave radios will be the only way to communicate across the globe, until other communication systems are restored.

Around the world, there will be two types of survivors. Those chosen to survive in specially prepared government arks and a number of self-reliant individuals living together in small, obscure, harmonious survival communities.

Planet X and the Kozai Mechanism

The Kozai Mechanism explains what happens to objects like Planet X with orbits that are perpendicular to the ecliptic. (See "Appendix D — Kozai Mechanism and Perpendicular Orbits" for more detailed information.) Comet Hale-Bopp is a perfect example. In 1997, its 4200 year perpendicular orbit was reduced to just 2,380 years! The same could happen to Planet X, especially if it is a Brown Dwarf. This would then mean the ultimate demise of the Earth in 3797, as predicted by Nostradamus. This is why Earth's governments are now searching the heavens for new extrasolar Earths at a feverish pitch.

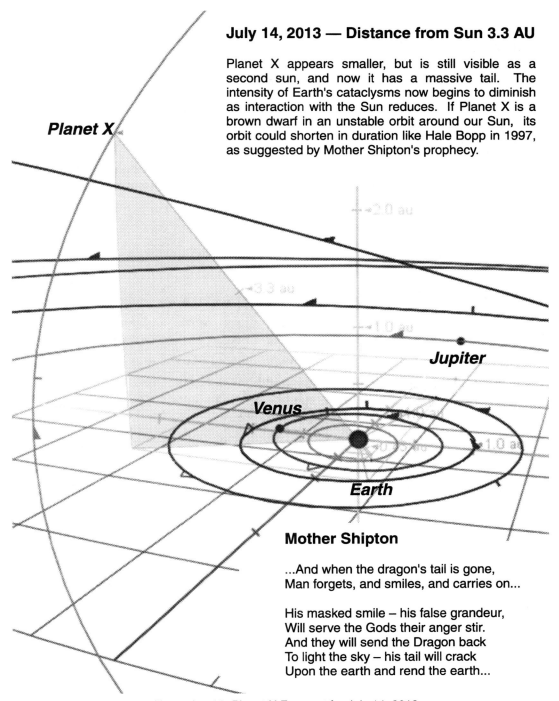

July 14, 2013 — Distance from Sun 3.3 AU

Planet X appears smaller, but is still visible as a second sun, and now it has a massive tail. The intensity of Earth's cataclysms now begins to diminish as interaction with the Sun reduces. If Planet X is a brown dwarf in an unstable orbit around our Sun, its orbit could shorten in duration like Hale Bopp in 1997, as suggested by Mother Shipton's prophecy.

Planet X

Jupiter

Venus

Earth

Mother Shipton

...And when the dragon's tail is gone,
Man forgets, and smiles, and carries on...

His masked smile – his false grandeur,
Will serve the Gods their anger stir.
And they will send the Dragon back
To light the sky – his tail will crack
Upon the earth and rend the earth...

Illustration 10: Planet X Forecast for July 14, 2013

Forecast for July 15, 2013

In "Chapter 4 – 2012 Flyby Scenarios," we will look at a moderately severe Planet X flyby, which could very well be described in Nostradamus' prophecies *Les Prophéties* in Century 6: Quatrain 6 and commonly known as the "Bearded Star" prophecy. Illustration 7 offers a future view of the Bearded Star, which in this case is Planet X as it will be seen looking north from Paris, France on July 15, 2013.

In the illustration, the Bearded Star mentioned in Nostradamus' prophecies will be clearly visible almost due North as the Sun enters the constellation of Cancer. It will appear near the North Pole Star and will appear small and reddish with a long tail.

When this prophecy is viewed in context with the Last Pope prophecy of St. Malachy, a hopeful possibility emerges that humanity escapes the horrific loss of life depicted in "Chapter 4 – 2012 Flyby Scenarios."

The Vision of St. Malachy

Saint Malachy was a 12th century Catholic priest who became the archbishop of Armagh, Ireland. He was canonized (declared a saint) after his death by Pope Clement III in 1199.

Several miracles were attributed to him, but the one he became most famous for was a vision, in which he was shown the identity of the last 112 last popes of the Holy Roman Catholic Church. For each, he saw a designation, which he characterized in only a few words; the longest designation was for the 112th and last Pope.

"In extreme persecution, the seat of the Holy Roman Church will be occupied by Peter the Roman, who will feed the sheep through many tribulations; when they are over, the city of seven hills will be destroyed, and the terrible or fearsome Judge will judge his people. The End." —*Saint Malachy (1094-1148)*

In his Bearded Star prophecy, Nostradamus confirms the last Pontiff's demise, C6:Q6 "The great one of Rome will die, the night over."

When viewed together, the prophecies of Nostradamus and St. Malachy tell us that, despite much war and suffering, much of France and Italy will have survived the peak interaction period between the Sun and Planet X. This clearly suggests that this next passage of Planet X will more closely resemble the best case scenario in this book.

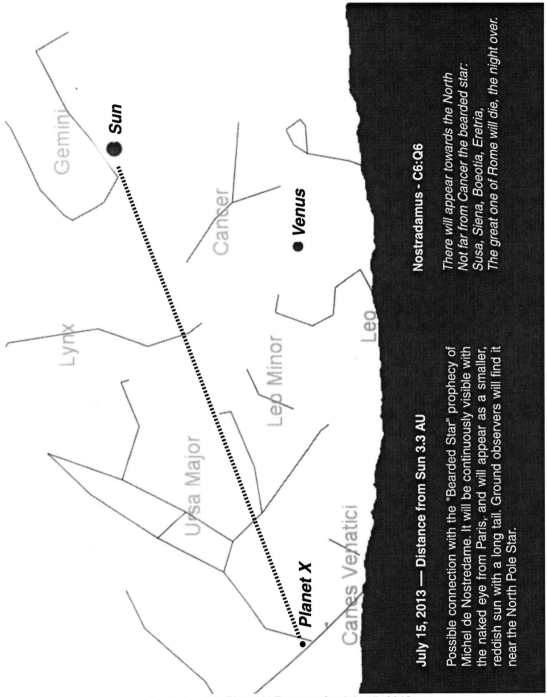

July 15, 2013 — Distance from Sun 3.3 AU

Possible connection with the "Bearded Star" prophecy of Michel de Nostredame. It will be continuously visible with the naked eye from Paris, and will appear as a smaller, reddish sun with a long tail. Ground observers will find it near the North Pole Star.

Nostradamus - C6:Q6

There will appear towards the North
Not far from Cancer the bearded star:
Susa, Siena, Boeotia, Eretria,
The great one of Rome will die, the night over.

Illustration 11: Planet X Forecast for July 15, 2013

Forecast for July 4, 2014

July 4, 2014 will be the next Independence Day of a new millennium, as Planet X recedes from the inner core of our solar system. It will be almost directly above the North Pole of Earth at a distance of nearly 6 AU from the Sun as the survivors gladly leave their subterranean havens behind. In the light of a new day, they will celebrate the healing of our planet and our souls. Yes, there will still be residual aftereffects, but by this time, they will begin to diminish, and in doing so, bring the hope of a better future.

- Earthquakes, volcanic eruptions, floods and tsunamis will become less numerous and decrease in severity.

- The one monotonous winter and summer season that has dominated Earth's weather will begin to show the hint of seasons, as the ash and dust in the atmosphere begin to settle.

- Thanks to man-made greenhouse gases, the nuclear winter brought on by volcanic activity will yield at a quicker pace towards more favorable conditions.

- Raised from the seas as a result of volcanic uplifts, new coastal regions will offer rich new farmlands with mineral-rich soils that will nourish new life and restore health.

Likewise, things are slowly returning to normal elsewhere in our Solar system, but how long will this last? That is difficult to say, because drastic changes in the orbit of Planet X could occur during the flyby. If that happens, what can future generations expect?

If the orbit of Planet X is altered during the flyby, like the 1997 flyby of Comet Hale-Bopp was, then Nostradamus' predictions that the Earth will die in 3797 AD are wholly consistent with the Kozai Mechanism. (See "Appendix D — Kozai Mechanism and Perpendicular Orbits" for more detailed information.) It is also consistent with the warning of the British Seeress Mother Shipton, when she talks of the gods sending the dragon back, 'to rend the earth'. A warning that echoes Earth's doom in 3797 AD.

Regardless of what you may think of America's government, it is working with other nations to find new Earths in distant solar systems. Proving, exploring and colonizing the likely candidates will take centuries, and the good news is that we've already begun.

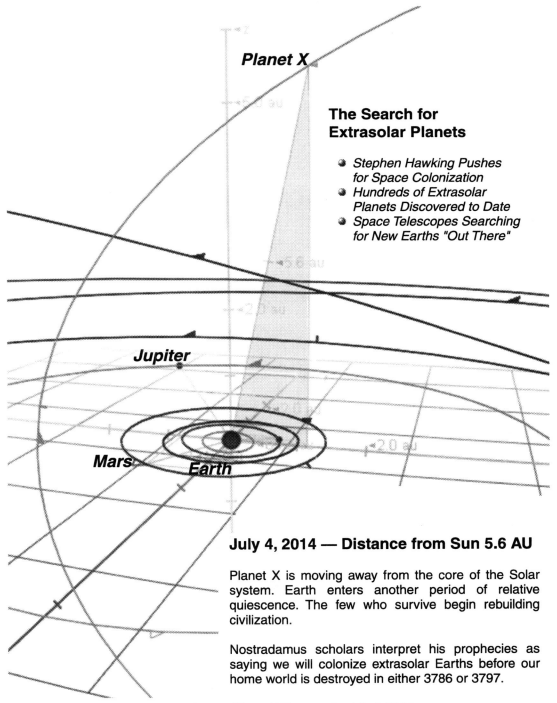

Planet X

The Search for Extrasolar Planets

- *Stephen Hawking Pushes for Space Colonization*
- *Hundreds of Extrasolar Planets Discovered to Date*
- *Space Telescopes Searching for New Earths "Out There"*

Jupiter

Mars **Earth**

July 4, 2014 — Distance from Sun 5.6 AU

Planet X is moving away from the core of the Solar system. Earth enters another period of relative quiescence. The few who survive begin rebuilding civilization.

Nostradamus scholars interpret his prophecies as saying we will colonize extrasolar Earths before our home world is destroyed in either 3786 or 3797.

Illustration 12: Planet X Forecast for July 4, 2014

3

Historical Accounts of Previous Flybys

What we call Planet X today was known to the ancients by many different names, and there is a very substantial historical record of previous flybys in both folklore and wisdom texts. The three most notable wisdom texts are the *Holy Bible*, *The Kolbrin Bible* and the Sumerian texts as translated by Zecharia Sitchin in his landmark book, *The 12th Planet* and therein referred to as Nibiru.

Of the three, the most comprehensive source of historical accounts and prophecy is contained in *The Kolbrin Bible*, a secular anthology. Penned by numerous Egyptian and Celtic authors, it was written in two parts, each in the same time period as the Old and New Testaments, respectively. (See "Appendix B — History of *The Kolbrin Bible*" for a more detailed history of this work.)

The direct correlations between these secular and non-secular texts are both stunning in scope and language. Likewise troubling is their equally-dire, prophetic warnings for our future. A complete discussion of all the accounts, prophecies and correlations between the two would require a book in itself. Therefore, this chapter will briefly discuss many of the more notable correlations and prophetic warnings.

Filtering Concepts through the Passage of Time

When reading ancient historical accounts and prophecies, it is easy to become frustrated, as these texts often lack a clear correlation to the present reality of our own lives. Consequently, we often use something akin to "Kentucky windage," a slang term used by shooters to describe a process whereby we adjust our aim in order to hit a distant target.

A good example is the creation of the State of Israel. Before 1948, many Christian Scholars explained the Bible prophecies regarding the re-establishment of Israel as a Jewish state in the context of a greater Christian Church. Given the political realities in those days, that reasoning made sense to those who could not imagine such a thing happening. Yet it did. Ergo, they rationalized the prophecies instead of reading them literally, and they were wrong for two reasons. First, they invented context where none existed before and second, because they lacked the patience to wait out the prophecy. Or in other words, if something does not make sense today, leave it be until it does.

Those reading the Planet X accounts and prophecies of the ancients decades ago would not have been able to fully understand them in a modern sense, as the scientific harbinger signs discussed in the first chapter of this book only became available within the last few decades. However, we do have this data, so now we can fully understand the prescient warnings of the *Holy Bible* and *The Kolbrin Bible* as they were written.

The most stunning warning is found in a direct correlation between the *Holy Bible* and *The Kolbrin Bible*. Both use the exact same name for Planet X, which they refer to as the "Destroyer."

Holy Bible: New Century version

- **Jeremiah 25:32 & 48:8** "Disasters will soon spread from nation to nation. They will come like a powerful storm to all the faraway places on earth…The **DESTROYER** will come against every town, not one town will escape…The Lord said this will happen."

The Kolbrin Bible: Egyptian Texts of the Bronzebook

- **Manuscripts 3:3** "When ages pass, certain laws operate upon the stars in the Heavens. Their ways change; there is movement and restlessness, they are no longer constant and a great light appears redly in the skies."

- **Manuscripts 3:4:** "When blood drops upon the Earth, the Destroyer will appear, and mountains will open up and belch forth fire and ashes. Trees will be destroyed and all living things engulfed. Waters will be swallowed up by the land, and seas will boil."

- **Manuscripts 3:6:** "The people will scatter in madness. They will hear the trumpet and battlecry of the **DESTROYER** and will seek refuge within dens in the Earth. Terror will eat away their hearts, and their courage will flow from them like water from a broken pitcher. They will be eaten up in the flames of wrath and consumed by the breath of the **DESTROYER**."

While "Wormwood" passages from the "Book of Revelations" are often cited by Planet X prophecy researchers, the most disturbing *Bible* prophecy comes from "The Book of Joel," which is part of the Jewish Tanakh, and the Old Testament of the *Holy Bible*.

Some 2,400 years ago, Joel predicted a terrible destruction that will befall Israel's enemies in a future cataclysm. This prediction clearly correlates with the scientific Planet X flyby scenarios we'll examine in the next chapter.

It also correlates with the Celtic prophecy written after the death of Jesus and which is noted in the second part of *The Kolbrin Bible*. It is important to note that while the Egyptians and Hebrews called Planet X the Destroyer, it was known to the Celts through their own folklore as the "Frightener."

When the prophecy of the Hebrew prophet Joel and those of the ancient Celts are read together, a profound and inescapable correlation occurs.

Jewish Tanakh, and the Christian Old Testament

- **Joel 3:15** "The Sun and the moon shall be darkened, and the stars shall withdraw their shining."

- **Joel 3:16** "…the heavens and the earth shall shake…: but the LORD will be the hope of his people, and the strength of the children of Israel."

- **Joel 3:19** "Egypt shall be a desolation, and Edom [western regions of present day Jordan and Saudi Arabia] shall be a desolate wilderness…"

The Kolbrin Bible: Celtic Texts of the Coelbook

- **The Silver Bough 7:18** "…I am the prophet to tell men of THE FRIGHTENER, though many generations will pass before it appears. It will be a thing of monstrous greatness arising in the form of a crab…its body will be RED…It will spread destruction across the Earth, running from sunrise to sunset…"

- **The Silver Bough 7:21** "…There will be no great signs heralding the coming of THE FRIGHTENER, it will come when men are least prepared… …It will be a time of confusion and chaos."

- **The Silver Bough 7:22** "I have warned of THE FRIGHTENER, I have done what I am charged to do…"

Up to this point, the prophecies have all spoken about a Planet X cataclysm in our near future, but is there proof that it has been here before? Yes!

The Kolbrin Bible: Egyptian Texts of the Bronzebook

- **Creation 4:5** "…God caused a sign to appear in the Heavens, so that men should know the Earth would be afflicted, and the sign was a STRANGE STAR."

◢ **Manuscripts 33:5**   "...FOUR TIMES THE STARS HAVE MOVED TO NEW POSITIONS and twice the Sun has [appeared to] change the direction of his journey. TWICE THE DESTROYER HAS STRUCK EARTH and three times the heavens have opened and shut. Twice the land has been swept clean by water."

The vast numbers of secular accounts, such as these, which are contained in *The Kolbrin Bible,* clearly establish this ancient Egyptian-Celtic anthology as the preeminent source of Planet X history and prophecy. Naturally, this begs a logical question. "Why haven't we heard of it before?"

Why *The Kolbrin Bible* was Revealed

The first part of what is now *The Kolbrin Bible* was first penned by the ancient Egyptians follow the Exodus as *The Great Book.* It was later translated by the Phoenicians from hieratic, the simpler, cursive form of hieroglyphic writing, into their own language, and copies were distributed as far North as Britain.

Recognizing many similarities to their own folklore, the ancient Celts embraced the work and actively taught it. Following the death of Jesus, Joseph of Arimathea (his great uncle on the side of Joseph) founded the Glastonbury Abbey in Britain, which then became the repository for these texts, as well as those authored by Celtic priests in their own language.

In 1184 CE, English King Henry II ordered an attack on the Abbey, because he viewed these Egyptian and Celtic texts as heresy. The Egyptian accounts of the Exodus differed dramatically from the Hebrew accounts. Likewise, early Celtic Christians loved Jesus as their "Lord and Master," but rejected him as a savior, as indicated in two biographical sketches of Jesus contained in the book, in which he is directly quoted in this regard.

The Kolbrin Bible: Celtic Texts of the Coelbook

◢ **Britain 2:13**   "Jesus was then asked if He was one with God, and He answered... 'I have proclaimed all men My brothers, and if I have said I am even as God, then truly I have raised them up also...'"

◢ **Britain 2:24**   "A man asked, 'Where is God? Jesus... said, '...Split a billet of wood, and God will be there. Lift up a stone, and you will find Him.'"

Following the attack on the Abbey, the surviving Celtic priests secreted the remaining texts to Scotland where they were translated into Old English and eventually merged to create the original *Kolbrin.* After WWI, this work was later updated to Continental English and finally revealed in 1992 by a senior member of this secret society after the fall of the Soviet Empire and the warlike rise of radical Islam. These end times harbinger signs were predicted by the Egyptians some 3600 years earlier.

Given the dire Planet X warnings of both *The Holy Bible* and *The Kolbrin Bible*, what can we expect in 2012 in the familiar terms of the worst case and best case scenarios? Both have happened before and were documented by both texts.

Historical Worst Case Scenario

The first recorded European to set foot on the islands of Hawaii, (America's 50th State,) was British explorer Captain James Cook in 1778. Tourists visiting the island today are often regaled with a deluge story unique to the island.

When Cook began explaining the Biblical story of Noah and the flood, the Hawaiians told him that they already had a similar story. The only difference was that their Noah was spelled "Noa." Some think it is a convenient yarn made up by tour guides pandering for a good tip, but the fact is that there are literally hundreds of deluge stories all around the globe.

When the deluge accounts in the *Holy Bible* and *The Kolbrin Bible* are correlated, the similarities are striking.

Noah's Flood, Deluge Correlations	
THE HOLY BIBLE **(King James Version)**	**THE KOLBRIN BIBLE** **(21st Century Edition)**
Gen. 6:5 – 8 ...the wickedness of man was great in the earth...grieved [the Lord] at his heart..."I will destroy ... man ... beast ... creeping thing ... fowl ..." but Noah [whose great-grandfather was Enoch (in German, "Henoch")] found grace in [his eyes] ...	GLN:4:13, 16 ... from afar off came three men of Ardis ... worshippers of The One God ... went to Sharepik, now called Sarapesh [which the Holy Bible calls Zarapheth] and said "... The shadow of doom approaches because of wickedness." ... [but] Sisuda, the King ... shall not perish. [Sisuda] ... sent for Hanok ...
Gen. 6:14 – 16 [Build] ... an ark of gopher wood. [Give it] rooms ... pitch it within and without ... [300 cubits long X 50 cubits wide X 30 cubits high] ... [Give it] a window [1 square cubit above the water line] ... [and] ... a door [in the side] ... with lower, second and third stories	**GLN:4:18, 19** The ... ship was [300 cubits long X 50 cubits wide], finished off above by 1 cubit (1 cubit over the water line) ... three storeys ... without a break ... hatch [in the side] ...

Noah's Flood, Deluge Correlations	
THE HOLY BIBLE **(King James Version)**	**THE KOLBRIN BIBLE** **(21st Century Edition)**
Gen. 7:10, 11, 12, 17, 18, 24 ... after seven days, the waters ... were on the earth ... all the fountains of the great deep ... opened, ... windows of heaven ... opened ... rain ... forty days and forty nights ... flood ... forty days ... [bore] up the ark ... waters prevailed [150 days] ... ark went upon the face of the waters	**GLN:4:28** The swelling waters swept up to the mountain tops and filled the valleys. [They] came in great surging torrents ... the DESTROYER passed away [which should have taken several weeks at least], and the great flood remained seven days [afterward] Then the waters spread out calmly ... great ship drifted ... brown scum ... debris. **OGS:3:22, 23** Then ... came a high wave wall of dark, white-fang-edged waters ... carried everything ... as a broom sweeps the floor ... fruits of the land, house debris, trees, bloated dead animals and humans floated upon the wild, wide waters ... earthy, brown, foamy scum ... great downpouring of rain which stopped after seven days ... surging seas tore between the high mountains ... [Their ancestors] saw the swimming house, made fast against the sea, come up to the land, and out from it came men and beasts from Tirfola [North American continent].

Scientists today tell us that such a global deluge is impossible, as there is simply not enough water on the face of the earth to cover all the land masses. Even if there were "forty days and forty nights" of rain, as the *Holy Bible* tells us, there simply would not be enough rainfall to flood the continents.

However, what the scientists do not examine is the possibility of a surge — in lieu of a deluge. This is where the deluge accounts in *The Kolbrin Bible* lend the *Holy Bible* phrase of "forty days and forty nights" an undeniable prescient brilliance. This also incidentally ties in perfectly with the pole shift prediction of Edgar Cayce, the sleeping prophet. Cayce made two pole shift predictions. The first was the harbinger event prediction, which has been fulfilled, and the second which is the future pole shift itself.

In a pole shift, the continents move about the molten core of our planet most like the loosened peel of an orange. After that, the North and South poles shift to a new location, or completely flip over.

To imagine the consequences of such a catastrophic event, assume that you're driving down the highway in a 50-year old car with a friend, when one of your tires suddenly blows out. Because of the high speed at which you're traveling, you lose control and slam head-on into a bridge embankment. The car, which is solid, immediately stops.

You unfortunately are a bit more fluid, and lacking the restraints of modern cars, you and your passenger fly head-first through the windshield of your car and splash into whatever is ahead of you. With regards to a global deluge caused by a Planet X flyby, the very same mechanism comes into play. Except in this case, the continents are the solid cars, and the oceans are you and your passenger.

Interestingly enough, speed will largely determine survivability in both cases. The more slowly the event unfolds, the greater your chances are of surviving it.

If the pole shift Cayce predicts does happen during the flyby of Planet X, then pray the whole process takes no less than the "forty days and forty nights" spoken of in the *Holy Bible*. If the pole shift completes in less time than that, the loss of life will increase exponentially. Keep in mind that Noah's Flood, or what is known globally as The Great Deluge, followed a pole shift!

The Kolbrin Bible: Egyptian Texts of the Bronzebook

- **Gleanings 4:24** "…the DESTROYER… opened its mouth and belched forth fire, hot stones and a vile smoke. It covered the whole sky above and the meeting place of Earth and Heaven could no longer be seen. In the evening, the places of THE STARS WERE CHANGED, THEY ROLLED ACROSS THE SKY TO NEW STATIONS; THEN, THE FLOODWATERS CAME."

- **Gleanings 4:28** "The swelling waters swept up to the mountain tops and filled the valleys. They did not rise like water poured into a bowl, but came in great surging torrents…"

Cayce and others predicted that this pole shift would happen in 2000, which it obviously has not — as of yet. That being said, there is nothing to suggest to he was wrong about the event itself, and in the grand scheme of things, the universe has its own calendar. In the meantime, let us all pin our deepest hopes and most solemn prayers on the best case scenario.

Historical Best Case Scenario

The Jewish people have celebrated Passover annually since the time of Moses to remember the bitterness of slavery and their miraculous escape from bondage in Egypt. It is the first of the seven annual festivals celebrated by Jews, and it is considered by most to be Israel's foundational feast. It is also called the Feast of Unleavened Bread, and the other six feasts celebrated by Jews build upon the celebration of Passover.

For the Egyptians, the Exodus was a time when their own pantheon of gods failed them miserably. Although they slaughtered better than half of the Jews on the land bridge at the Red Sea, the nation lost an army and a pharaoh in the process. Worse yet, the plagues of Exodus were part of a global catastrophe, and following the Exodus, Egypt had to fight off a massive invasion from the South.

In the aftermath, a studious new pharaoh and his academics and scribes embarked upon the most ambitious anthropological study of the ancient times. They interviewed the wisest of the wise from the many lands and peoples within Egypt's trading spheres with one singular goal in mind. They did it to find clues that would lead them to the one true God of Abraham, which they reasoned was not the god that led the Jews out of Egypt. Rather, it was a lesser god, which nonetheless was mightier than those of Egypt.

The result of this effort was a 20-volume encyclopedia-length work titled *The Great Book*. All that remains of this work are contained in the first six books of *The Kolbrin Bible*. As you read the correlations between the Hebrew accounts of the Exodus and the Egyptian accounts, keep the following in mind:

- The Hebrew account documents the righteous victory of a nation.

- The Egyptian accounts in *The Kolbrin Bible* document a bitter defeat. They are as brutally honest as the conclusions in America's own 9-11 Commission Report.

- After 9-11, Americans reaffirm their relationship with the being that they call the One true God of Abraham. The Egyptians, on the other hand, were left empty-handed, with a bankrupt belief system. A fate certainly worse than 9-11.

If we are to be blessed in 2012, the worst we can expect is another 10 plagues of Exodus. Rather than being the result of a vengeful God intent on punishing a hard-hearted pharaoh, these plagues will result from the same natural disasters caused by solar flares, asteroid impacts and brutal meteorite showers.

Exodus Correlations	
THE HOLY BIBLE **(King James Version)**	***THE KOLBRIN BIBLE*** **(21st Century Edition)**
Ex. 7:20 – 25 "... Moses lifted up the rod ... smote the waters ... in the river in the sight of Pharaoh and ... his servants ... all the water ... in the river ... turned to blood ... fish ... died ... the river stank ... Egyptians could not drink ... blood throughout Egypt ... (plague lasted 7 days)"	**MAN:6:11,12, 14** "Dust and smoke clouds darkened the sky and coloured the waters upon which they fell with a bloody hue. Plague was throughout the land, the river was bloody and blood was everywhere [red ash mixed with water]. The water was vile and men's stomachs shrank from drinking. Those who did drink from the river vomited it up, for it was polluted. ... The fish of the river died in the polluted waters;"
Ex. 8:6 – 16 "... Aaron stretched out his hand over the waters ... frogs came up and covered the land ... Moses cried [to] the Lord because of the frogs ... frogs died [from] houses, ... villages and ... fields"	**MAN:6:12-14** "Vermin bred and filled the air and face of the Earth with loathsomeness ... worms, insects and reptiles sprang up from the Earth in huge numbers ..."
Ex. 8:17 – 19 "... Aaron ... smote the dust of the earth ... it became lice in man and upon beast ... Pharaoh's heart was hardened." **Ex. 8:24** "... grievous swarm of flies into ... house of Pharaoh ... servants' houses ... all ... of Egypt ... corrupted by ... swarm of flies. (did not affect Israelites)"	**MAN:6:14** "The fish of the river died in the polluted waters; worms, insects and reptiles sprang up from the Earth in huge numbers."
Ex. 9:3 – 7 "... upon thy cattle, ... horses, ... camels, ... oxen and sheep ... shall be a very grievous murrain (fatal bovine disease) ... all the [animals] of Egypt died. (did not affect Israelites)"	**MAN:6:12** "Wild beasts, afflicted with torments under the lashing sand and ashes, came out of their lairs in the wastelands and caveplaces and stalked the abodes of men. All the tame beasts whimpered and the land was filled with the cries of sheep and moans of cattle."
Ex. 9:10 – 11 "... They took ashes from the furnace ... stood before Pharaoh and ... sprinkled it up toward heaven ... it became a boil breaking forth with blains upon man and ... beast..."	**MAN:6:12** "The dust tore wounds in the skin of man and beast ..."

Exodus Correlations	
THE HOLY BIBLE **(King James Version)**	**THE KOLBRIN BIBLE** **(21st Century Edition)**
Ex. 9:23 – 25 "Moses stretched forth his rod ... and there was hail and fire mingled with the hail [such as never before when Egypt was a nation] ... The hail smote all ... of Egypt that was in the field, [man, beast, herb and tree] (did not affect Israelites) "	**MAN:6:13-14** "The face of the land was battered and devastated by a hail of stones which smashed down all that stood in the path of the torrent. They swept down in hot showers, and strange flowing fire ran along the ground in their wake. As the DESTROYER flung itself through the Heavens, it blew great gusts of cinders across the face of the land."
Ex. 10:13 – 15 "Moses stretched forth his rod ... [God] brought an east wind [which] brought locusts ... rested in the coasts ... very grievous ... no such locusts before or after ... covered the earth ... ate ever herb and fruit that the hail left ... left nothing green ..."	**MAN:6:14** "Great gusts of wind brought swarms of locusts which covered the sky."
Ex.10:22 – 23 "And Moses stretched forth his hand toward heaven; and there was a thick darkness in all the land of Egypt three days: They saw not one another, neither rose any from his place for three days: but all the children of Israel had light in their dwellings."	**MAN:6:14** "The gloom of a long night spread a dark mantle of blackness which extinguished every ray of light. None knew when it was day and when it was night, for the Sun cast no shadow. The darkness was not the clean blackness of night, but a thick darkness in which the breath of men was stopped in their throats. Men gasped in a hot cloud of vapour which enveloped all the land and snuffed out all lamps and fires. Men were benumbed and lay moaning in their beds. None spoke to another or took food, for they were overwhelmed with despair. Ships were sucked away from their moorings and destroyed in great whirlpools. It was a time of undoing."

Exodus Correlations

THE HOLY BIBLE (King James Version)	THE KOLBRIN BIBLE (21st Century Edition)
Ex.11:2 - 12:30 "Speak now in the ears of the people, and let every man borrow of his neighbour, and every woman of her neighbour, jewels of silver, and jewels of gold. And the LORD gave the people favour in the sight of the Egyptians. Moreover the man Moses was very great in the land of Egypt, in the sight of Pharaoh's servants, and in the sight of the people. ... Thus saith the LORD, About midnight will I go out into the midst of Egypt: And all the firstborn in the land of Egypt shall die, from the firstborn of Pharaoh that sitteth upon his throne, even unto the firstborn of the maidservant that is behind the mill; and all the firstborn of beasts. And there shall be a great cry throughout all the land of Egypt, such as there was none like it, nor shall be like it any more. (did not affect Israelites who put lamb's blood on their doorposts and lintels)Israel needs to take a lamb for every house on the 10th day of the month ... lamb without blemish ... male of the first year ... from the sheep or the goats ... keep it until the 14th day ... congregation of Israel shall kill it in the evening ... take of the blood ... strike it on the two side posts and upper door post of the house, wherein ... shall eat it. Eat it in haste, [clothed, with shoes on and staff in hand] ... it is the Lord's Passover. For I will pass through the land of Egypt this night and ... smite all the firstborn, man and beast. The blood shall be ... a token ... when I see the blood, I will pass over you, and the plague shall not be upon you ... [God] smote all of the firstborn of Egypt, from the firstborn of Pharaoh to the firstborn of captives in the dungeon, and all of Egypt's cattle. Pharaoh rose up by night and all his servants ... a great cry in Egypt ... not a house where there was not one dead."	**MAN:6:19, 21, 22, 24** "On the great night of the DESTROYER's wrath, when its terror was at its height, there was a hail of rocks and the Earth heaved as pain rent her bowels. Gates, columns and walls were consumed by fire and the statues of gods were overthrown and broken. People fled outside their dwellings in fear and were slain by the hail. Those who took shelter from the hail were swallowed when the Earth split open. The land writhed under the wrath of the DESTROYER and groaned with the agony of Egypt. It shook itself and the temples and palaces of the nobles were thrown down from their foundations. The highborn ones perished in the midst of the ruins and all the strength of the land was stricken. Even the great one, the first born of Pharaoh, died with the highborn in the midst of the terror and falling stones. The children of princes were cast out into the streets and those who were not cast out died within their abodes. There were nine days of darkness and upheaval, while a tempest raged such as never had been known before. When it passed away brother buried brother throughout the land. Men rose up against those in authority and fled from the cities to dwell in tents in the outlands. The slaves spared by the DESTROYER left the accursed land forthwith. Their multitude moved in the gloom of a half dawn, under a mantle of fine swirling grey ash, leaving the burnt fields and shattered cities behind them. Many Egyptians attached themselves to the host, for one who was great led them forth, a priest prince of the inner courtyard."

Exodus Correlations	
THE HOLY BIBLE **(King James Version)**	**THE KOLBRIN BIBLE** **(21st Century Edition)**
Ex. 13:20 "And they took their journey from Succoth, and encamped in Etham, in the edge of the wilderness. And the LORD went before them by day in a pillar of a cloud, to lead them the way; and by night in a pillar of fire, to give them light; to go by day and night: Speak unto the children of Israel, that they turn and encamp before Pi–hahiroth, between Migdol and the sea, over against Baal–zephon: before it shall ye encamp by the sea. For Pharaoh will say of the children of Israel, They are entangled in the land, the wilderness hath shut them in. And Moses stretched out his hand over the sea; and the LORD caused the sea to go back by a strong east wind all that night, and made the sea dry land, and the waters were divided. And the children of Israel went into the midst of the sea upon the dry ground: and the waters were a wall unto them on their right hand, and on their left. And the Egyptians pursued, and went in after them to the midst of the sea, even all Pharaoh's horses, his chariots, and his horsemen. And it came to pass, that in the morning watch the LORD looked unto the host of the Egyptians through the pillar of fire and of the cloud, and troubled the host of the Egyptians, And took off their chariot wheels, that they drave them heavily: so that the Egyptians said, Let us flee from the face of Israel; for the LORD fighteth for them against the Egyptians. And Moses stretched forth his hand over the sea, and the sea returned to his strength when the morning appeared; and the Egyptians fled against it; and the LORD overthrew the Egyptians in the midst of the sea. And the waters returned, and covered the chariots, and the horsemen, and all the host of Pharaoh that came into the sea after them; there remained not so much as one of them. But the children of Israel walked upon dry land in the midst of the sea; and the waters were a wall unto them on their right hand, and on their left."	**MAN:6:25, 30, 31, 32, 35, 38** "Fire mounted up on high and its burning left with the enemies of Egypt. It rose up from the ground as a fountain and hung as a curtain in the sky. In seven days, by Remwar the accursed ones journeyed to the waters. They crossed the heaving wilderness while the hills melted around them; above, the skies were torn with lightning. They were sped by terror, but their feet became entangled in the land and the wilderness shut them in. They knew not the way, for no sign was constant before them. The host of Pharaoh came upon the slaves by the saltwater shores, but was held back from them by a breath of fire. A great cloud was spread over the hosts and darkened the sky. None could see, except for the fiery glow and the unceasing lightnings which rent the covering cloud overhead. A whirlwind arose in the East and swept over the encamped hosts. A gale raged all night and in the red twilit dawn there was a movement of the Earth, the waters receded from the seashore and were rolled back on themselves. There was a strange silence and then, in the gloom, it was seen that the waters had parted, leaving a passage between. The land had risen, but it was disturbed and trembled, the way was not straight or clear. The waters about were as if spun within a bowl, the swampland alone remained undisturbed. From the horn of the DESTROYER came a high shrilling noise which stopped the ears of men. The slaves had been making sacrifices in despair, their lamentations were loud. Now, before the strange sight, there was hesitation and doubt; for the space of a breath, they stood still and silent. Then all was confusion and shouting, some pressing forward into the waters against all who sought to flee back from the unstable ground. Then, in exaltation, their leader led them into the midst of the waters through the confusion. Yet many sought to turn back into the host behind them, while others fled along the empty shores. Then the fury departed and there was silence, stillness spread over the land while the host of Pharaoh stood without movement in the red glow Then, with a shout, the captains went forward and the host rose

After reading this chapter, you may be asking yourself, "can we survive?" Take heart; we have before and we shall again. It is why the ancients labored so hard to pass along their experiences, wisdom and predictions to us.

The Kolbrin Bible: Egyptian Texts of the Bronzebook

- **Manuscripts 3:9** "...the hour of the DESTROYER is at hand."

- **Manuscripts 3:10** "In those days, men will have the Great Book [earliest name given to the work] before them [upon its return], wisdom will be revealed, the few will be gathered for the stand, it is the hour of trial. The dauntless ones will survive, the stouthearted will not go down to destruction."

At the close of each of his Cut to the Chase Internet radio shows, Marshall Masters ends with "I'll see you on the backside." The "backside" will be the glorious years to follow after the next Planet X flyby, and it will belong to the stouthearted.

See you on the backside.

4

2012 Flyby Scenarios

When discussing Planet X with those new to the topic, the most common question they'll ask you is, "so if this is such a big thing, why haven't we heard about it already?" Be patient, because they've been hearing about Planet X since they were children. They cannot see that, because they lack the context. Not the facts.

As we saw in "Chapter 3 - Historical Accounts of Previous Flybys," Christians and Jews have been studying the last two flybys of Planet X for thousands of years. We know them as the Biblical allegories of Noah's Flood and Exodus. In a scholarly sense, these Biblical allegories document the birth of a nation and its right to exist.

For Planet X researchers, they encapsulate abstract scientific ideas with bigger-than-life characters and spellbinding narratives so powerful that they endured the millennia with unquestionable success. The data has always been there in the *Holy Bible,* and thanks to the secular writings of *The Kolbrin Bible*, we have a key to unlock the knowledge.

Unlocking the Planet X Scenarios in the Holy Bible

Noted Planet X historian Greg Jenner says, "*The Kolbrin Bible* is the Rosetta Stone of Planet X." (See "Appendix B — History of *The Kolbrin Bible*" for a more detailed history of this work.) Not only does this ancient wisdom text offer us a Rosetta Stone path to the Holy Bible, it also connects us to a broad range of other folklore and secular prophecy. Or as the ancient Romans so aptly put it:

Uno itinere non potest perveniri ad tam grande secretum. *The heart of so great a mystery can never be reached by following one road only.*

For those willing to embrace such a philosophy, a global examination of all the historical accounts of the last two flybys of Planet X yields a very clear pattern. On a micro view, the last two flybys wrought global cataclysms upon the Earth. These events are described in the Biblical stories of Noah's Flood and Exodus, but do they stand alone? No!

On a macro view, the folklore and wisdom texts of virtually every indigenous culture in the world tell similar stories. Regardless of the allegories used, all coincide in time and description with the Noah's Flood and Exodus accounts in the Holy Bible.

Of specific interest are the striking correlations between the Hebrew accounts in the *Torah* (Old Testament) and the Egyptian accounts in *The Kolbrin Bible* of these two events. Both texts were penned at about the same time and often agree on key points.

For example, both the Hebrew and Egyptian accounts intentionally omit the name of the Pharaoh of Exodus and those of his family members; they both establish that Moses was a prince of Egypt and that the Egyptians freely gave the Jews precious metals and gems.

Dissimilarities exist, as well. For example, the Hebrew version tells us that Moses led most, if not all, of the entire host across the exposed land bridge of the Red Sea before Pharaoh's army was destroyed. In contrast to that, the Egyptian account tells us that better than half of the host was massacred before the waters flooded back over the land bridge. It further tells us that Pharaoh died at the Red Sea, and that shortly after this brutal military defeat, Egypt was invaded from the South by starving armies, who were also affected by the Ten Plagues.

We'll examine these Exodus aspects more carefully when we examine the best-case scenario later on this chapter, but first we need to take a careful look at the worst-case scenario, which is based on Noah's Flood.

When it comes to giving us a complete picture of what happened during Noah's Flood (Deluge), the Holy Bible and *The Kolbrin Bible* click together like a box of Legos to create a whole new understanding of exactly what happened and how it could happen again — to us! Why is this?

Much of the entire Egyptian account of what happened during the Deluge was lost in the arson of the Glastonbury Abbey in 1184. Luckily for us, the critical historical accounts of *The Kolbrin Bible* that were lost in that blaze can be found in the *Torah* (Old Testament), and within this link, we find a scientific explanation of "40 days and 40 nights" that works.

Worst Case Scenario — Deluge Surge with Pole Shift

A common red-herring rejection of the flood story in the Bible is that there is simply not enough water on the planet to cover all the continents. Another red-herring rejection is that

"40 days and 40 nights" of rain spoken of in Genesis is nothing more than a good monsoon at most. Certainly not a global flood — all true but ... these red-herring rejections only work when the Bible is scientifically analyzed out of context.

When science is correctly applied to the allegories contained in Genesis and the historical accounts in *The Kolbrin Bible*, a prescient explanation takes shape that is frightening in its scope.

Frightening? Yes, when one takes into account the pole shift prediction of Edgar Cayce, the 'sleeping prophet,' who first described a coming pole shift at the outset of this millennium during the late 1920's and early 1930's.

A pole shift is the result of the Earth's crust moving independently from the core of the Earth to change the location of the continents relative to the Earth's spin axis.

To help visualize how it works, imagine you've just removed the peel from an orange in one continuous piece. Next, wrap the peel back around the flesh of the fruit and imagine the surface of the Earth with deep ocean trenches and towering mountain ranges. Assuming the crust is the peel, and the flesh of the fruit is the Earth's core, a pole shift describes how the peel rotates to a new position over the flesh of the fruit.

A common misconception is that, during a pole shift event, the Earth literally flips head over heels, so to speak. While an extreme flip is theoretically possible, it would also be an extinction level event for all life on Earth. Even the cockroaches would disappear.

During the 19th and 20th centuries, various prophets predicted a pole shift for these times, but Edgar Cayce's prediction is the most remarkable, because it correlates perfectly with the Deluge accounts in the Holy Bible and *The Kolbrin Bible*.

Edgar Cayce

"...where there has been a frigid or semi-tropical climate, there will be a more tropical one, and moss and fern will grow."

What makes Cayce's prediction so compelling is that he is not saying there will be a head over heels flip. Rather, he is telling us the continents will move thousands of miles to different climate zones. Not by a difference of kind, but by a difference of degree. Assuming it takes at least "40 days and 40 nights" to complete the process, we can survive an event of this nature.

Or in other words, the time it takes, and not the distance of the shift, will largely determine whether we survive as a species — or not.

Time and Distance

According to *The Kolbrin Bible,* a pole shift with a distance similar to the Cayce prediction preceded the Deluge known to us in the Bible as Noah's Flood. *The Kolbrin Bible* likewise pinpoints the time frame, which is strikingly similar to the "40 days and 40 nights" mentioned in Genesis.

The Kolbrin Bible: 21st Century Master Edition

- **Gleanings 4:24**   "… In the evening THE PLACES OF THE STARS WERE CHANGED, they rolled across the sky to new stations [the pole shift occurs], then the floodwaters came [which caused the oceans to slosh across the land]."

- **Gleanings 4:27**   "…THE SHIP WAS LIFTED BY THE MIGHTY SURGE OF WATERS [the ancients actually described this as a surge — not a flood] and hurled among the debris, but it was not dashed upon the mountainside because of the place where it was built…"

- **Gleanings 4:27**   "The swelling waters swept up to the mountain tops and filled the valleys. They did not rise like water poured into a bowl, but came in GREAT SURGING TORRENTS [much like tsunamis, which come in a series of waves]…"

When we read *The Kolbrin Bible* account, we see no evidence of a sudden cataclysm, but just as the Holy Bible tells us, the event occurred slowly, over a period of weeks. Had it occurred in a matter of days, the Deluge would have been an extinction-level event (ELE). This is because the tectonic motion would cause massive earthquakes while destabilizing the atmosphere and oceans.

A pole shift that takes only a few hours would cause earthquakes off the Richter scale. Some of them could conceivably be as strong as a sunquake. A recently observed sunquake was triggered by an ordinary solar flare. The energy released in that event was roughly equivalent to a magnitude 11.3 earthquake. Or in other words, 40,000 X more energy than the 1906 earthquake that leveled San Francisco, California.

As these massive quakes turn the continents and sea floors of our world into seismic, wobbly gelatin molds, the atmosphere would scour the surface of the planet with winds in excess of 625 mph (1000 km/h), along with mile-high tsunami waves.

An ELE of this scale would be as devastating as the Cambrian-Ordovician extinction event, which occurred some 488 million years ago. Or worse yet, it would be as severe as Earth's first major extinction event, The Late Great Bombardment of 3.9 billion years ago, which killed over 99% of all life on the planet.

Should the worst happen, there would be little left of complex life on this planet and single cell organisms. Given that none of the predictions in ancient folklore and historical texts suggests this dire possibility for 2012, what can we expect, and is it survivable?

A Survivable Deluge

Deluge stories are found all across the globe, which proves that this global ELE is globally survivable as well.

To get a feeling for what happens, let us consider an example of a pole shift of 5000 km (3125 miles). This corresponds, for example, to the North American continent moving to the location where now the North Pole is.

TIME — Torah (Old Testament) — 960 Hours

- **Genesis 7:11** "… and the windows of heaven were opened."

- **Genesis 7:12** "And the rain was upon the earth FORTY DAYS AND FORTY NIGHTS. "

- **Genesis 7:17** "… the flood was forty days upon the earth; and the waters increased, and bare up the ark, and it was lift up above the earth."

- **Genesis 7:24** "…the waters prevailed upon the earth an hundred and fifty days."

DISTANCE — Edgar Cayce — 3,125 miles (5,000 km)

- "…where there has been a frigid or semi-tropical climate, there will be a more tropical one, and moss and fern will grow."

In the previous worst case example, the shift takes only a few hours during, which the Earth flips completely over, with the possibility of earthquakes as strong as sunquakes. A sunquake can deliver 40,000 times more energy than the 1906 earthquake that leveled San Francisco, California.

Now, let's stretch this doomsday event of just a few hours, into the Biblical timescale of 960 hours, and combine that with a distance suggested by Edgar Cayce's prediction of 3,125 miles (5,000 km). When we do that, the math clearly works to our advantage!

Biblical Time + Cayce Distance = Survival

Shifting a distance of 3,125 miles (5,000 km) over a period of 960 hours means that the poles would shift at a rate of 78 (125 km) miles a day. This would then give the event an average speed of 3.25 mph (5.2 km/h).

Does this mean we could survive a pole shift? Yes, because this time and distance would be comparable to the pace of the ground motion that occurred during the 1906 San Francisco earthquake. Granted, even an event of this magnitude will be devastating, but it will be survivable.

There is the possibility that it could be even milder, if the whole crust of the Earth moves in a somewhat synchronous manner. In this case, earthquake activity will still be severe, but not continuous, and those riding out the event in ships at sea or deep underground will have an excellent chance of survival. However, the greatest loss of life will be amongst those living on or near the shore.

What to Expect

The term "great surging torrents" in Gleanings 4:27 of *The Kolbrin Bible* tells us what to expect. The oceans will still slosh onto the land, and entire continents will be flooded; but it would not be a Sumatra-style tsunami. *The Kolbrin Bible* also tells us that the stars first changed place in the heavens, after which the waters rose.

Ergo, the pole shift begins with movement of the Earth's crusts. In response to this, the oceans surge across the land in a slow, but persistent rise. In a manner of speaking, it will be much like a slow motion slosh, like water sloshing out of a pail.

Consequently, the continents shift to new positions, but the oceans will lag behind them in an asymmetrical manner. In other words, the land and sea will not move as one.

Here, we find a scientific smoking gun to validate the 40 days and 40 nights of rain described in the Biblical story of Noah.

As a result of the asymmetrical movements of the land and sea, the atmosphere will likewise move separately from the other two. Consequently, humid air from above the seas will be pushed across landmasses and then upward, and the water from this air will return to the earth in perpetual, torrential rainfalls lasting throughout the event and for days following it.

The land motion will precede the water motion, but the air will catch up with the land a bit more quickly, since it has less mass and is more prone to friction effects. It will be literally dragged along. Humid air from above the seas will be pushed across land and upward, so the water from this air will come out in the form of torrential rainfall.

Death in the Deluge

In the deluge stories of the *Torah* (Old Testament) and *The Kolbrin Bible,* the protagonists and those close to them survive in floating arks made of wood. Despite the mocking disbelief of most, they nonetheless took action on the knowledge offered them, and prepared accordingly.

In a similar vein, the same is happening today. In "Chapter 10 — Arks for The Chosen," this book takes a present day look at the massive numbers of sea and land arks that are being built at this very moment by various governments.

Those who are chosen to populate these arks will endure a great period of fear. Those left behind will surely perish if they cannot make it to safe ground in time. This is because they will have to swim in turbulent water littered with debris and poisonous man-made chemicals. The common fate for both land mammals and marine life will be death by poisoning, blunt force trauma or crushing.

One may think that deep-sea marine life will be spared, but this will not be so. The turbulence of angry seas will hurl them upward at fantastic speeds, and they will die by decompression.

Virtually all species on the planet will suffer as natural habitats are destroyed. Likewise, most structures built by humans will be swept away, and civilization as we know it will cease to exist. Estimates vary, but a consistent number hovers around a 90% loss of life for all land species, including man. Most marine life will die, and all waters, sweet, brackish and salty, will be filled with rotting carcasses, debris, trees, rubble and such.

As grim as this worst-case scenario is, there is one hope. In Genesis 9:8, we're told that "… God said to Noah … 'I establish my covenant with you: Never again will all life be cut off by the waters of a flood; never again will there be a flood to destroy the earth.'"

May it be so! Now, let's move on to the best-case scenario.

Best case scenario - The 10 Plagues of 2012

Consider this question: How many home libraries already have a copy of *The Origin of Species* by Charles Darwin on the shelf? Likewise, how many will have a copy of *Aesop's Fables* or *Fairy Tales and Stories by Hans Christian Andersen* in the very same home today? Likewise, how many will have them in library a 100 years from now?

The point here is that scientific observations (whether you agree with them or not) tend to get a bit dusty as time marches on. Sure, we may still be reading Darwin in 100 years, but there will certainly be even less interest in the scientific texts Darwin was reading when he was alive. And there is very little of that interest now. Therefore, truths endure through allegories, folklore and storytelling.

All folklore, wisdom texts and mysticism rely upon the use of allegories to convey important facts within certain human events across the passage of time and generations. In this manner, the Bible story of the 10 Plagues of Exodus is an allegorical time machine with ten scientific observations organized in the following order:

Order	Hebrew Name	English Description	Exodus
1	Dam	Water Turns into Blood	7:14-25
2	Tsfardeia	Frogs	7:26-8:11
3	Kinim	Lice or Fleas	8:12-15
4	Arov	Dog Flies	8:16-28
5	Dever	Cattle Plague	9:1-7
6	Shkhin	Boils	9:8-12
7	Barad	Hail Mixed with Fire	9:13-35
8	Arbeh	Locusts	10:1-20
9	Choshech	Darkness	10:21-29
10	Makat Bechorot	Death of the Firstborn Son	11:1-12:36

All ten of these scientific observations have survived the ages because they were carefully encapsulated within a moving and very human allegory of how G-d punished a hardhearted Pharaoh, according to the Hebrew version of Exodus in the *Torah* (Old Testament).

When we compare that with the Egyptian version in *The Kolbrin Bible*, it allows us the unique opportunity to remove the time machine wrapper from the 10 plague events. By doing this, we can now decode the scientific observations of both the Hebrews and the Egyptians to view a complete picture of the global cataclysm that happened during the last flyby of Planet X. One that, relative to the pole shift and deluge described above, was far less severe.

To begin decoding the Hebrew version of Exodus, we must first start with the causality, which, according to the Egyptians, was not the punishment of a hardhearted Pharaoh. Rather, it was meteorite showers and impact events caused by Planet X, along with increased volcanism and earthquakes.

When we correlate the Hebrew and Egyptian accounts, we see that the 10 Plagues of Exodus are not stand-alone events. Rather, each is but one link in an unbroken chain of catastrophes, where each plague was a natural system failure caused by the effects of Planet X. Then, as with all catastrophic failures, each one piled upon the other in an unbroken chain of events, until the system as a whole finally gave way.

By examining each of these links in the Exodus chain of failure, we begin to see a very likely scenario for 2012. One based on historical fact!

1st Plague — Water Turns into Blood

Visit a local brickyard, and ask how they make those beautiful red bricks used to decorate the outside of our homes. The answer will be simple; "we add iron to the mix."

Keep in mind that Planet X is likely a brown dwarf, which means as an unborn sun, it will be surrounded by a large protoplanetary disk made up of various objects from the size of dust particles on up. Many of these will wind up striking the Earth as iron meteorites, as Planet X swings through the core of our system.

It was the iron in these meteorites that turned the water to blood, no differently than it gives decorative bricks a rich, blood red appearance. This made the waters of the Nile unfit to drink.

The same holds true for those who live in the country and rely on wells with unusually high levels of iron in the water. Even in low concentrations, it stains toilet bowls and makes the water unpalatable.

Now, imagine iron concentrations in the water that are 1,000 times worse. That is essentially what happened during the 1st plague. It was the in the iron meteorites that turned the water to blood. It also made it unfit to drink, but that was not the only problem caused by these meteorites.

2nd Plague — Frogs

In August 2004, University of Arizona researchers found that Schreibersite, an iron-nickel phosphate found in iron meteorites, could help explain the abundance of phosphorus on Earth.

Phosphorus is a very common substance in the universe, and phosphorus compounds are used in matches and incendiary bombs, artillery shells and mortar rounds.

Given that that the 7th Plague was hail mixed with fire, we have a spot-on confirmation that Planet X smote Earth with meteorite showers containing high concentrations of phosphorus-laden Schreibersite.

Therefore, the Schreibersite in the meteorites not only turned the waters of the Nile into a blood-red ecological disaster, it was also partly responsible for fouling the water for humans and cattle. Regrettably, it also proved to be a windfall for algae.

Blue-green algae blooms are common to many parts of the world and readily found in Egypt and America. The primary nutrient for Blue-green algae is phosphorus, and the meteorite storms that pelted the Earth caused a phenomenal increase in blooms.

As Blue-green algae blooms, it does two things that are deadly to life. It removes oxygen from the water, while at the same time releasing a deadly neurotoxin called microcystin. In lower levels, microcystin is a powerful irritant, and as levels began to build up, it reached a point where it so badly irritated the skin of the frogs living in the waters of the Nile that they eventually left the water en masse.

3rd Plague — Lice

The *Torah* uses the word *'Tsfardeia'* to describe common frogs, but the word also includes all species of frogs and toads. This is an important distinction for two reasons. First, because this means the toads left the water because of the building levels of microcystin from the Blue-green algae blooms.

Second, because lice are a primary source of the toad's diet, with the absence of a major predator, the lice population quickly grew to plague level.

4th Plague — Dog Flies

In America, Dog Flies are commonly known as stable flies. In areas like Western Florida and Louisiana, these blood-sucking flies can cause a lot of grief for people, pets and livestock.

As the algae continued to replace the oxygen in the water with growing levels of microcystin, the various water species of the Nile began to die off. This set off the ideal conditions for a plague of Dog Flies.

Unlike the frogs and toads, the marine life of the Nile was condemned to a miserable death, and many kinds of insects began to thrive on the rotting, floating carcasses near the shores of the river.

However, a principle factor for the plague of Dog Flies was again the microcystin in the water. This is because it denied livestock and animals their primary defense against a dog fly outbreak, which is to stand in water up to their necks. Hence, the blood-sucking Dog Flies were given a veritable slow-moving feast of tortured animals to feed upon.

5th Plague — Cattle Plague

Malaria kills as many as 3 million people each year, and it is the fourth largest killer of children five years of age and younger in the third world. Hardest hit are the young children in Sub-Saharan Africa.

Like the blood-sucking female Anopheles mosquitoes that infect us with the Malaria parasite, the 'Arov' (Dog Fly) spreads death in the very same manner. Their American equivalents, the stable flies are known to transmit diseases such as anthrax, Equine Infectious Anemia (EIA) and anaplasmosis to animals. Plus, the bite wounds often become sites for secondary infections.

This brings us to the reason why the Hebrew cattle escaped this plague. The Egyptians watered their livestock at the Nile. There, they faced three deaths:

1. They could not drink the water because of the iron from the meteorites.

2. The microcystin in the water kept them from immersing themselves in the water to fend off the dog flies. Worse yet, the microcystin levels rose to a concentration that is fatal to humans and livestock.

3. The combination of dehydration and Dog Fly bites reduced their immune systems, thereby setting them up for plague parasites.

The Hebrews knew something was wrong with the water, so they kept their animals clear of the river. Therefore, the Egyptian cattle became the prime targets for a plague that spread quickly, thanks to a massive outbreak of Dog Flies.

6th Plague — Boils

Aside from drinking water, the Nile also served as bathing water, laundry water and a sewer to the people. Water that contains microcystin from blue green algae blooms irritates human skin and, in massive doses can cause death. In these conditions, any minor lesions on the hands and feet from hard work will immediately get infected and cause boils, which are very hard to treat.

However, a plague of boils would need even more than this. Within the Hebrew accounts in Genesis, we find that clue in the word 'Shkhin' (usually translated as "boils").

According to the ancient Hebrews, Shkhin was a type of skin disease caused by soot, and soot is a real killer even today. Nearly 2 million children and adults in the 3rd world die each year from the smoke and soot generated by un-vented indoor cooking fires.

Soot is a killer, because it contains active coal, which is, chemically speaking, very reactive. Not only will it irritate and damage the lining of your lungs, it will also damage your skin and irritate it just as badly as the microcystin of the algae. In terms of Shkhin boils, any skin lesion that is under attack from high levels of microcystin in bathing water will become incredibly difficult to treat, even by today's standards.

7th Plague — Hail Mixed with Fire

Although the 10 plagues of Exodus as described in the *Torah* (Old Testament) are highly factual, they were obviously sequenced for dramatic effect. In terms of cause-and-effect the 7th plague should be the first of the plagues due to the interdependencies of the first 6 plagues.

Keep in mind these plagues were not occurring in perfect linear order, but in unequal, yet parallel time frames. However, for an allegory such as the Exodus story in the *Torah* (Old Testament) to be successful over time, it must have a simple linear design. One that is easy for the reader to comprehend and remember.

Unlike previous generations, those of us living today have the science and the understanding to reconstruct the complex 3-dimensional event matrix of the Exodus. Even so, we are tempted by Earth-centric explanations that sound eminently logical on the first pass, but they can only sustain their validity through intricate exceptions.

One such scientific explanation of the 7th plague is the theory that the eruption of Santorini in the Mediterranean caused the 7th plague. However, Egypt is too far away from Santorini to have suffered a lava impact from the eruption. While this volcanism theory offers one explanation, it is built upon a broken chain of cause-and-effect.

Again, we come back to the Hebrew account in the *Torah* (Old Testament), which tells us that the 7th plague was hail mixed with fire, and this is directly corroborated by the Egyptian account in *The Kolbrin Bible*.

⚜ **Gleanings 4:24** "... riding on a GREAT BLACK ROLLING CLOUD came the Destroyer ... The beast with her opened its mouth and belched forth FIRE AND HOT STONES AND A VILE SMOKE..."

The description given in *The Kolbrin Bible* of a hailstorm mixed with fire clearly attributes it to the presence of the Destroyer. Therefore, a rain of fire falling upon the Earth results from a meteorite storm — not volcanism.

Further, this is the only way to explain the iron and phosphorus compounds (such as Schreibersite) that rained down upon the Earth and initiated the first 6 plagues in a simple, unified way. In other words, once you attribute the 7th plague to meteorite storms wrought by the Destroyer, everything fits together without the need for problematic exceptions.

Ergo, *The Kolbrin Bible* is not only "the Rosetta Stone of Planet X" as Planet X historian Greg Jenner put it; it also meets the criteria of Occam's razor, which is often paraphrased as "All things being equal, the simplest solution tends to be the correct one."

8th Plague — Locusts

The Hebrew and Egyptian accounts of Exodus protagonists both focus on Moses and the unnamed Pharaoh of Exodus as the main protagonists. In fact, both texts go to great lengths to avoid the given name of the Pharaoh of Exodus and his family.

Where they differ is in the scope of the event. The Hebrew version is mostly focused on Moses and Pharaoh and little else. Consequently, the plagues are attributed to G-d punishing Pharaoh for being so hardhearted. The resulting impression is that this is a national event, as opposed to a regional or global event.

On the other hand, the Egyptian account clearly tells us that the 10 Plagues of Exodus impacted their own nation, as well as those bordering it. In other words, Exodus was, at the very least, a broad scale, regional event, and the 'smoking gun proof' of that is the 8th plague. This was not just a swarm of locusts, but the worst plague of locusts in the history of humankind.

When you consider that a typical swarm of locusts in Africa can eat approximately 80,000 tons of vegetation a day, multiplying that into a Biblical-scale event boggles the mind. Therefore, in order to find the cause-and-effect linchpin between such a massive plague of locusts and Planet X, we must determine what triggers the swarming behavior in locusts. This is no simple task.

Throughout the history of humanity, the compulsion to find an explanation as to why locusts swarm has tasked many a great thinker. However, the usual suspects of sight, smell and sound never yielded an authentic answer.

According to Dr. Steve Simpson of Britain's Oxford University they never will because after 25 years of exhaustive research he has found the cause. A genetic response triggered by crowding.

What Simpson found is that locusts have a very unique way of coping with dwindling food resources. Instead of competing against each other, they bump into each other.

As their food resources shrink they all converge on what remains. This is when they literally fly into each other and strike a genetic swarm spot located on the back leg. Once crowding has caused these genetic hotspots to be struck often enough, the swarming behavior is initiated.

Therefore, in order to trigger a Biblical-scale locust plague, there had to be a regional if not global loss of habitat. Evidence of that is clearly found in *The Kolbrin Bible:*

> ◢ **Manuscripts 6:13** "Trees, throughout the land, were destroyed and no herb or fruit was to be found. The face of the land was battered and devastated by a hail of stones, which smashed down all that stood in the path of the torrent. They swept down in hot showers, and strange flowing fire ran along the ground in their wake."

Again, we are led back to the 7th plague, hail mixed with fire. This tells us that not only did the waters of the Nile turn to blood from meteorite showers, the African continent was inundated with a iron-rich dust and other calamities that caused deforestation, crop failures and massive loss of habitat.

At the time of Exodus, Imperial Egypt straddled the Nile in a verdant swath of rich vegetation. As the locusts from neighboring regions began swarming due to a sudden depletion of their food supplies, what remained of Egypt's lush farmlands and fruit orchards after the meteorite showers became a dotted patchwork of vegetation oases for converging swarms of locusts.

9th Plague — Darkness

The three days of darkness could have been due to a cloud of smoke from the volcanic eruption on Santorini; that is, given favorable assumptions and a minimal number of problematic exceptions to the theory.

When we read the Egyptian account of the 9th plague in *The Kolbrin Bible*, we see an entirely different explanation:

> ◢ **Manuscripts 5:5** "The Doomshape is like a circling ball of flame which scatters small fiery offspring in its train. It covers about a fifth part of the sky and sends writhing, snakelike fingers down to Earth. Before it the sky appears frightened, and it breaks up and scatters away. MIDDAY IS NO BRIGHTER THAN NIGHT… "

The Egyptians also had multiple names for Planet X, which they referred to as the Destroyer. The term "Doomshape" could be another name for the Destroyer, or it could reference a large satellite in orbit around Planet X. Either way, the message is clear. It filled the atmosphere with so many global dimming particles that it literally blocked the sunlight for three days.

From a cause-and-effect point of view, it would be more logical follow the 7th plague with the 9th plague and to make them the 1st and 2nd plagues of Exodus, respectively.

10th Plague — Death of the Firstborn Son

Of all the plagues, the 10th and last plague has puzzled critical thinkers for millennia. How could one discern the firstborn sons as well as the firstborn of livestock for a silent death in the dark of the night? So for starters, what poisoned them?

The answer to that takes us directly back to what caused the 2nd Plague of Frogs and Toads. Algae blooms. Not only do these blooms fill the water with deadly levels of microcystin, but they also remove the naturally occurring oxygen from the water as they produce dimethyl sulfide. This is a chemical that oxidizes (combines with oxygen) into sulfur dioxide.

Sulfur dioxide is as lethal to humans and livestock as cyanide gas, because it is equally toxic. Evidence of the level of lethality is the 945 men and seven women gassed to death between 1930 and 1980 in American prisons. All were executed with cyanide gas.

Not only is sulfur dioxide as lethal as cyanide gas, it is also a 'heavy' gas. It concentrates near the floor, because it is heavier than most components of air. This would have made it a very lethal substance for those lying near or on the ground floor.

It was a common practice amongst the ancient Egyptians to allow their first born sons to sleep on a bed close to the coolest part of the home — the ground level. The rest of the family would then sleep on the roof, which was usually the second coolest part of the house. Likewise, the firstborn of livestock were usually penned up near the home whenever grazing areas were inaccessible.

Consequently, the firstborn sons were exposed to a much higher concentration of sulfur dioxide as they slept, in contrast to their families above. Likewise, the firstborn of livestock were smaller and shorter than their fully grown parents and were thus exposed to higher concentrations of sulfur dioxide as they slept.

Not only were the firstborn sons and the young of livestock exposed to high concentrations of sulfur, they too were more susceptible to it. Human adults and cows have more developed bodies and can absorb significantly more sulfur dioxide than firstborn (this should rather state 'young', all kids are more susceptible, not just the ones born first).

If a similar scenario unfolds in 2012, it will be made worse by man-made pollution that is pumping significant amounts of sulfur dioxide into the atmosphere. This is because man-made pollution and global warming are already creating optimal conditions for huge algae blooms in many places around the world.

The Global Message of Exodus

On one hand, we can limit our view of Exodus as an important feast that Jews celebrate each year to remind them of how their ancestors were delivered from bondage. On the other hand, if we unwrap the event from the allegory of the Torah (Old Testament) we can easily see a simple, timeless message of survival buried deep within the allegory.

It tells us that time-and-again, the Hebrews survived the plagues because they employed simple preventative measures. The Egyptians, on the other hand, were blindsided by each of the plagues, as a result of their own arrogance and hubris. Not according to the Hebrew accounts in the Torah, but to their own accounts in *The Kolbrin Bible!*

For this reason, the story of Exodus gives each one of us alive today, regardless of race, creed or belief, an urgent warning. We can choose to survive the next flyby of Planet X in the manner of practical Hebrews, or we can die like blindsided Egyptians.

It's the simple things in life!

Part 2 – Reading the Signs

"The intuitive mind is a sacred gift, and the rational mind is a faithful servant.

We have created a society that honors the servant, and has forgotten the gift."

—*Albert Einstein (1879 – 1955)*

Those who say "I'll cross that bridge when I come to it" risk finding themselves in long queues. Standing alongside countless others, they'll likewise pray the bridge remains passable until their turn.

Beyond the far shore, those who prepared might pause long enough to gaze back upon the queues — or not.

5

Surviving What Comes

Paradigms describe how we see the world, and the vast majority of those living in the industrialized world rely upon a materialistic, consumer paradigm. Consequently, when something scares us, we look to see if there is something we can buy or acquire that will help us deal with it. In many cases, this paradigm serves us well, but in the times to come, it lacks the breadth and flexibility to be a true survival paradigm.

In terms of creating a survival paradigm, this chapter is the mortar, and all of the other chapters are the bricks. It offers a high-level how-to strategy for creating a catastrophic survival paradigm.

For those in the midst of the unsettling throes of sudden Planet X / 2012 awareness, reading this chapter may be a little bit frustrating.

If you feel this frustration, that's OK. It is entirely natural and is no reflection upon you. Part 1 is written to address your immediate concerns, so you can return to this chapter when you're ready. After all, one must first gather the bricks before making the mortar, so feel free to revisit Part 1 now.

On the other hand, those of you who've already passed through the throes of sudden Planet X / 2012 awareness, looking at how the mortar is made might be of interest to you. If so, you're ready for the big picture that we call the 5 stages of catastrophism.

The 5 Stages of Catastrophism

Those who research Planet X and 2012 issues for several years will progress through each of the 5 Stages of Catastrophism.

Stage	Description	Level of Awareness
1	Deflection	"I haven't got time for this crap."
2	Internalization	"Oh crap!"
3	Externalization	"Share the crap!"
4	Acceptance	"Crap happens."
5	Enlightenment	"The Universe is unfolding as it should."

Each has its own level of awareness which is often described with "crap," a word you may feel to be offensive at this point. However, before you finish reading this section, you'll see why it works so well.

As we discuss each stage, you'll quickly spot your current level of awareness. Knowing where you are in relationship to others is essential to your own personal survival.

Stage 1 – Deflection

There is an old saying that there are three types of people in the world. The first two are a tiny minority that makes things happen and a larger minority that watches things happen. The third type is the vast majority, and they could care less about what does happen.

This stage is called deflection, because this is an active state. We see things that are in conflict with the comfort or continuity of our lives, and so we usually deflect them by looking the other way. When that does not work, we disparage the messengers with ad hominem attacks that play upon our prejudices, emotions and self-interests. An excellent example is the Bible story of Noah's Flood.

Instead of saying, "you may just have something there, Noah. What's available in the way of staterooms above the waterline?" they mocked and ridiculed him. Then with their last breaths, they were treading water, beating their fists on the hull of the Ark and screaming, "We're sorry for all the terrible things we said about you, but could you please open up? We're drowning. We're drow... We're d.... W... ... ..."

This is where we all must say, "there, but for the grace of God go I," because most of us who become aware of what is to happen in the coming years started out at this very stage.

Why we're different is that something came along completely out of the blue, and it ripped the blinders off our heads. When that happens, there is no going back to the idle bliss of deflection, and this leaves you with four simple options:

1. You deflect your newfound awareness with prescription medications and alcohol. Eventually, your liver will pack it in, but there's always the next option.

2. You pray away your newfound awareness. At first, you'll whisper; then, you'll raise your voice, and finally, you'll raise your fists. All of this is to no avail, because when it comes to Planet X and 2012, it seems that God's answering machine reached its message limit eons ago.

3. You finally accept your newfound awareness, and in that moment of epiphany, you enter stage 2, internalization.

4. Yes, this stage is really a tough one, but before you lament your newfound awareness, consider this. What's coming is nature's way of culling the herd, and now, you hear it coming in time to do something about it. Most never will.

Stage 2 – Internalization

Until Planet X and 2012 become a clear and present danger, the one question that has long been the quintessential harbinger for stage 2 is "Am I nuts?"

If you're wracking your brain with this question, relax. It is one of the self-correcting mechanisms our materialistic societies drill into our psyches from day one to keep us from veering off the path as obedient taxpayers and consumers. Consequently, many of us wrestle with this dilemma in the calm of the night.

Like the character Ebenezer Scrooge in *A Christmas Carol*, we still hope to write off the first ghostly visit from his deceased partner, Marley, with something like "a bad dream, caused by something I ate that disagreed with me." So during the day, we haunt the Internet during lunch breaks and when we have a spare moment, and what we find comes home to roost in the still of the night.

We lay in bed, and once our eyes adjust to the faint moonlight filtering into the bedroom, we begin tracing every nuance in the ceiling above our heads as catastrophic scenes play themselves out in our imagination.

Just as surely as Scrooge was visited by the three ghosts of Christmas all one night, we replay the same scenes each night in our mind. Then one night, the awareness internalizes, and we know we're not nuts. That's when we know we've crossed the threshold, because we now feel the urge to sound the alarm.

Stage 3 – Externalization

As the old saying goes, "misery loves company," and this pretty much sums up stage 3. Until Planet X and 2012 becomes a clear and present danger, this is the most miserable stage of all, because it infects one's life with a terrible loneliness.

While sounding the alarm is a noble thing to do, those in stage 3 tend to forget that most everyone who hears the alarm will be solidly ensconced in stage 1, with it's "I haven't got time for this crap" level of awareness. The result is predictable. Your spouse enrolls for 20 hours of night school classes at the local junior college, you mysteriously drop off of everyone's Christmas card list, and your social calendar starts to look like the dark side of the Moon.

All the while, you're still lying in bed, doing your stage 2 thing, looking up at the bedroom ceiling (which you've memorized in excruciating detail by now) and running the catastrophe scenarios through your head. Then one night, something wonderful happens. You have another epiphany. It's time to repaint the ceiling and make peace with your awareness.

Stage 4 – Acceptance

You'll know you've arrived at stage 4, when you start sleeping as you did before you entered stage 2. In this stage, you know you're not nuts, and that even if you must be alone with this awareness, you must still deal with it. This is when you know in every fiber of your being exactly what poor old Noah went through. Given that Noah did the right thing, that's something you can take comfort in.

During stage 4, you'll separate Planet X and 2012 from your daily life. For those who ask, you'll have brief answers, and good ones at that, because this is a time when you regain control of your life, through the accumulation of knowledge and thought. This will be a powerful time in your life, as it will forever alter your view of the world.

In the past, you may have taken walks through forests before, gossiping on a cell phone or chatting about mundane matters with a friend. Now, you notice the little things. You'll notice squirrels foraging for nuts, a new patch of flowers and much more.

Colors and scents carried on the wind become more vibrant and nourishing. You take it all in, knowing that this simple moment will become a treasured memory in a future time, when the Earth and all her children will endure bleaker days.

In terms of creating your own survival paradigm, you can remain in stage 4 indefinitely, because you've accomplished that part of the journey most vital to survival. This is because you've honed the three essential skills that often decide who is going to live and who is going to die.

1. You can assess your situation quickly.

2. Formulate a plan based on the best possible options.

3. Take immediate and decisive action on that plan.

Consider this; when the cataclysms start happening more quickly and with more severity like a woman in labor, most people expect that they will not be pacing the floor in the waiting room wondering.

They will all be in stage 1, and dragged kicking and screaming through a process that has taken you months or years to work your way through. Except they'll have hours, or at best, days. If they are your loved ones and those for whom you care, you can be the Noah that opens the hatch for them, and they'll follow you. As for the rest?

This is a hard part. You may not be able to save any more than your family and loved ones. The others will not know you, and they will be disoriented by the sudden compression of catastrophic awareness. You can expect this to make them panicky, argumentative and dangerous. Like Noah, you must listen to these poor souls banging their fists on the hull of your ark until all there is left is the creak of unyielding timbers, because if you cling to life, you can only hope to save those you can.

For a few, there comes a fifth and final stage.

Stage 5 – Enlightenment

At the beginning of this section, you were presented with a table, such as the one below, where the first four stages of awareness all used the word "crap," because in these four stages, you're focused on yourself. Ergo, the whole experience is crappy, relative to the more pleasant rewards of a happily-naïve material existence.

Stage	Description	Level of Awareness
1	Deflection	"I haven't got time for this crap."
2	Internalization	"Oh crap!"
3	Externalization	"Share the crap!"
4	Acceptance	"Crap happens."
5	Enlightenment	"The Universe is unfolding as it should."

So why is stage 5 crap free? This is because advancing from stage 4 to stage 5 is about moving towards a change in perspective. Instead of moving ever closer to the dynamics of the cataclysm, you move away from it.

In a manner of speaking, you're no longer walking in the forest. Rather, you sitting atop a high mountain peak with the whole valley spread out before you. This is when you realize the universe is unfolding as it should, but what does that really mean?

It means that you quit filtering the world through the various prisms of our present day belief systems and accept the world about you at face value, warts and all, and without judgment. This is not to say that good becomes evil, and vice versa.

Rather, you see the world again as a young child. It is what it is. Then as a reasoning adult, you will be able to pass through the confrontation and abuse of the coming cataclysm with a far greater clarity of mind and purpose. When this happens, you will possess what could be called the Zen of evolutionary cataclysms.

The Zen of Evolutionary Cataclysms

In human terms, a monumental lesson we're about to learn is why our civilizations rise quickly, degrade slowly and then fail catastrophically. Service to self.

Service to self is a cancer, not a cure, and civilizations that take root in a service to self foundation carry within them the seeds of an early demise. As alien as this may sound, once you accept this notion, your world view changes.

Instead of living in service to self and all the fear that paradigm creates, you begin to live in service to others. When that happens, you're empowered with hope, because you're in it for the species, because you've found a harmonious balance between the needs of the self and the needs of others.

Is this a radical new way of thinking beyond our grasp? No. In fact, the service to others paradigm has enabled numerous indigenous cultures to survive the millennia.

While some amongst us berate them as ignorant savages, we've yet to withstand the very same test of time. Ergo, our unsustainable consumption societies are truly none the wiser, which is not to say we do not possess wisdom. In fact, we possess great wisdom! Case in point is Albert Einstein when he said, "If the bee disappeared off the surface of the globe, then man would only have four years of life left."

News flash. The bees are now disappearing as the result of something called colony collapse disorder (CCD), which is just as much a mystery to us as the disappearance of London's sparrows. Einstein saw this coming half a century ago, and now that it's happening, we're still laughing through re-runs of M*A*S*H. Meanwhile, indigenous cultures are observing these aberrations with great concern.

This is not because we're evil people. It is because we've failed as a culture to fully grasp the concept that the most important survival tool we could ever possess is the universal desire to seek harmony within ourselves and with all that is about us. The very reason why indigenous cultures do survive for millennia.

We must find a harmonious way to incorporate what has worked for them together with our newfound technological capabilities. Once we do, we'll be ready to take our place amongst the stars, and that, in a nutshell, is what 2012 is really all about. A horrifically painful wakeup call that will jolt us into the next stage of our evolution.

If you are feeling anguish because every human on the face of this planet cannot see this simple reality now, it is because of how we've been taught to see the world for hundreds of years.

Dominion View vs. Ecosystem View

Each of us has the choice to view the world about us as a dominion, or as an ecosystem. In simple terms, a dominion is something you exploit. An ecosystem is someone's home.

An easy way to understand the fundamental difference between these dramatically different ways of seeing the world about us begins with the dominion view.

Dominion View

The desired result of the dominion view is to identify, isolate and use some part or aspect of the world about us to satisfy our own wants and needs. In a manner of speaking, we see the world through the lens of a 35mm camera with a powerful zoom lens.

We zoom out and scan the world before us, and then, when we find something of interest, we zoom in on it and then begin the intensive process of zooming, framing and focusing the image until it meets with our expectations. At which point, we snap the picture and move on. What's done is done.

The Achilles heel of this dominion-style world view is that while we're focused on what we wish to exploit, the rest of the world is blurry and out of focus. If we see something large and blurry moving off in the corner of the viewfinder, we repeat the process again. Zooming in, framing and focusing in on the new image.

Consequently, we often miss new opportunities, which of course is the whole point of advertising. It grabs our limited attention, so that we'll zoom in on whatever new opportunities the advertisers are pushing at us. These can also include developing threats, such as: Quick, look here to learn more about breast cancer or protecting your assets.

In terms of more general threats to society, we're so busy focusing on whatever it is we need to exploit or acquire that we simply cannot move our cameras fast enough to take it all in. So, we rely on others to do it for us. Or we try our best to be self-informed, within the limitations of our 35mm zoom lens, dominion view of the world.

The end result is that when catastrophe does strike, it often takes us totally by surprise, because we're zoomed in somewhere else. To get a first-hand idea of what this is really like, spend a full day at home with a zoom lens camera.

Wherever you go in the house, or whatever you do, see it through the camera, and only through the camera. But that's not how we see the inside of our homes, is it? Of course not. Our home is our ecosystem, and we expect those who enter our home to respect it and all who dwell in it.

Ecosystem View

With an ecosystem view of the world, you're not separated from the world about you by a zoom lens. Rather, you're a part of this world, so everything about you, near and far, is in focus. Consequently, you see new opportunities and threats developing that you would have otherwise missed.

Respect the opportunities, because you're in someone else's home, and good guests do not leave a mess. Likewise, you're more likely to see distant threats far sooner than you would with a dominion view, as well as safe pathways around those threats.

In the world of cataclysm, taking threats head-on is the last thing you want to do. If you dial 9-11 in 2012, it could be a long time before someone even answers the phone, if ever. Worse yet, if matters degrade into an exchange of gunfire, there will be no emergency rooms stocked with painkilling and lifesaving drugs. Rather, you'll be living in a world where even a small scrape or a sore tooth can be the start of a slow and painful death.

By adopting an ecosystem view of the world, you're not becoming a tree-hugger, if that is how you define environmentalists. You're employing the very basic human skill that saved 100% of all the simple natives during the December, 2004 Indian Ocean Superquake and tsunami.

The moment they felt the ground shaking beneath their feet, the "ignorant natives" as some "civilized" folks would call them stopped whatever they were doing, because they're raised with an ecosystem view of the world. This is why they grabbed their children and started running for high ground, screaming something that would probably translate into "feet, don't fail me now."

Meanwhile, some dominion thinkers with their air-conditioned homes, cars, education and money stood transfixed as the ocean drew back, exposing the seabed. Others ran after it to pick up the stranded fish.

While the "ignorant natives" were giving thanks that not one of them died, the dominion thinkers were burying their dead and asking God, "why?" When there is no answer, we often call it "irreconcilable grief." Or we say "somebody is going to hang for this," which brings us to the notion of governments and conspiracies.

Governments and Conspiracies

Conspiracies are the first oldest profession, and government conspiracies abound. Anyone that tells you to the contrary is either profiting from them or is a mindless twit. They do exist, and with layers upon layers, replete with a global cast of heroes, villains and opportunistic ne'er-do-wells of every imaginable shape and form.

Yes, being aware of conspiracies is helpful; nonetheless, squandering precious time on them can work more against your chances of survival than the conspiracies themselves.

Therefore, the best thing to do with conspiracies is to give them wide berth. This is ever so much easier to do with an ecosystem view of the world, because it helps you to stay focused on your own personal zone of survival.

Or, you can fall into a dominion view trap which is much like doing laps in the indoor swimming pool of a sinking ocean liner. You can analyze conspiracies with endless back and forth arguments, but no matter how much water you pound, you always wind up where you started. Yet, the process is seductive so you persist.

As you do, the ocean liner continues to slowly founder, but you're too distracted to notice it, because the water in the indoor pool remains level at the surface. Reassured by this, you continue doing laps, even though things seem to look a bit off kilter.

Then suddenly, your head bounces off the floor of the swimming pool. This is not good, because the ship has finally lost whatever remained of its buoyancy, which brings you to three certain conclusions about conspiracies and foundering ships:

- On the downside, the pool water now has a salty taste, which tells you that what was once a slow foundering is now a fast death plunge to the ocean floor.

- On the upside, cheer up. It will be mercifully quick, and you're dressed for the occasion.

- Take the long view. You body will nourish sea life that will eventually be swept up in a drag net and used in some libido-enhancing, oriental soup.

The point here is that the cataclysm coming our way will be so powerful that it will sink most conspiracies and their conspirators. In terms of Planet X and 2012, we're all passengers in a foundering ship. Leave the 1st class cabins to the conspirators, and find a way to get to the boats.

This, of course, begs an interesting question. Given that we've yet to board the ship, when should one start looking for the lifeboats? The answer is that you start looking today, through the power of your own imagination.

Programming Your Brain for Survival

An old adage tells us, "what doesn't kill you makes you stronger." Granted, those most likely to tell us this are usually trying to kill us at the same time. Yet, the logic stands, because this coming cataclysm will be unstoppable and beyond human control. For decades, governments and power cabals have been preparing for this event on a scale that few could imagine.

The operative word here is "imagine." To illustrate the point, let's assume the following. You've decided to respond like a government, and the first thing you do is to build a 9-foot fence around your back yard, so as to block prying eyes.

During the cover of night, you play music with a boom box just while building a nice bunker in your back yard. When it is finished, you stock it full of supplies, food, fuel, weapons and ammunition, and you seal it up. Just for extra measure, you build a gazebo over it and then refinance the house to buy a brand new Hummer. Now, you're set, and you go on about your life, confident in knowing that you've got the best secret survival plan in the neighborhood.

As luck would have it, the guacamole hits the fan while you and the family are out of town visiting relatives, and sheer chaos ensues. Power lines are down, the Red Cross is running out of supplies, the National Guard is patrolling the streets, and the stores are out of everything. You're lucky; you topped off the tank in your Hummer before the chaos, and now you've got just enough fuel to make it home to your bunker. No worries.

The going is rough because bridges have collapsed, and tornadoes have ripped out huge chunks of paving, but that's where a Hummer shines. You pat yourself on the back. What a great investment.

After clearing the last check point, your Hummer starts to cough. Starved for fuel, it barely gets you into the driveway before the engine fails. That's OK. You've barely made it home, but you've got 100 gallons of fuel in the bunker. Again, you pat yourself on the back as you and the family jump out of the Hummer and run around to your back yard. No worries.

The next thing you know, you're standing there looking at the pile of debris that was once your gazebo and what's left of your bunker, which is nothing. Everything is gone, and as the reality of it sinks in, your wife nudges you in the ribs and motions for you to look up.

There, looking down on you from the 9' fence, are your neighbors. They're aiming your guns at you, loaded with your ammunition, and they've only got one question. "Where's the other bunker?"

How do you tell them there is no other bunker?

So how did you get here? You reacted like a consumer – not like a survivor. Consumers dig bunkers, fill them with supplies and buy practical survival vehicles like Hummers. Then, they feel free to resume their usual routine, knowing in the back of their minds they have a plan. Survivors, on the other hand, use the luxury of time in a very different way.

Programming Your Neural Network for Survival

Survivors begin surviving by first sitting under a tree and contemplating that, which is about to happen. For consumers, this seems like a silly waste of time, especially when you know there is a freshly stocked bunker under your gazebo and a shiny new Hummer in the driveway.

Yet, the survivor already knows what every military planner expects. Once the shooting happens, events on the ground dictate the rules. This is why military planners spend so much time visualizing the battlefield in their mind with war games. By doing this, they create a framework of ideas and concepts that will enable them to rapidly and decisively respond to what will become a fluidic and fast-moving situation. After they feel they've identified as many variables as possible, they know what they need, and that's when they go shopping.

There is another benefit of these war games. As you create them, you also create new neural networks in your brain. In a literal sense, you hardwire your brain to perform in these circumstances. In order to make this work, you must visualize yourself dealing with all of the variables in this war game scenario.

If you are serious about surviving the natural catastrophes most likely to beset your geographic area, as well as those you'd normally never expect, now is the time to use your imagination like a war gamer.

Identify as many threats and threat combinations as possible that make sense to you. Then, find a quiet place where you can be alone with your thoughts, and then use your imagination to explore each of them, one by one.

Close your eyes, and then, using your imagination, begin by seeing yourself doing whatever you do in the course of a normal day. Then, imagine the event. Perhaps it begins with sirens and the sight of co-workers fleeing the building. Or perhaps you're having a BBQ in the backyard with your family when you begin to feel the Earth shake deep beneath your feet.

As the visualization unfolds, see yourself responding to what is happening. Be honest in evaluating your response. If you see yourself not knowing what to do, make a mental note of that, and find the information you need to fill that gap. A lot of this information is freely available on the Internet and with local agencies.

Once you have the information you need in-hand, it's useless to you unless you have it in-mind. So find your quiet place, and use your imagination to re-run the scenario again. Once you honestly feel that you see yourself handling this particular scenario as you can, play it through to the next day, then the next week, the next month and so on.

Also keep in mind that 2012 is not an absolute date. It is a relative reference to a tribulation that will last for a period of years. You must think of it in that context.

Personalizing the Process

Another aspect of all this is that each of us comes to it in our own way. There is no "one-size-fits-all" approach to this. After you work through your first scenario, tweak the process in a way that makes you feel right with it. Also, find a pace that does not interrupt your life, but one, which you can follow on a consistent basis.

Although this form of contemplation would appear to be depressing at first glance, what you will begin to feel is a strong sense of empowerment that will help offset the weight of such unpleasant thoughts. As awkward as this may sound, do you really want to find yourself undergoing on the job training, in the midst of a catastrophic event because you relented to that old colloquialism of "we'll cross that bridge when we come to it?"

Crossing that Bridge When You Come To It

When that old colloquialism nags at you to put dreary thoughts aside and to dwell on more pleasant thoughts, visualize that future bridge in your mind. Not the well-maintained bridges we use today, but tattered structures packed with fleeing refugees from rail to rail.

The human flood is virtually impassable, and so the queue stretches far behind the military checkpoint you'll have to pass through, as well. That is, if they let you.

One of the saddest "we'll cross that bridge when we come to it" chapters in American history comes from the turbulent days of the Civil War. With support for the war waning, President Lincoln gave General Sherman the go-ahead to launch his historic march to the sea that would cut a swath of destruction through the heart of the South. Always on the move, Sherman was ever-pressed for provisions to feed his troops; his supplies further taxed by the thousands of African slaves following his army to freedom.

Faced with dwindling supplies, the situation for Sherman's army was growing desperate, and this spawned tragedy. It happened when a battalion of men, led by Union general Jeff Davis (no relation to the confederate president), reached Ebenezer Creek in South Carolina. The water was too deep and fast to wade across, so Davis ordered his men to construct a pontoon bridge.

After he had moved all his troops to the opposite bank, Davis ordered his men to cut the ropes before the freed slaves could cross, stranding around 5,000 women, children and elderly men, with the confederate army close behind.

In a cruel instant, Davis severed their path to freedom, and desperate to be free, hundreds of the slaves rushed into the turbid stream and drowned while his troops watched in horror from the opposite bank. A few made it across, but most did not. Those who could not brave the water were later put to death by the Confederate troops or returned to slavery.

When Sherman later learned about the incident at Ebenezer Creek, he steadfastly defended what Davis had done as a "military necessity." Consequently, Davis was never reprimanded or brought to trial. Keep this in mind the next time you're discussing Planet X and 2012 with a friend, and they say, "I'll cross that bridge when I come to it."

If you feel the urge to explain the finer points of military necessity to them, ignore it. Your friend is still in stage 1 deflection, and if you press the point, they'll likely rebuke you with "I haven't got time for this crap."

Survival is a personal responsibility, and there is one more thing you can do to enhance your survival skills. One thing you can begin doing today is to watch television news reports in a whole new way.

Reading the News Inside the News

American media enjoy an unfettered freedom of the press with mundane news stories; especially those featuring attractive, but unfortunately dead white females. From a corporate perspective, the beauty of these stories is that they are cheap to produce and generate phenomenal advertising revenues. An added bonus when you consider that investigative news budgets are slimmer than ever before.

Above the level of dead white females, things start to get relative. This is when the consolidation of the media into the hands of a few moguls has paid off handsomely for those who manipulated the U.S. Federal Communications Commission to break with decades of policy, so as to allow that consolidation to happen. Expect filtering and disinformation on key stories.

Are the reporters of the same ilk as the managers who tell them what they can and cannot report? Some are not entirely comfortable with the sellout. Case in point was what happened during Hurricane Katrina.

America was shocked to see people packed in the hot misery that played out in the New Orleans Superdome. Pleading for help, stranded victims were largely ignored by state and federal leaders, who were busy pointing fingers in every direction except the Superdome.

The basic problem was these folks were mostly poor tax burdens. Before Katrina, they would happily tell you that they'd never vote for a Republican president, even if their lives depended on it. Sadly, that belief actualized as a self-fulfilling prophecy. Had they been Republican bankers, their plight would have lit a bonfire under President Bush's backside.

Just when things were getting truly hopeless, something unthinkable happened, and by two TV reporters for the Fox News Network, no less. Framed by the sweltering Superdome in the background, America watched the tears stream down Geraldo Rivera's face.

His pleading, almost poetic monologues were powerful, and beside him was one very furious Shepard Smith. The two went toe-to-toe with Bill O'Reilly and Sean Hannity, who from their cool and comfortable studio in New York, were dismissive of the whole matter. No doubt because corporate executives were telling them to do so. Nonetheless, Rivera and Smith refused to back down.

Anderson Cooper of CNN made a similar plea, but it was Fox that got the undivided attention of the White House. Bush's most favorable network had two loose cannons on deck, and neither of them would shut up. Now, there would be hell to pay. Something had to be done, and the buck stopped — somewhere — finally.

The lesson to be learned from Katrina is simple. If those who run the government see you as an asset, you're treated as such. Whereas, if they see you as a liability, you're likewise treated as such.

President Bush was simply acting in a manner that was consistent with the history of governance, and Rivera, Smith and Cooper changed the accounting. They forced him to cut his losses short. It's just that simple. Like they say in the Mafia movies, "it's only business," and after this remarkable episode passed, we slid back into the usual, mundane 24/7 coverage of attractive, but unfortunately dead white females.

Still the same, there is a load of great information on TV, especially stories about weather and habitat change. To get the most out of them, watch them like a deaf person. Turn off the sound and turn on the closed captioning. Then play something soothing like Debussy's Claire de Lune on the boom box, and take written notes. You'll be amazed at what you really can notice when you're not listening to theme music that's designed to pump up your heart rate.

Do not worry about missing anything. They'll repeat it again-and-again. Best of all, you will not be distracted by talking heads struggling to stretch 6 minutes of hard news into 60 minutes of watered-down analysis. What you really want are the repeating visuals; the video segments and graphics that are continuously repeated with something new occasionally thrown in. Over time, you'll begin to notice different things, especially when you surf the news channels.

To help you develop this ability, the next two chapters offer special News Inside the News tips for monitoring reports on atmospheric and oceanic events.

6

Reading Signs in the Atmosphere

NASA has announced they expect Earth to heat up to a level beyond anything this world has seen in the last one million years. Assuming our hominid ancestors were trying to walk upright one million years ago, we're talking about Earth changes modern man has never experienced. As a result, NASA speculates that we may see a rise in sea level of up to 25 meters. The key word here is "speculate," even though the evidence to support the NASA statement is already visible.

Now, the exception has become the rule, and during the last decade, freak storms have begun appearing out of the blue. They rage for relatively short times, leave trails of near-total destruction, kill a lot of people — and then vanish.

Forecasters tell us that we've experienced major storms like these in the past and show us historical charts with multiple dates. The fine distinction they gloss over is that the event dates in their charts are separated by decades and centuries. In doing so, they conveniently sidestep the fact that, during the last decade, we've seen this separation of time compress into months and years.

One result of this compression is that we've already had one year that, on a global basis, was a clear harbinger sign of the times to come. Like an engine sputtering to life, the first coughs came with the extra-tropical European storms of 1999. The second and even larger cough was a pandemic of deadly weather in 2005.

Extra-tropical European Storms

In autumn, Western Europe commonly suffers from extra-tropical storms, and some are intensely violent. They are called extra-tropical storms because the mechanism that creates and fuels them is the very same mechanism seen in Atlantic hurricanes passing through the Caribbean, such as Hurricane Katrina in 2005.

Extra-tropical storms are caused by the onset of winter, and the period between November and February is traditionally a season of stronger storm activity for most of northwest Europe.

These storms incubate when the atmosphere cools more quickly than the ocean below. This releases heat into the atmosphere, which in turn feeds instabilities in the atmosphere; they then morph into powerful extra-tropical storms. Especially hard hit are the British Isles, but these types of storms have been the norm throughout recorded history.

That would change in the autumn of 1999, when a highly unusual storm depression moved in from the Atlantic Ocean towards Brittany (the westernmost peninsula of France). Fed by relatively warm ocean air, a fast-moving storm system developed. Before reaching shore on December 26, it deepened quickly, and European meteorologists dubbed it Lothar.

Extra-tropical Storm Lothar

Being at a moderate latitude, France is no stranger to Christmas storms. The same mechanism that drives these holiday season storms in Europe, also drives tropical hurricanes as well. Temperature differences between the sea and the air above it are the engine of this mechanism.

A normal pattern of development for such a storm, once it reaches land, is that it begins to lose its 'engine'. When the storm is over the ocean, the engine is revved up by the energy generated by the warmer water beneath it and zooms along at a fast pace. Once it reaches land, the energy source is land, which is cooler. This starves the storm of energy, and so, it begins to sputter.

The speed at which it sputters out depends on how fast the storm is traveling when it makes landfall. When it is over the ocean, it is fed by a warm, slick ocean that gives it power and speed. On the other hand, land is cool and coarse, so the storm naturally begins to sputter, because it is starved for energy while simultaneously having to deal with increased friction.

This has always been the normal pattern of storm development until Lothar hit France in December 1999. In the lull between Christmas and New Years, Lothar defied logic and history.

Instead of sputtering out as it moved onshore into the cool and coarse landscape of France, it kept acting just as though it was still over the ocean. European meteorologists were stunned by the storm's behavior. Its mechanism raced on unchecked, gaining both in intensity and speed.

In just over 6 hours, Lothar ravaged approximately 900 kilometers of the French country-side between Brittany on the west coast and the Lorraine region on the border between France and Germany. The destruction it left in its wake was a clear harbinger sign of what Hurricane Katrina would do to New Orleans in 2005.

Tropical storms and hurricanes automatically conjure up mental images of devastating wind speeds, and this is what happened with Lothar. While over the ocean, it sped up to ma-jor tropical storm strength (11 Beaufort), and then once it made landfall, it developed into a hurricane-strength (12 Beaufort) monster. Consequently, the impossible happened before our very eyes as Paris was slammed by 109 mph (175 kph) wind gusts.

By the time Lothar reached the Black Forest in southwest Germany, at the northern edge of Switzerland, it had grown in horrific proportions with measured wind gusts up to 149 mph (240 kph), and in the process, claimed scores of victims and left a good portion of France without electrical power for nearly a week.

The destruction was so pervasive that the French authorities had to declare a state of emergency for Paris and its surroundings. They likewise deployed their military to maintain order and to help clear the rubble, and as the French began to pick up the pieces, they ner-vously hoped that Lothar would be remembered as a one-time, freak event. It wasn't long be-fore nature would shred that tentative hope apart.

Extra-tropical Storm Martin

During hurricane seasons, people are used to seeing hurricanes ranked according to the Saffir-Simpson scale. A class 1 hurricane will do some damage, but a class 5 is the mother of all bad news. As Hurricane Katrina approached New Orleans and the Gulf Coast in 2005, it built itself to a class 5. Once it made landfall, it lost enough energy and strength to become a class 3 hurricane, but one big enough to knock out the levees and flood New Orleans.

To put this in a European perspective, Lothar slammed through France with all the vi-cious energy and strength of a class 2 hurricane. Even for storm-hardened Floridians, a class 2 hurricane is something to fear when it is headed your way.

This is why Europe's guts went into a collective twist just days after Lothar cut its swath of destruction across the Northern half of France. Another extra-tropical storm rolled in right behind Lothar, surprising everyone, most especially the meteorologists, who dubbed it Mar-tin. With all the strength of a class 1 hurricane, it slammed through the Southern half of the country.

Coming in from the Atlantic, as Lothar had done, Martin made landfall just north of Bor-deaux and raged across the country from west to southeast. Like its bigger brother Lothar, Martin left a trail of destruction and woe right up to the foot of the Alps with its exceptionally strong winds and beating rains.

Although it packed a marginally smaller punch than Lothar, Martin was far more deadly. Between the two storms, the European death toll reached 140, and the material damage in France alone exceeded 5 billion Euros.

The results of Lothar and Martin were unsettling questions that remain to this day for Europeans. Were these two storms freakish, random events? Or, do they signify a fundamental change in storm behavior for the European continent?

For everyone else, the question is broader in scope and portends even greater dangers. Extra-tropical storms Lothar and Martin both occurred during the 1999 solar maximum, which peaked in September of that year. The next solar maximum will occur in 2012, which implies a relationship between solar output and these anomalous storms.

NEWS INSIDE THE NEWS

Extra-tropical European Storms

Regardless of where you live, tracking extra-tropical European storms will give you invaluable trending data. As these forecasts are announced, create your own simple map of the storm's geographic footprint, and note the following data:

- **Point of Origination:** When did the storm form in the season, which is between November and February?

- **Ocean Path and Intensity:** What direction is the storm traveling in, and how much strength is it accumulating?

- **Point of Landfall:** The exact direction, speed and intensity at the point of landfall.

- **Land Path and Intensity:** From the point of landfall, track the storm's strength, change in speed and direction. Be especially keen to track areas where the storm maintains a steady level of intensity and speed and areas where there is a marked increase.

In the years leading up to 2012, we will see solar activity never witnessed in recorded history, so the comfortable distinctions of geography will fade as we approach the next solar maximum.

Will storms everywhere gain strength as they make landfall, instead of sputtering out, as they always have in the past? The first step in examining this broader question is to shift our focus from the cool and coarse Western shores of Europe, across the Atlantic to the balmy shores of the Caribbean.

Atlantic Hurricanes

Without doubt, Hurricane Katrina in 2005 was a horrific wake up call for America. It cut a wide swath of death and devastation through America's Gulf Coast region, leaving New Orleans flooded and helpless. It is keen to note that professional forecasters not only underestimated the 2005 season; they grossly overestimated the 2006 season, as well.

One explanation for this is that forecasters rely on statistical data to help them interpret future trends. The glaring discrepancies between their 2005 and 2006 forecasts suggest that there is a fundamental factor buried in the data that is now changing in a way never seen before. The impact of this change became self-evident during the 2005 Atlantic hurricane season.

The 2005 Atlantic Hurricane Season

The hurricane season for the Atlantic normally runs from the end of June until mid-November, early December. The 2005 Atlantic hurricane season was the most active in recorded history, and Arlene, the first named storm, formed on June 8.

While the 2005 season would be more active, the overall intensity was expected to be less than the preceding 2004 season and end two months earlier than the previous 2004 season. Of the 7 major hurricanes that made landfall, Dennis, Emily, Katrina, Rita, and Wilma were the most deadly and likewise, anomalous record breakers.

Hurricane Dennis

Dennis formed on July 4 and grew to a Category 4 storm. It was the first major hurricane of the season to make landfall, striking Florida as a Category 3. It claimed 89 lives and caused $2.23 billion dollars in damage. However, what made it truly distinctive was that it was the first serious hurricane to make landfall in the US so early in the season. In a typical hurricane season, hurricanes do not make landfall before August.

Hurricane Emily

Emily formed on July 10 and grew to a Category 5 storm. It was the first Category 5 hurricane to form in the Atlantic basin before August. It first slammed into the Yucatan peninsula, the Mexican holiday peninsula, and by the time it had made its last landfall in the state of Tamaulipas in northern Mexico, it had claimed 9 lives and $550 million dollars in damage. All of this happened before the first storm would have hit the shore in a 'regular' seasonal build-up.

Hurricane Katrina

Katrina formed on August 23 as the third most powerful hurricane to ever hit a US coastline and the sixth most powerful to have ever formed in the Atlantic basin. It left New Orleans flooded and flattened the coastal areas of Louisiana and Mississippi. The deadliest hurricane in US history since the 1928 Okeechobee Hurricane, it claimed 1,836 victims and caused $84 billion dollars in damages.

Despite the havoc it wreaked on America's Gulf Coast, Katrina was not a natural record breaker like Dennis and Emily, but it did garner a unique distinction as the first major global-warming hurricane in history. Boston Globe reporter Ross Gelbspan said as much in an opinion-editorial article, and his thoughts were quickly echoed by Britain's deputy prime minister, John Prescott, and Germany's environment minister, Jürgen Trittin.

Although many climatologists were quick to disagree with this assessment, their lack of a solid predictive track record prevented them from quashing the idea early on. In fact, the aftermath of Katrina would create a highly receptive audience for Al Gore's global warming movie, *An Inconvenient Truth.*

Hurricane Rita

Rita formed on September 17 and was the third Category 5 hurricane of the season. The fourth-most intense Atlantic hurricane ever recorded, it will be remembered as the most intense tropical cyclone ever observed in the Gulf of Mexico.

On September 24, it made landfall near the Texas-Louisiana border and caused extensive damage to the coastlines of Louisiana and Texas. It eventually claimed 113 lives and caused $11.7 billion dollars in damage.

Hurricane Wilma

Wilma formed on October 15 and was the fourth Category 5 hurricane of the season. Only two Category 5 hurricanes have ever developed in the month of October, and Wilma was third. The twenty-second storm of a record-breaking season, it was also the most intense hurricane ever observed in the Atlantic basin. It devastated parts of the Yucatán Peninsula and southern Florida and left 63 victims and $28.9 billion dollars of destruction in its wake.

Other 2005 Atlantic Hurricane Season Firsts

With one small exception, the 2005 season broke all standing Atlantic hurricane season records.

- **Number of Storms:** With 28 totals storms, the 2005 season broke the standard record of 21 tropical storms, hurricanes and Category 5 hurricanes in any one season.

- **Number of Hurricanes:** Of the 28 storms, 15 were named hurricanes, breaking the previous record of 12 named hurricanes in any one season.

- **Number of Category 5 Hurricanes:** The previous all-time high had been 2 category 5 hurricanes in any one season. That record was smashed by 4 storms in 2005.

- **First use of "V" and "W" Names:** This was the first storm season to see the names Vince and Wilma.

- **First use of the Greek Alphabet:** The season outlasted the English alphabet designations, so the last 6 named storms were: Alpha, Beta, Gamma, Delta, Epsilon and Zeta.

- **Longest-lasting December Hurricane:** Epsilon set the record. It formed on November 29 and dissipated on December 8.

- **Longest-lasting January Hurricane:** Zeta set the record. It formed on December 29 and dissipated on January 6.

The only record this season did not break was the number of Category 3+ storms, which stands at 8. This season saw only 7.

Comparing the Seasons

The official 2004 Atlantic hurricane season started on June 1, 2004 and ended on November 30, 2004. In terms of activity, the season was above average, as compared with the previous seasons; it was notable for its accumulated energy, which was one of the highest on record.

The official 2006 Atlantic hurricane season started on June 1, 2006 and ended on November 30, 2006. Forecasters were initially certain that 2006 would be another violent season, much like 2005. However, it turned out to be a surprising non-event, as none of the hurricanes made landfall in the US.

Unlike the 2005 season, which started on June 8 and ended on January 6, both the 2004 and 2006 seasons started on June 1 and ended on November 30. These June to November dates represent the standard period of each year when most tropical cyclones are expected to form in the Atlantic basin.

Although the 2005 season did get off to a slightly late start, it nonetheless kept on raging for 2 more months than usual, breaking every record in the book, save one, and claiming thousands of victims in the process.

So how do we explain this? Meteorologists tell us we've entered a regular period of increased hurricane activity, which could continue for another two decades. This is assuming that they're right about what constitutes a "regular period." Given they were so far off the mark in forecasting the 2006 season, this explanation is no better than a roll of the dice in a Las Vegas casino.

We really need to know if there is a shift in the way Atlantic hurricanes develop and move through the Caribbean. Like the counter-intuitive changes we witnessed in the storm mechanisms that propelled extra-tropical storms Lothar and Martin, will future hurricanes become counter-intuitive as well? Instead of weakening as they approach landfall, just as we expect them to do, they'll suddenly gather devastating energy just before making landfall.

While Atlantic hurricanes are the most documented and researched hurricanes in the world, other regions of the world will also suffer from a change in activity, most notably that of typhoons.

The Typhoons and Hurricanes of 2005

In the Pacific region, hurricanes are known by different names. They're known as typhoons, cyclones and Willie-Willies. While the names are different, these Pacific and Indian Ocean storms are just as deadly and destructive as their Atlantic counterparts.

A good example of this was the 1997 season: 11 of 24 named storms turned into category 5 super-typhoons. These major storms are sadly underreported by the Western media, because they are usually not mentioned until the number of deaths reaches some kind of enigmatic, news-value tipping point.

However, there is a good deal of information on the Internet, and one such report featured satellite imagery from September 20, 2005. It showed seven simultaneous hurricanes and typhoons around the globe:

- Two were moving towards Japan and China in the West Pacific.

- Three were in the East Pacific, moving from Mexico towards the Hawaiian Islands.

- Two hurricanes were in the West Atlantic, one of which was Rita just before it made landfall.

As stated earlier, Rita set a record as the most intense tropical cyclone ever observed in the Gulf of Mexico and claimed 113 lives.

The Threat of Global Superstorms

When we look at the statistics of both the Atlantic and the West Pacific of the last decade and see this stunning number of simultaneously active storms, the conclusion becomes evident that the weather changes towards increasing violence. In the 2004 sci-fi blockbuster, *The Day After Tomorrow*, the Earth is violently thrown into another ice age spawned by man-made global warming.

NEWS INSIDE THE NEWS
Atlantic Hurricanes

In addition to tracking the counter-intuitive behavior of recent extra-tropical European storms, similar tracking is necessary with Atlantic hurricanes. Create your own simple chart (or spreadsheet) for each hurricane season, and note the following data:

- **Storm Formation and Path:** Note the storm's formation date and the path it follows.

- **How Does it Develop?** Not all storms are powerful enough to be named. If the storm is named, note on your chart where and when it was named and how it developed.

- **Point of Landfall:** Of particular concern is that hurricanes can move more deeply into moderate latitudes before landfall. Make clear notes on latitude and longitude.

- **Rainfall:** Note where the storm makes landfall and the amount of rainfall attributed to it.

- **Duration:** Note when the storm dissipated and the amount of time it remained strong.

- **Simultaneous Storms:** As you build your Atlantic hurricane chart, monitor the other areas of the world for named typhoons and cyclones, especially those appearing at or about the same time as named Atlantic storms and hurricanes.

In the film, polar melting changes the salinity of the world's oceans and disrupts the North Atlantic current, causing water temperatures in the North Atlantic to plunge.

One immediate impact of this sudden change is felt in Southern California, as we observe Los Angeles being devastated by tornadoes. Later in the film, major storm systems form over Siberia, America and Europe, and when they link up, the result is a global superstorm.

While this disaster scenario was hotly debated by scientists, many acknowledged that its basic premise was plausible, even though most felt it pushed outside the envelope of what could actually happen within a given period of time.

Nonetheless, one key point in this film that is directly relevant to this discussion of extra-tropical European storms, Atlantic hurricanes and Pacific typhoons, is that we've entered a period, in which disparate regional storm events can now become components of a broader global event.

Given that the American media does a poor job of reporting cyclonic storms in the Pacific and a marginally better job of extra-tropical storms in Europe, you'll need to be on the lookout for alternative media sources on the Internet to track these events. Only in this way will you be able to spot emerging trends for possible counter-intuitive storms and global superstorms long before the American media reports them.

Taking another clue from *The Day After Tomorrow*, a much closer examination of tornado trends is equally advisable.

Tornadoes

Not only have hurricanes started to grow more violent in the last decade, so has the average number of tornadoes striking in the US each year. When you boil down the statistics, the picture that forms shows tornadoes claiming more lives and causing more damage in the last decade. They are doing these things, not only because there are more of them, but also because they're becoming more severe and are occurring under more freakish circumstances.

The Number of Tornadoes

There is an undeniable increase in numbers of tornadoes per year during the last ten years, relative to the average of the last 30 years. Specifically, the last decade shows a 23% increase in the average number of tornadoes. Consequently, averages for the last ten years represent the most active period for tornadoes since the second half of the 20th century.

Most recently, the years 2004 and 2006 produced well above even the ten-year average number of tornadoes, and the relatively 'slow' year 2005 still was at the 10-year average. Further proof of a clear trend, and a deadly one, at that. The number of people killed by tornadoes in 2006 was 65, an annual death toll greater than that for any of the three previous years.

As we move closer to 2012, this trend will increase, resulting not only in an increase in Category 5 hurricanes and typhoons that make landfall each year, but in the number of F5 tornadoes that are sure to devastate cities everywhere, as well.

The Hell of an F5 Tornado

In 1996, movie goers in Oklahoma City packed the theaters to see the film, *Twister*. It was a time when Hollywood was really beginning to flex its muscles with computer-animated special effects, and to this day, *Twister* remains a must-see film for all those with a serious interest in the topic. However, for Oklahomans, it would be more than a spectacular special effects film; it would be a harbinger of the monster that would shred large parts of Oklahoma City in 1999.

The Oklahoma City Twister and the Fujita Scale

The twister that slammed into Oklahoma City on May 3, 1999 was so brutal that it did something most scientists believed was impossible until then. It broke the record on the Fujita scale used to classify tornadoes.

A key point to remember with the Fujita scale is that the size of a tornado is not necessarily an indication of its intensity. Rather, wind speed is the real indicator. Named after a Japanese meteorologist who did groundbreaking research on tornadoes, it reaches all the way up to F12, corresponding to the speed of sound.

F-Scale Number	Intensity	Wind Speed	Types of Damage Done
F0	Gale	40-72 mph	Some damage to chimneys, and branches broken off trees.
F1	Moderate	73-112 mph	The beginning of hurricane wind speeds that peel road surfaces and push mobile homes off their foundations.
F2	Significant	113-157 mph	Considerable damage. Roofs torn off frame houses, and mobile homes are demolished. Light object missiles, such as boards, that punch through walls.
F3	Severe	158-206 mph	Well constructed homes lose their roofs and walls. Trains can overturn, and trees are uprooted.
F4	Devastating	207-260 mph	Well-constructed houses are leveled to the ground, and cars are thrown.
F5	Incredible	261-318 mph	Strong buildings are lifted off foundations and carried considerable distances to disintegrate, while cars and trucks fly through the air like speeding missiles.
F6	Inconceivable	319-379 mph	The heavy damage is already done by the F4 and F5 winds surrounding an F6.

Anything beyond F5, such as an F6, cannot be properly established with engineering studies, other than possible land deformations, such as ground swirls. Ergo, an F6 presents a simple, chilling reality. A tornado that reaches this intensity level will leave nothing behind to study, which is exactly what happened to Oklahoma City in 1999.

The Oklahoma City F6

On May 3, the tornado first touched down a few miles southwest of Oklahoma City and quickly transformed itself into an F5 monster. As it moved across the outskirts of the city, its maximum diameter on the ground swelled to nearly a mile.

Doppler radar tracked it with wind speeds up to 319 mph (512 kph), which put it at the threshold of an F6 classification on the Fujita scale. It left a broad swath of total destruction and killed over 40 people, and most of those who were killed were either caught by surprise, due to the speed at which the tornado came, or did not have any way to shelter themselves against this kind of violence.

These were the very kinds of tornadoes depicted in the film, *The Day After Tomorrow*. As 2012 approaches, these F5+ level tornadoes could become tragically commonplace, and in places where we would never expect – until now. Places like California and Europe.

Tornadoes in America and Europe

In terms of a global rash of anomalous weather, 2005 was a nexus point with the most deadly Atlantic hurricane season in recorded history and simultaneous typhoons in the Pacific.

Statistically speaking, the 2005 tornado season was above the 30 year average, but, relative to what was happening in both the Atlantic and the Pacific, not significant. That is "statistically speaking," which is one way to overlook a new and unsettling tornado trend with the significant activity that occurred in California in January and February of 2005.

In January 2005, four minor tornadoes hit California on the 8th through the 11th. Before Californians could laugh them off with their usual bravado, on the heels of these 4 minor twisters came two killer tornadoes on the 12th and 13th. In terms of location, time of year and frequency, this 6-twister cycle was anomalous, to say the least. This is because California does not often get hit by this type of violent weather, especially not for six days in a row!

While the overall number of twisters in the 2005 tornado season was low, relative to the previous three years, there was a new twist. A geographic redistribution of twister events. Tornadoes happened in locations that did not make sense.

As to the usual tornado-prone areas, some saw no activity at all, while others were battered without mercy. Had these anomalies been limited to America, they could have been easily rationalized away, but similar anomalies were happening in Europe, as well.

It is not widely known in America, but Europeans also see a significant number of tornadoes each year. Unlike the twisters that routinely tear through America's Mid-western tornado alleys, most European twisters never touch down. Hence, tornado deaths and damages in Europe are considerably less than those in the US.

However, in the last decade, Europe, like America, has seen an overall increase in the number of tornadoes and a similar geographic redistribution of twister events. During the 2005 season, several tornado reports caught attention of the media in Europe, and a few of these twisters struck in remarkable locations.

NEWS INSIDE THE NEWS
Tornadoes

The media are more likely to report tornadoes that touch down with F2 strength, which cause significant loss of life and damage. Create your own simple map for each tornado season, and note the following data:

- **Significant Tornadoes in America:** Note the location and strength of F2+ tornadoes in America, associated storm activity, lives lost and the amount of damage. Do not limit yourself solely to tornado-prone areas.

- **Significant Tornadoes in Europe:** Note the location and strength of F2+ tornadoes in Europe, associated storm activity, lives lost and the amount of damage.

- **Extra-tropical Storms in Europe:** Note storms that have occurred prior to major twister events in Europe.

- **Simultaneous Events:** Track named Pacific typhoons and cyclones and Atlantic storms and hurricanes that make landfall during peak tornado periods.

In the beginning of September, several strong tornadoes touched the ground in and around Barcelona on two days with F2 and F3 strength. They formed in a complex of thunderstorms, which battered the Northeast of Spain for several days in a row. This storm complex generated many tornado sightings. While Barcelonans are used to seeing tornadoes, never before had this many strong twisters touched ground inside the city limits, and on consecutive days, no less.

The tornado reports from California and Barcelona are just two examples of apparently changing tornado behavior. On one hand, this change in behavior could be due to increasingly unstable atmospheric conditions. On the other, 2005 could have been the harbinger of a broader global trend as we approach 2012. Especially when catastrophic floods are factored into the equation.

Catastrophic Flooding

While tornadoes, hurricanes and typhoons conjure fear in our hearts with sound-level speed, the simple fact remains that flooding kills more people and causes more damage. What hurricane Katrina did to New Orleans in 2005 is a perfect example. Offshore, the storm loomed as a Category 5 monster, but it decreased to a Category 3 when it struck New Orleans and burst the levees. The worst of the damage and most casualties resulted from the flooding from the storm surge and broken levees, rather than the winds that hit New Orleans.

Another example of broad-scale, geographic flooding happened during the summer of 2002, when central Europe was inundated by severe flooding. The disaster took weeks to build, as a chain of exceptional rain-falls pushed water levels in rivers, such as the Danube and Elbe, above their banks.

These rain-falls caused a regional flood encompassing Germany, Austria, the Czech Republic and Slovakia and claimed over one hundred lives and caused billions of euros in damage. Further to the East, Russia likewise suffered from flooding that Summer, but not to the same extent.

Catastrophic Flooding in Europe in 2005

As hurricanes were wreaking havoc in the Atlantic basin, Central America and the Northern Gulf Coast area of America, Europe was suffering another freakish flood. Unlike the 2002 flood that had caused much death and damage to Germany, Austria, the Czech Republic and Slovakia, the 2005 floods hit deep in central Europe, and this time, Romania and Bulgaria would suffer.

During the summer of 2005, parts of Romania were flooded 6 times, and in the later half of September, both Romania and Bulgaria received more than twice the normal amount of rainfall for that season. This brought rain-driven floods that were so severe that they blanketed entire regions. The flooded areas were vast enough to be photographed from space.

Flooding also occurred in Switzerland, Austria and Germany when rivers fed by the runoff from several days of torrential rains hitting the Alps. Swollen beyond capacity, these rivers, along with many of the tributaries to the Danube and the Rhine, overran their banks. This caused flooding in many countries and resulted in mud slides that would later claim dozens of lives.

While the European storms of 2002 had been extensively reported in America, the European floods of 2005 were clearly overshadowed by the devastation caused by Katrina. This is not to say that a lack of media attention warrants the dismissal of an obvious, anomalous trend in the frequency of severe floods in Europe.

Extreme rainfall

As was proven by the rain-driven European floods of 2002 and 2005, excessive amounts of protracted rainfall can be even more disruptive to life than strong winds. Likewise, a short duration of extreme rainfall can generate similar results in a very short time, and two such extreme rainfalls occurred in 2005; one in the Netherlands and one in India.

On the night of June 29, 2005, a thunderstorm pummeled the Dutch town of Gorinchem with 4.5 inches (113 mm) of rain in just over 90 minutes. The most amazing aspect of this storm was that it fell on the center of the town and up to a distance of 10 miles away in nearly any direction. The rainfall beyond the outskirts of the town's 10-mile extreme zone amounted to less than .86 inches (20 mm) that night.

Gorinchem is not a modern city. Its existence dates back to the middle ages, and throughout the centuries since, none of Gorinchem's city planners or managers ever conceived of the possibility of such an extreme event. Consequently, the sewage system was quickly overwhelmed, and significant damage was sustained during the flooding of local streets and basements.

The incredible speed, with which the sewage system was rendered useless became clearly obvious after the storm, thanks to calculations based on recorded precipitation radar images. The calculations showed that, at its peak, the thunderstorm was dumping rain on the city at a pace of over 8 inches (200 mm) per hour!

Given that a relatively heavy monsoon day in India will drop half that amount of rain on a broader area in a given day, this clearly tells us that what happened to Gorinchem is, at least, a troubling aberration. Especially in light of what has been happening to the monsoon seasons in India for the last 10 years.

Statistically, the average amount of annual monsoon rainfall in India hasn't changed in the last ten years. What has changed is the distribution, according to Indian meteorologists. Their analyses of monsoon storms occurring over large portions of central and eastern India have determined that storms producing at 4 or more inches of rainfall a day are twice as many in this century as they were in the last. Whereas, those producing more moderate rainfall are happening less often. The result is that, while the volume of water remains the same, the distribution has undergone a significant change.

Further to which, the occurrence of freakish downpours similar to the one that hit Gorinchem are now happening more often in India, as well. Case in point is what happened over Mumbai on July 26, at the outset of the 2005 monsoon season.

More commonly known to Westerners as Bombay, this vibrant Western India city is the home to 13 million of India's most affluent citizens. What happened to the nation's largest city and financial capital was mind boggling. It suffered a torrential rainfall of 37 inches (940 mm) of water in just 24 hours!

The result was a human catastrophe that paralyzed the city and broke the standing record for the greatest amount of rainfall in a single day that dated back to 1910. While official estimates put the death toll at approximately one hundred, it is believed that hundreds more died because of the massive flooding.

Look for Global Trends

For centuries, the weather has always been discussed from a local-centric point-of-view. What is happening to our town, state, national region or country. As technology has progressed, we've begun looking at larger regions. However, we've only begun to think of the weather with a more a holistic, planetary view.

Those who argue with this planetary view are typically the same ones arguing against the proposition that our planet is warming. Meanwhile, the media is attempting to present a balanced viewpoint, which means our awareness of what is happening to our planet's weather will continue to stagnate in nonsensical debate until enough global misery exists to end this paralysis once and for all.

While we can no longer deny that human action plays a role in the change of our climate, we must avoid the pitfall of overstating the case, so as to drown out the naysayers. Yes, our emissions are not helpful to our planet's biosphere, but to arbitrarily halt our investigation at this point is to blindside ourselves to the other causes.

The most notable of these causes is the steady increase in solar activity and the destabilizing weather pattern it is generating in the oceans that cover more than 70 percent of the surface of our planet.

Admittedly, a holistic, nuts-and-bolts understanding of global weather science is elusive for everyone — to include scientists and naysayers alike. Therefore, we can monitor atmospheric anomalies, such as those, which happened in 2005. In doing so, we can begin to see an interconnected global view.

As we move closer to 2012, that data will begin to evidence global patterns that will make us stand up and take notice when a small Dutch town like Gorinchem is flooded.

Improving Survival Odds with a Global View

On a personal level, make a point of becoming more globally aware of what the weather is doing. Harvest facts to create your own simple database, and in time, you will see patterns that make sense to you.

If they do not make sense to the professionals, just remember that when you toss a coin, you have a 50/50 chance of calling it right. That's usually better odds than you'll get with a professional weather forecaster.

Look at it this way. If you wanted to become a day trader, the best way to test your stock picking hunches is to paper-trade. This way, you can safely test your ideas on paper before you commit your hard earned cash. In the same vein, by putting your life in the hands of television gurus, you're letting them paper-trade with your life.

If that doesn't set right with you, then start doing your own analysis in a way that makes sense to you. When the time comes to toss a weather coin in the air, you're not going to do any worse by trusting your own instincts. In fact, trusting your instincts could put you and your family well along the way to safe ground, while everyone else stays home, glued to their television sets.

7

Reading Signs
in the Oceans

In the previous chapter, you learned how to monitor the news inside the news to track how our climate has begun showing more extreme behavior. In the last decade, storms have begun to behave differently, doing more damage and appearing in unfamiliar places. These anomalous weather changes are the first symptoms of broader, more alarming trends in our oceans.

The oceans cover 71% of the surface of the Earth; they store tremendous amounts of heat and absorb billions of tons of gas from the atmosphere each year. As a major heat buffer system for our atmosphere, oceans play a crucial role in the distribution of heat around our planet. They are both the thermostat of our atmosphere and the lungs of the Earth, and they are nearing a catastrophic tipping point.

This tipping point is largely man-made, and when we reach it, we'll see an onset of catastrophic events that will happen far more quickly and severely than in recent history. So much so, that many experts will be half in shock by what they're seeing in their own numbers and half in shock at the prospect of wrecking their professional careers by sounding an early alarm.

These trends will be so massive that waiting to be the last to know is not an option. Building on what you learned in the Atmosphere chapter, you also need to start following the news inside the news for the early signs of our oceans, as they draw near to their catastrophic tipping points.

Current Climate Model Forecasts

Despite humanity's incredible surge of scientific knowledge, we've yet to understand our oceans at a holistic level. Despite our powerful satellites and research ships, we're still like the proverbial blind man trying to understand an elephant for the first time. We have a handful of this and a handful of that, but we're a long way away from getting our hands on the whole thing.

In the same vein, present global climate model forecasts for the 21st century are largely based on decades of observations and research, leading up to the end of the twentieth century.

That was a period of relative quiescence, when compared to present times. This is why our present current climate models are optimistic, because they do not factor in the buffering capacity of the oceans, and therefore, they do not factor in a tipping point.

This does not only make them inaccurate. It makes them *dangerously* inaccurate, because they are based on faulty worst-case expectations. A good example is the sinking of the *RMS Titanic*.

Failed Expectations

The *Titanic* was said to be "virtually unsinkable," because it was built with a double bottom hull and used state-of-the-art watertight bulkheads with electrically triggered hatches to control.

This method of construction was intended to allow the ship to survive partial flooding as water filled up to three sealed compartments. The naval architects assumed that if the ship were to sink, it would be slow, even foundering; that would give the crew and passengers plenty of time for a rescue.

What actually happened was that the front of the ship flooded in four compartments. Even though the compartments were vertically sealed by waterproof bulkheads, the tops of the compartments were not sealed.

As the ship slowly sank by the head, the water filled in each compartment until it reached the top of each bulkhead, where it would then spill over into the next compartment. Much like the small, terraced waterfalls in our gardens, where the water falls from one level to the next, until it falls into the pond at the bottom.

Prior to reaching its tipping point, the flooding progressed slowly enough for the lights to remain while the musicians played. However, moments after the *Titanic* reached its tipping point — that's when the stern rose up into the air, and the hull split in two — the bow of the mighty *Titanic* was carving out its final resting place on the seabed.

The reason why the ship's compartments were not sealed at the top and why it did not carry enough life boats was a failed assumption based on naïve, self-serving expectations of the worst case scenario.

A Modern Day Titanic

While the disaster scenario in the 2004 film, *The Day After Tomorrow,* was considered to be too extreme, the scientific criticism of the film was intended to soothe growing concerns that the Earth could be violently thrown into a man-made ice age.

While the effort to play down the catastrophic scenario in the film continues, museums continue to display the mummified remains of 10,000 year old giant woolly mammoths. These creatures were literally flash frozen to death with fresh grasses in their mouths. Furthermore, this freezing process happened so quickly that DNA recovered from these 10,000 year old specimens, is of sufficient quality for genetic breeding.

Despite the scientific criticism heaped on *The Day After Tomorrow*, it nonetheless pointed out three salient facts:

1. Evidence exists to prove that such events happened in the past.

2. We are presently monitoring unsettling trends in our oceans.

3. We lack the experience to understand the full extent of the danger we now face.

When all three are taken together, we have unsettling trends that conservative scientists insist require further close study before we make any big conclusions. A bona fide "let's not rock the boat" approach that guarantees a steady stream of funding.

Those scientists who are willing to sound the alarm and rock the boat are quickly branded as alarmists, and their careers are often sidelined. We know these things happen. Our popular culture tells us so.

A good example is the 1978 film, *Superman.* The film opens with Superman's father, Jor-El, played by Marlon Brando, warning the elders of Krypton that their sun is about to explode. Unwilling to accept that possibility, they ignore him, which at face value, is rather strange for such a technically advanced society.

Silenced, but still confident in his own analysis, Jor-El sends his infant son, Kal-El, to Earth to ensure his survival, and Krypton's sun does explode. Of course, this only proves that being right about such things is no reward.

In the days to come, each of us will find our own Jor-El moment. It will be a time when we see what we see, and so we cannot be dissuaded by naïve mocking; a time when we each must be willing to act, independently if we must.

The Lungs of the Earth

The human body has two lungs, each of which provides us with half the oxygen our bodies draw from our blood. In a similar manner, one could say the Earth has two lungs, as well. One is comprised of the various trees, shrubs, grasses and other plants, with which we're all so familiar.

Through the process of photosynthesis, they take in water and carbon dioxide or CO_2 and produce oxygen and sugars. Taken altogether, the plants of the world produce one quarter of the oxygen, upon which we depend for life, as they dispose of the CO_2 we exhale as waste.

Earth's other lung is phytoplankton, the very foundation of the sea's food chain, and current estimates show our oceans hold up to 80 times the amount of CO_2 that we have in our atmosphere.

Given the clear-cutting of invaluable rain forests, spreading global desertification and other factors, the phytoplankton in our oceans is more important to us than ever before. Especially when you consider that CO_2 levels in our upper atmosphere are soaring to unprecedented levels and that CO_2 is the 'strongest' greenhouse gas in the Earth's atmosphere.

Why CO_2 is the "Strongest" Greenhouse Gas

CO_2 is the 'strongest' greenhouse gas in the Earth's atmosphere for two reasons. First, it has strongest heat absorption of all the greenhouse gases, and is therefore a crucial factor in the development of our climate. This is why CO_2 levels in the atmosphere offer the clearest indicator of imminent climate changes.

The second reason why CO_2 is different from other major greenhouse gases is that it does not have a full transfer cycle.

Other critical warming gases, such as water vapor, offer a full heat transfer cycle. This process occurs within the normal surface temperature ranges on Earth, whereby the gas absorbs heat, then after that, it condenses back into a liquid state, transferring that heat into the sea or land.

With CO_2, there is a dependent heat transfer cycle. That is, unless you're at the South Pole, where temperatures can drop below -109.12 Fahrenheit (-78.4 Celsius), at which point CO_2 turns into a solid.

Like water vapor and methane, CO_2 absorbs heat. However, the heat cannot be transferred back to the land or sea until it is absorbed and converted by phytoplankton or plants. This is why the phytoplankton in our oceans, which absorb vast amounts of CO_2, is of vital importance to us.

What is disturbing, is that Earth's phytoplankton is under attack from man-made pollution and being starved of a necessary life-giving mineral — iron.

Where Has the Iron Gone?

Vitamin makers often tout ads about "iron-poor, tired blood" and how their supplements will help you avoid the fatigue and decreased immunity of anemia. Unlike rare elements, iron is one of the most abundant metals on Earth, and phytoplankton needs it every bit as much as we do.

In the human body, iron is used to make hemoglobin, the substance that carries oxygen through the blood to all the cells in the body. Phytoplankton uses iron to absorb CO_2, and when they become anemic, they suffer as we do.

The iron they depend upon occurs naturally in the seas. Most of it comes from desert sands that are carried out over the oceans by the winds. When these sands fall into the sea, these natural iron salts within them dissolve naturally in sea water.

The great concern now is that, despite the abundance of iron in the world, phytoplankton in huge areas of our oceans is not getting the iron it needs. In fact, since the 1980's, scientists have monitored a steady loss of iron in all the ocean basins across the planet, with the sole exception of the equatorial Atlantic basin.

The result is that we're seeing a steady decline in the volume of phytoplankton in our oceans, as compared with the usual levels in previous decades. The most likely culprit of this iron loss is the potassium and sodium phosphates in our laundry detergents.

The detergents we put in our washing machines use these phosphates to get our clothes clean. Phosphates make the dirt particles in our clothes slicker, so they can easily be extracted during the rinse cycle and flushed down the drain.

From our laundry drains, these phosphates make their way into our rivers, and then into our seas, where they keep on doing their job. This is the crux of the problem.

Laundry Phosphates Are Killing Our Oceans

Man-made laundry detergent phosphates are deadly to phytoplankton, because of how they interact with the naturally occurring iron salts in our oceans. Detergent phosphates bond with naturally occurring iron and form a completely different kind of iron salt that does not dissolve well. It literally falls to the sea floor like useless sand.

Consider this. In our previous example about the *Titanic*, we saw how the ship sank because the water could easily flow over the tops of the bulkheads that separated the ship's watertight compartments. Now, let's apply this example to phytoplankton anemia.

Our atmosphere and the oceans are all part of a perfect natural system. Had the naval architects who designed the *Titanic* been influenced by nature's example, the watertight compartments would have been sealed at the top.

We're depriving the phytoplankton of iron simply because we like to wear clean shirts to work. Consequently, we're stripping away nature's watertight seal at the top of the compartments bit-by-bit.

In other words, to keep us breathing, the oceans have to keep breathing, too. This is why our pollution of the oceans is an important contributor to the acceleration of climate change. We not only see evidence of this in our atmosphere, we also see it at the most fundamental level of life, our oceans.

Plankton are dying, and vast stretches of sea are now lifeless, save for Algae. When the Algae and pollution force their way into productive waters, massive fish die-offs begin to happen. A permanent dead zone already exists in the north of the Gulf of Bothnia, between Sweden and Finland.

Critics will claim this is fear-mongering and then point to the fact that the Gulf of Bothnia is a closed arm of the ocean. What they'll choose to ignore is that seasonal and permanent dead zones will become common in open stretches of sea, as well.

NEWS INSIDE THE NEWS

Ocean Life and Natural Systems

Tracking fishing reports and fish prices, as well as reports of erratic sea animal behavior, will give you insight into the biological state of the oceans. As these are announced, note the following data:

- **Fishing quota and size:** Over-fishing shows itself by the decreasing average size of fish caught and fishing grounds moving away further from land.

- **Whale beaching:** Where most whales beach is where the state of plant life in the water is worst. Whales feed on plankton, and lack of plankton sends them searching for it. Lack of food disorients them and causes them to beach themselves.

- **Algae growth:** Where algae bloom, all other life dies off, leaving a lifeless sea beneath the waves. No more oxygen is made by plankton there.

- **Oil spills:** When oil is spilled, it sinks to the sea floor and kills all life there, robbing fish and sea animals of their food. This disrupts the food chain and kills the sea.

One such seasonal dead zone now exists beyond the mouth of the Mississippi river. More are certain to follow, and entire regions of sea will just die.

This will affect the amount of fish we can catch for our own consumption, which is already pressed, as we've already fished out 90% of the ocean's largest fish species. Our fish markets still give us the appearance that our oceans still contain a virtually unlimited supply, but the fact is that we're using huge factory ships and drag nets to squeeze out the remaining 10% of large fish species. Fish that also happen to be of vital importance to the health of the world's coral reefs.

However, the most critical threat is what is happening to plankton. They represent the base of the food chain of the sea, and their fate will impact all other life in the oceans. Most noticeable is how this has already affected the largest creatures on Earth, the whales. Many now venture near land, searching for food, and wind up beaching themselves. Weakened and unable to get back out into open water, some are saved by compassionate people, but most still die. The point here is that we're not all bad.

While more nations are striving to be more prudent stewards of their fisheries, others continue to plunder the oceans. Predatory fishing nations like China will continue to blindly plunder one fishery after another, until they all fail.

Then, desperate to feed their growing masses, they'll begin marauding into well-managed, protected areas, which will surely fuel heated confrontations, but those will not last for long, because we'll be more interested in fighting for air, rather than fish.

CO_2 and Oxygen

If man-made and natural forces conspire to push our oceans over the tipping point, there will be a massive release of CO_2 into the atmosphere, concurrent with a reduction in oxygen. Let's look at the percentages.

At present, the Earth's atmosphere has a low CO_2 concentration of approximately 0.038%. If it surges to:

- 0.5%, we can take it for long periods of time.
- 3.0%, we can take it for short periods of time.
- 2.5% and remains at that level or higher, we die.

Likewise, if phytoplankton quits absorbing CO_2, it'll also stop producing oxygen, which means there will be less oxygen in the atmosphere for us to breathe.

At present, the amount of oxygen in Earth's atmosphere is 21%; if it sinks to:

- 17%, a candle flame will no longer burn, but we can live on that.
- 14% we slowly lose consciousness.
- 11% we die.

Humanity is tampering with a complex system that is vast, but not limitless, although it appears that way.

Like any other system, it has its own catastrophic tipping point. While we know it is stressed, we do not know enough about it to assume it does not have a tipping point, at which it stops being slowly choked to death by our thoughtless hubris.

If we push it over that tipping point, everyone would first feel the buildup of CO_2 and the effects of asphyxia and then suffer oxygen deprivation. The canaries in this future coal mine will be the old, the infirm and those with weakened cardiopulmonary systems.

At first, it will be a quiet dying, much like the 2003 European heat wave. In one of Europe's hottest summers on record, 14,802 people, mostly elderly, died in France.

For those living at high altitudes, the CO_2 levels will be more tolerable, but there will be a more noticeable loss of oxygen. The reverse will be true for those living at sea level, except those living at sea level will have a whole extra dimension of grief to consider.

CO_2 and Sea Level

A massive release of CO_2 stored in the ocean could push the CO_2 level in the atmosphere above 2%. If this happens, temperatures could rise by more than 18 degrees Fahrenheit (10 degrees Celsius.) This would result in the melt-off of all permanent ice on Earth within a few years, at which point there would be no glaciers or polar caps left.

The accelerated melting of the major ice masses on land is exactly what we see happening and is borne out by a May 2007 report by the National Center for Atmospheric Research (NCAR). That report states that sea ice is being depleted at three times the predicted rate and that our polar regions are the hardest hit.

If we continue to underestimate the rate at which we're losing ice sheets, we'll only blindside ourselves to a coming global positive feedback loop, where problems layer one upon another until they cause a catastrophic failure.

One way of seeing this in your mind is to imagine a terrible, great ogre with massive hobnailed boots standing at one end of a small stone bridge.

You're standing on the middle of the bridge, and he's at the end, when he stomps his great boot with a great thud that sends a tremble through the bridge. You feel the tremble, but it fades away. Still angry, the ogre stomps his boot again, and again the process is repeated. Still, the bridge remains as solid and as safe as ever.

This infuriates the ogre, so he begins stomping his boot as fast as he can. Now, the tremble from the first stomp is still passing through the bridge when the second stomp comes, and likewise for the third, fourth and so on.

Unable to shed the vibrations, the bridge begins to resonate as the tremble from one stomp magnifies the tremble from the next. As the ogre continues to stomp, it all builds into a resonance that is too powerful for the bridge to handle. It eventually breaks apart, collapsing into the stream, taking you along with it.

Now, let's think of our ogre's hobnailed boot as a source of CO_2 and that each stomp is an unnatural release. What happens next?

The Resonance of Failure

For the sake of argument, let's assume that the Greenland Ice Sheet is the first to feel the CO_2 tremble of an ogre's stomp. This is a logical place to start, because north of the equator, our great concern is the Greenland ice sheet. Scientists have determined that it would not only melt rapidly, but that it would also slide off in huge chunks.

As our CO_2 ogre starts his stomping, we begin to see a massive Greenland ice sheet melt-off. As huge sheets of ice literally slide off, sea levels will begin to rise. If the entire Greenland ice sheet melts into the sea, we could see an average rise of sea level of as much as 21.33 feet (6.5 meters.)

At this point, our eyes would turn to Antarctica, our Southernmost continent. Almost 90% of all sweet (fresh) water on Earth lies on Antarctica, locked in ice and snow. This frozen sweet water is important to us, because it reflects solar radiation. When it is gone, the exposed land and the water from ice melt-offs will absorb the solar radiation.

As less solar radiation is reflected by ice and snow, more heat will be absorbed by the land and oceans, which in turn will create a positive feedback loop that could eventually cause all of the permanent ice on Earth to melt.

Should the ice caps of Antarctica, Greenland and all the glaciers in mountain regions melt away, sea levels could rise to upward of 65.62 feet (20 meters), with disastrous consequences for every low-lying area near the ocean shores. Additionally, the ocean water, itself, will warm up. As a result of this warming, the water expands, and it will rise even further. A good example of what this would mean for cities like New York was graphically illustrated in the 2001 film, *Artificial Intelligence* by Steven Spielberg.

The first nations to be hardest hit will be those in low-lying coastal areas, such as Bangladesh, which would disappear into the sea almost entirely, with a tragic loss of life.

Industrialized nations would feel the impacts, as well. In America, entire cities in the Gulf States regions, like New Orleans, would disappear, along with the major coastal cities, such as Miami, Florida. Europeans would feel it, too.

London would become uninhabitable, and entire parts of countries in Western Europe, such as Belgium, The Netherlands and Denmark will disappear, along with their rich agricultural lands.

Everyone will be affected, regardless of whether they live in coastal or inland regions. Those that are flooded out of their homes will flee as refugees to safe ground. Most will be unprepared, and this is when a logistical and economic nightmare will ensue.

If you live inland and can ignore what is happening to the world's permanent ice and rising sea levels, you will eventually be blindsided by a flood of hungry and thirsty refugees.

The first amongst them will be grateful, but those who follow will take by force that which they lacked the foresight to set aside. They'll come at you like an unstoppable swarm of locusts, but not for long.

Things Could Get Even Worse

As our oceans and atmosphere change, our global climate will become more violent and more extreme at moderate latitudes, and this could trigger a slow-down or even a full halt of the North Atlantic Gulf Stream. If that happens, the severe cooling scenario in the motion picture, *The Day After Tomorrow,* which experts feel is unlikely, though not impossible, could very well become reality.

After some time, however, the current will restore itself; human action right now helps to push the climate off a stable point of balance, but the climate will restore itself in time. The question is just how many of us will be there to see that. Remember, we're making the same mistake as the owners of the *RMS Titanic* in reverse. They saw no danger in not sealing the tops of the watertight compartments to keep the incoming sea water from flowing over them, and we know the result.

Nonetheless, in the absence of knowing the exact tipping point, at which our oceans respond suddenly and catastrophically to our short-sighted behaviors, we keep chipping away at nature's perfect system and removing the seals at the tops of our own watertight compartments.

So here you are, standing on the dock with a boarding ticket, and above you looms a ship that experts have assured you is "virtually unsinkable." Yet, there are other ways to get where you're going, and for the moment, you're free to choose.

NEWS INSIDE THE NEWS

Ocean and Atmosphere Trends

Whether you live inland or near a coast, keeping track of changes in the oceans and atmosphere will help you anticipate near future threats and take action in advance of those who will choose to ignore these vital trends.

- **Where do you live relative to the sea:** How far you live below sea level or above it. In 2012, this will be a deciding survival factor for coastal dwellers.

- **What is your level of protection:** If you live behind dikes or levees that protect you from a rise in water level, evaluate their state of maintenance.

- **How many people are around you:** Determine how many people are around you who rely on the same protection against the water that you do. They will be competing with you for resources in case there is trouble.

- **How often do you have flooding problems:** Find out whether there are other sources of water that may cause you trouble, like rivers and sewage systems, and how many times they overflow to find trends. Find out how the disposal of excess water is arranged near you and whether you are in harm's way in case of flooding from anything other than the sea.

- **Weather records:** Look for record-breaking weather, cold or warm, wet or dry. Keep a watch on statistics of unusual weather phenomena; they come directly from a change in sea water temperature.

- **Sea water temperature:** Changes in average sea water temperature will indicate an upcoming climate change. Warmer sea water will lead to more violent storms; colder water will lead to more droughts.

- **Ice sheet break-up:** Reports on the breaking up of ice sheets or the breaking off of chunks of ice from Greenland or Antarctica. They indicate a rise in global temperature.

Part 3 – What our Governments are Doing

"You cannot escape the responsibility
of tomorrow by evading it today."

—*Abraham Lincoln (1809 – 1865)*

Governments are like extended families. Good, bad or otherwise, they all share one primordial goal — to survive. Do not be assuaged by their hyperbole.

Rather, imagine the one question that tasks those of great power as they sit for their portraits: "*When my heirs view this painting, what will they think of me?*" Everything else is secondary; including the rest of us.

8

Solar Storm Monitoring

The greatest threat we will face from Planet X is its interaction with our Sun. After Planet X passes through the ecliptic, we will begin to see violent solar storms as the Sun begins to respond to its presence. Any one of them could deliver a knockout body blow to the communications networks and power grids that provide the foundations of our industrial might — and worse.

The dangerous behavior of the Sun in the years ahead is now a major threat to the industrialized nations. It has spawned a multi-national effort to bolster our solar activity defense system. Consequently, America's NASA, Europe's ESA and Japan's JAXA space agencies are working together to position a fleet of 7 solar observatories in space by 2008. And these are just the ones they are discussing publicly!

When we take into account the number of solar observatories that will be collectively used to monitor our Sun through the perilous years ahead, we see a well-coordinated effort. No matter what you may think of your government, know this; they're spending your tax dollars wisely; so let's see what they're using our tax dollars for.

Earth's Space-based Solar Observatories

When we go to the hospital, physicians will run several different tests in order to gain a clear overall view of what is happening in our bodies. The same holds true with our Sun, and to achieve this aim, we need to carefully monitor 5 different radiation wavelengths: Gamma, X-Ray, X-UV, UV and Visible.

Mission Name AGENCY *Launch*	Mission Target	Gamma	X-Ray	X-UV	UV	Visible
Ulysses ESA, NASA *1990*	Charting the Sun's poles	fil	fil			
SOHO ESA, NASA *1995*	Solar atmosphere and solar flares warning		fil	fil	fil	fil
Hinode NASA, ESA, JAXA *2006*	Interaction of Solar magnetic field and corona		fil	fil	fil	fil
STEREO NASA *2006*	Solar behavior and dynamics of CME's			fil		fil
Proba-2 ESA *2007*	Solar observation and space weather monitoring			fil	fil	
Solar Dynamics Observatory NASA *2008*	Magnetodynamics of the Sun			fil	fil	fil
Solar Orbiter ESA *2010 or 2015*	High-resolution study of the Sun			fil	fil	fil

Scientists tend to split hairs when defining these 5 different radiation wavelengths. This chapter will present a broad-brush overview of the 5. This will give you a broad-brush working concept of the science that will help you interpret the news inside the news as the media begins to report on live data from these solar observatories.

Measuring Radiation

When measuring radiation wavelengths, two common scientific terms, nanometers and microns, are typically used.

Nanometer (nm): One billionth of a meter.

- Gamma = Anything below 0.1 nm
- X-Ray = 0.1 nm to 50 nm

▵ X-UV = 50 nm to 200 nm

▵ UV = 200 nm to 380 nm

▵ Visible light = 380 nm to 780 nm

Micron: One millionth of a meter.

▵ Infrared (Near Infrared) = 780 nm (0.780 microns) to 10 microns

▵ Far Infrared = 10 microns to 200 microns

The solar observatories discussed in this chapter only monitor the Sun in the nanometer bandwidths. The space-based telescopes discussed in the next chapter observe the heavens in both bandwidth ranges.

Solar Monitoring in the Nanometer Ranges

By monitoring the following five nanometer bandwidths described above, scientists and astronomers will be able to create a comprehensive diagnostic picture of the Sun in real-time.

Gamma Rays — Monitoring the Sun's Inner Furnace

This is the radiation that comes from decaying isotopes, such as uranium and plutonium. Nuclear plants create gamma radiation as a normal course of business. Gamma radiation tells us what is taking place within the fusion (fusion produces neutrons, their collision into other matter produces the heat we feel and radiation, too) furnace of the Sun.

Measuring this radiation tells us if this activity is trending upwards, downwards or remaining relatively stable. In a simple sense, monitoring gamma radiation is like taking the Sun's pulse. Ergo, a higher pulse rate indicates a greater overall level of systemic excitement.

X-Rays — Predicting Cosmic Lightning

Actual X-Rays can only be created by man-made devices. In science, this term is used to describe radiation that occurs naturally within this same bandwidth and which is used to measure certain types of high-speed collisions between atoms.

The more violent these collisions are, the more X-Rays are generated at shorter (harder) bandwidths. These more violent collisions are caused by increases in the electromagnetic fields affecting these atoms.

After Planet X crosses the ecliptic, we will begin to see a sharp increase in X-Ray emissions as sprite (cosmic lightning) interactions begin to happen between Planet X and the Sun.

X-UV — Forecasting Solar Storms

This bandwidth allows us to measure the ionization of an atom via its inner electrons. Unlike the X-Ray bandwidth, which focuses on high-speed atomic collisions, X-UV focuses on low-speed atomic collisions. It gives us a real-time capability to forecast the kinds of solar flares and coronal mass ejections (CME) that could paralyze our communication networks and power grids.

UV — Measuring the Sun's Reaction to Planet X

Unlike X-UV, UV measures the ionization of an atom via its outer electrons. This gives us two important views at the atomic level. First, we see how the bond of inner electrons to the nucleus is increased as the outermost electrons are stripped away. This in turn changes a star's chemical composition and electrical interactions.

By monitoring shifts in the Sun's UV output, we will be able to determine the degree, to which it is perturbed by Planet X during the flyby.

Visible Light — Knowing When to Sound the Alarm

The visible light bandwidth is what we see with our eyes. It is created on the surface of the Sun and gives us a way to measure the ultra-low speed collisions between atoms. Within this bandwidth is also a wealth of information about the magnetic field fluctuations occurring on the Sun's surface.

When a coronal mass ejection (CME) occurs, the visible light bandwidth not only allows us the opportunity to observe it using space-based and ground-based telescopes, it also gives us the speed and direction of the ejected plasma. Using these observations, we can know if the plasma is coming at us and how soon it will arrive.

The heated plasma from a perfect solar storm can reach the Earth in as little as 18 hours. Without warning and unprepared, a perfect solar storm would certainly throw us back into another agrarian age.

Solar Observatories

An overall picture emerges from the missions and plans that have just begun or are due to begin in the immediate future. This unprecedented effort to monitor our Sun tells Planet X researchers that our governments really do get it. They understand that the more warning time we have in advance of an incoming solar eruption, the better chance we have.

Ulysses (ESA, NASA)

Since its launch in 1990, Ulysses has studied the Solar wind from all sides, as well as behavior of the Sun's poles. It is also being used to create a three dimensional map of the Sun's heliosphere. Such a map would allow the Sun's dynamics to be thoroughly studied, so as to develop an unprecedented understanding of how the Sun works.

In December 2006, Ulysses passed below the Sun's South Pole. It detected strong magnetic activity at a level that corresponds to the level of solar maximum. However, it was almost solar minimum then. This behavior of the Sun has yet to be explained and could suggest that something could be stirring up the Sun's South Pole. Starting November 2007, it will pass over the Sun's North Pole; this should provide us with a comparison between the poles. It will be interesting to see whether they are equally active or the activity is just on one side.

SOHO Solar and Heliospheric Observatory (ESA, NASA)

SOHO was launched in 1995, and this venerable old spacecraft has fed a nearly steady stream of breathtaking images of our Sun, thanks to its Lagrange point orbit at 1 million km from Earth.

Because SOHO neither orbits the Sun nor the Earth it is officially designated as a space probe. Satellites such as the ones we use for our cell phones and cable televisions orbit the Earth. The Lagrange point that SOHO orbits is between Earth and the Sun at 1 million km from Earth.

SOHO primarily observes solar activity and provides an early warning system for solar eruptions aimed at Earth. It gives us about 20 minutes warning time to shut down vulnerable satellites and direct astronauts to radiation shelter during a solar storm.

Originally slated for deactivation in 2006, the venerable SOHO mission was recently extended to 2009. Its mission profile was also updated to re-create images of conditions on the far side of the Sun. This new data will help us advance our ability to predict strong Solar activity in the future.

It is interesting to note that the mission extension was due in part to a very clever software fix by NASA in 1998. In June of that year, the space probe's 3 gyroscopes failed one-by-one. Instead of abandoning SOHO, NASA engineers developed a software solution that eliminated its need for gyroscopes. Soon after the software was uploaded to the satellite, it was able to fully resume its mission. NASA does have its moments.

Hinode (ESA, NASA, JAXA)

The Japanese mission Hinode (formerly known as Solar-B) studies the interaction between the Sun's magnetic field and its high-temperature ionosphere. The mission's goal is to achieve a better understanding of what drives our Sun's long-term luminosity changes.

Previously in the book, we noted the global warming and weather perturbations happening to most of the planets in our solar system. This is because increased solar output is putting an extra energy load on the planets in our solar system. One result of this increased solar output is what we presently see happening to Earth's climate.

Thanks to the incoming Hinode data streams, scientist will be more able to understand atmospheric perturbations caused by the extra energy loading of increased solar output.

STEREO Solar Terrestrial Relations Observatory (NASA)

Of all the solar observatory missions to become operational between now and 2008, NASA's STEREO mission is the most ambitious, because it consists of two spacecraft.

One of the STEREO twins is ahead of Earth in its orbital path. The other trails behind the Earth, also on the same orbital path. When used together, they will create something never before seen in the history of humankind … 3-D images of the Sun!

The 3-D images will certainly be stunning to laymen and scientists alike, but the really powerful aspect of this 3-D imagery will come in the form of enhanced CME (Coronal Mass Ejection) monitoring and forecasting. This improved forecasting ability will help us to better anticipate the effects of solar eruptions so that we can do all that is possible to minimize the damaging effects.

Proba-2 (ESA)

Proba-2 is a Belgian made microsatellite, launched in 2006 to study the behavior of the Sun. It is unique in that it has a mass of only 265 lb (120 kg). Hence, the term microsatellite.

The mission of this microsatellite is to study the Sun in the far ultraviolet range, which makes it highly useful in the study of how Planet X will excite our Sun during its flyby through the core of our system. However, the Proba-2 offers another benefit that may be of greater importance.

Once Planet X crosses the ecliptic, our Sun will become increasingly violent, and many of our solar observatories could be impaired or destroyed in the ensuing solar storms. However, replacement microsatellites, such as Proba-2, could be built and launched far more quickly than larger, more sophisticated satellites and space probes.

Solar Dynamics Observatory (NASA)

After the Solar Dynamics Observatory (SDO) is launched in 2008, it will be used to observe the Sun's outer atmosphere to help us to better understand the Sun's influence upon the Earth. It will do this by simultaneously observing the Sun with multiple instruments, in small periods of time, small scales of space and in many wavelengths.

In essence, the SDO is NASA's replacement to the venerable SOHO, which is scheduled to be deactivated in 2009 and will become Earth's new primary early warning system for solar flares. It will also study the magnetic topologies that lead to these violent eruptions on the Sun.

The SDO will be far more capable than SOHO. Like the SOHO, it will be used to observe solar flares in real time, but in addition to that, it will also be used to attempt observations of solar flares before they erupt.

Solar Orbiter (ESA)

The old colloquialism, "from the frying pan into the fire," is an apt description for the ESA Solar Orbiter. Once deployed, it will station much closer to the Sun than any other solar observatory, at 0.21 AU. A single AU (astronomical unit) is Earth's average distance to the Sun, so at 0.21 AU, the Solar Orbiter will orbit halfway between the Sun and Mercury, which is 0.4 AU from the Sun. A hot spot, for sure!

The Solar Orbiter is presently scheduled for launch in 2015, but NASA is urging ESA to push up the launch to 2010, as this solar observatory is a perfect companion to NASA's own SDO, which will become operational in 2008. This is because it can augment SDO observations with 'in situ' (a Latin phrase meaning *in the place*) observations.

NASA is right. Given the life-or-death consequences of solar super-flares, we need to increase our maximum warning time by 2010 — not by 2015.

9

Planet X and
New Earths

In "Chapter 8 — Solar Storm Monitoring," our focus was turned inwards towards one single object: our Sun, and how it will respond to the flyby of Planet X through the core of our solar system.

In this chapter, we'll reverse the focus outwards towards the furthest reaches of our own solar system and far beyond. We'll be looking for Planet X, other similar objects in distant star systems and for new extrasolar Earths.

The Kolbrin Bible tells us that Planet X will be unlike any other object we've ever seen, and in 1930, we thought we had first glimpsed it after Clyde Tombaugh of Lowell Observatory discovered the Planet Pluto. However, that notion ended with the discovery of Pluto's moon, Charon, by astronomer James W. Christy of the U.S. Naval Observatory in 1978.

What made Christy's discovery significant is that Charon gave astronomers a precise way to determine the mass of Pluto, which happens to be 1/400th that of the Earth. Ergo, Pluto, which is smaller than Earth's own Moon, could never have been the mysterious Planet X that astronomers have searched for since the discovery of Neptune in 1846. In fact, it was recently demoted from the status of a planet to that of a dwarf planet.

Another possible consequence of Christy's discovery of Charon was a 1992 NASA press release, in which they said, "Unexplained deviations in the orbits of Uranus and Neptune point to a large outer solar system body of 4 to 8 Earth masses, on a highly tilted orbit, beyond 7 billion miles from the Sun."

NASA Press Release 1992

"Unexplained deviations in the orbits of Uranus and Neptune point to a large outer solar system body of 4 to 8 Earth masses, on a highly tilted orbit, beyond 7 billion miles from the Sun."

Or, was this "1992 Planet X smoking-gun" NASA press release triggered by something else, as many Planet X researchers believe? The answer to that question does not begin with what our governments are looking at with our rapidly growing fleet of space satellites and probes. Instead, it begins with the manner, in which they peer through the darkness of space.

Earth's Space-based Solar Observatories

Seeing Neil Armstrong take his first step on the lunar surface was a hard act to follow, but we've done it. After the last manned mission to the moon, the public's attention refocused on the dozens of unmanned space probes our governments are using to explore the planets of the Solar system and beyond.

These missions included the Voyager, the Pioneer and also the Venera missions to Venus, and the Viking, Mars Observer and Pathfinder missions to Mars. The Galileo mission went to Jupiter and its moons, and the on-going Cassini mission is looking at Saturn and its satellites.

One by one, the planets are studied in more detail, and the images we see on our televisions amaze us. However, what we cannot see with the human eye has become increasingly more important.

Since 2000, there is clear evidence of a new sense of urgency in the launch of space missions. In "Chapter 8 — Solar Storm Monitoring," we saw how ESA, NASA and JAXA have dramatically stepped up their efforts to observe the Sun. They've likewise increased their exploration of the Solar System, sending probes to hit comets, land on asteroids and to find new Earths in distant solar systems.

Missions and plans to study planets

During the last few years, however, the number of missions aimed to study outer space has seen a strong increase by the American (NASA), European (ESA) and Japanese (JAXA) space agencies.

Mission Name AGENCY *Launch*	Mission target	UV	Visible	Infrared	Far Infrared
IRAS NASA *1983*	All-sky survey of sources of infrared radiation			fil	
HST (Hubble Space Telescope) NASA *1990*	Deep Space exploration	fil	fil	fil	
SST (Spitzer Space Telescope) NASA *2003*	Deep Space exploration			fil	
COROT ESA *2006*	Stellar seismology Extrasolar planet search		fil		
ASTRO-F JAXA *2006*	All-sky survey up to 10 times more sensitive than IRAS			fil	
Herschel Space Observatory ESA *2008*	Formation of galaxies Chemical composition of surface of bodies				fil
WISE NASA *2009*	All-sky survey up to 1000 times more sensitive than IRAS			fil	

The observations made by these probes are telling us that something is changing or about to change. Hence, the focus of our governments has shifted from pure research to measuring something of a more serious nature.

Measuring Radiation

When measuring radiation wavelengths, two common scientific terms are typically used, nanometers and microns.

Nanometer (nm): One billionth of a meter.

    UV = 200 nm to 380 nm

⬛ Visible light = 380 nm to 780 nm

Micron: One millionth of a meter.

⬛ Infrared (Near Infrared) = 780 nm (0.780 microns) to 10 microns

⬛ Far Infrared = 10 microns to 200 microns

Obviously, infrared is the dominant radiation bandwidth used in this urgent, new research. Assuming that Planet X is a brown dwarf, an unborn twin sun to our own Sol, using these four radiation bandwidths together offers us a broad profile of this mysterious object.

UV — Planet X Presence and the Sun

We measure UV bandwidths to determine changes in a star's chemical composition and electrical interactions. As a brown dwarf, Planet X is essentially a smoldering star. While it once had enough mass to ignite briefly, it wasn't large enough to trigger the fusion of hydrogen that keeps stars like our Sun shining for billions of years. In a manner of speaking, you could imagine a brown dwarf as a smoldering charcoal briquette in a backyard BBQ. It continues to generate heat as it slowly dies.

Recent discoveries suggest that an Earth-sized planet in a tight orbit around a brown dwarf could actually receive enough UV radiation and light to sustain life. However, the big interest in brown dwarf research is focused on measuring the UV activity between brown dwarfs and the larger companion suns they orbit.

By observing the UV output of extrasolar brown dwarfs and the larger companions they orbit, we will be better able to determine the degree to which our Sun will respond to Planet X during the most critical phase of its flyby.

Visible Light — Building a Reliable Ephemeris

The visible light bandwidth is what we see with our eyes, and it gives us a wealth of information about the magnetic field fluctuations occurring on the Sun's surface. This data will be invaluable in forecasting and detecting coronal mass ejections (CME), along with the speed and direction of the ejected plasma.

In terms of Planet X, the visible light bandwidth serves an even greater purpose, because this is the bandwidth used by the greatest number of professional and amateur telescopes. This means that, once Planet X can be observed in the visible light bandwidth, data will begin to stream in from astronomers from around the world.

At first, the observations will trickle in from countries in the Southern Hemisphere, such as Australia, New Zealand and Chile, but as Planet X approaches the ecliptic, that trickle will turn into a flood of high-quality observation reports.

The data from all of these governmental, professional, academic and amateur observations will be processed by the most powerful computer networks on Earth to create the most accurate Planet X ephemeris possible.

An ephemeris is a device or chart used by astronomers to give them positions of an astronomical object in the sky at various times. Few of us ever use an ephemeris to locate a star or comet at night, but those of us who follow prognosticating astrologers to learn about our chance for love, wealth and so forth use them. This is because astrologers rely upon specialized ephemerides to cast our horoscopes.

Building an ephemeris for two objects can be easily done with a hand calculator. However, developing an accurate, long-term ephemeris for Planet X will make forecasting love and wealth with absolute certainty look like child's play. This is because knowing exactly where Planet X will be and when it will be there during its flyby through our system requires a 12-object solution. Tackling this problem will require all the visible light observation data and computer resources humankind can bring to bear.

Infrared (Near infrared) — Observing Planet X at a Distance

The infrared bandwidth is expressed as heat and warmth. We often see examples of infrared technology in news broadcasts where we see our war fighters using infrared devices to track enemy troops and vehicles at night, so they can destroy them.

Like the warm engine in an enemy tank at night, the natural heat generated by Planet X makes it stand out like a sore thumb in the infrared bandwidths. This is why many Planet X researchers believe that the infrared cameras on the IRAS telescope were the first to detect Planet X at the outermost realms of our solar system in 1983. If so, Earth- and space-based infrared telescopes have been "unofficially" observing it on and off since then.

The only problem with observing Planet X vis-à-vis its infrared bandwidth emissions is that we can easily detect its heat signature, but learning more about this mysterious object in this bandwidth is virtually impossible, due to its protoplanetary disk.

Far Infrared — Peering Through a Protoplanetary Disk

A protoplanetary disk is essentially a cloud of dust and gas that surrounds a Sun. Our own Sun ignited to life and began to rotate from within a protoplanetary disk, which then continued to form the celestial bodies, such as planets and asteroids, of our solar system.

When Planet X first ignited, it too came from a protoplanetary disk, but on a much smaller scale, even though it could conceivably be 4 AU in diameter (four times the distance between the Earth and the Sun).

If you happen to be caught in a blinding sandstorm in one of Earth's great deserts, you'll be lucky to see a few feet ahead of you. The dust in a brown dwarf's protoplanetary disk has the same effect on visible light, which is why Planet X will need to be much closer to Earth before we can see it with the naked eye, as we do Saturn.

Likewise, this same protoplanetary disk prevents us from seeing any great level of detail in Planet X itself, aside from its heat bloom. This is where far infrared gives us a huge advantage. Virtually unfazed by the distortions of Planet X's protoplanetary disk, this bandwidth gives us a way to peek through the dust cloud surrounding this mysterious object while it is still far away. Thanks to far infrared bandwidth observations of space-based observatories, we'll know a great deal about Planet X long before astronomers on the Earth can begin to observe it in the visible light ranges.

Observing Planet X in Space

Any dust around Planet X will make observation in the wavelength range of visible light very difficult to impossible until it starts to brighten noticeably. At present, we have few options but to search for it in the UV, visible, infrared and far infrared spectrums with space telescopes, especially since it does not move in the ecliptic plane.

IRAS — the First "Unofficial" Sighting of Planet X

Launched in January 1983, the Infrared Astronomical Satellite (IRAS) was a joint project of the US, UK and the Netherlands to map the sky with a built-in infrared telescope. Placed in orbit around Earth, it operated for 10 months before a malfunction forced its shutdown. During that time, it managed to find over 350,000 different sources of infrared radiation, and it mapped 96% of the sky twice.

The formal reason for the termination of the IRAS mission was a critical malfunction in the satellite's cooling system. However, according to John Maynard, a former US intelligence officer turned government whistleblower, this "official" explanation was not the actual reason for the eventual shutdown of the IRAS satellite.

According to Maynard, the IRAS astronomers detected a massive heat bloom at the furthest reaches of our Solar System, far below the ecliptic, several months into the sky survey. In order to create the best available ephemeris at that time, American ground controllers declared the "official" cooling system malfunction and ceased sharing data with academic project partners in Europe. Controllers then used the remaining navigation thruster fuel aboard the IRAS satellite to continue private observations of this new object until it was fully spent.

Astro-F — A New, More Powerful IRAS

Also known as Akari, the Astro-F was launched by Japan in February 2006 to study protoplanetary disks around stars within 1,000 light years of Earth. It is 10 times more sensitive to infrared radiation than IRAS was in 1983, and it will give us greater detail on the structures within a protoplanetary disk, such as the one that surrounds Planet X.

It also has the far infrared capability to enable it not only to see protoplanetary disks, but also to look at the stars, themselves. This capability will help in finding cooler, darker stars that cannot be seen within their dust disks in the range of visible light.

SPT — Looking Up at Planet X from Due South

In "Chapter 8 — Solar Storm Monitoring," we learned that our growing fleet of space-based solar observatories is vulnerable to the ravages of a perfect solar storm. In the event several are damaged or destroyed, we will be able to launch microsatellite replacements such as the Belgian made Proba-2.

However, to ensure that we can maintain continuous monitoring of Planet X, a plan B was needed. In 2004, America began construction of a plan B observatory, the South Pole Telescope (SPT).

In late 2006, a fleet of specially equipped C-130 transports began flying pre-assembled SPT components to the Amundsen-Scott South Pole Station, which sits nearly atop the South Pole. Assembled under the harsh polar conditions, the SPT became operational in February of 2007.

Conditions at the South Pole are hard on personnel and equipment, and building this telescope elsewhere, such as Chile, would have been far more economical, especially when you consider what it takes to man and supply the SPT on an ongoing basis. In fact, even a space-based observatory becomes an affordable option, relative to the cost of building and maintaining the SPT.

However, when you set aside the operability issues, the SPT is the perfect instrument at the perfect place and at the perfect time. The reason is simple; this infrared telescope is ideal for tracking something like Planet X. Should we lose our space-based assets, the SPT will keep us focused on Planet X throughout the most hazardous segments of its flyby.

Herschel Space Observatory — Peeking Into the Stuff of Planet X

Scheduled to launch in 2008, The Herschel Space Observatory is built to study the molecular chemistry of the universe via the light of the far infrared and sub-millimeter portions of the spectrum.

Its mission is to find new information about the oldest, most distant stars and galaxies, as well as younger stars much closer to home. It will be able to look through clouds of dust to help observe the chemical composition of the atmospheres and surfaces of comets, planets and satellites.

Once it becomes operational, it will be able to gather significant data on Planet X and the many small objects and gases that will precede it and follow it. Of equal value will be its ability to gather information about Planet X's comet-like tail, which has been extensively documented in the historical accounts of *The Kolbrin Bible,* as well as other ancient texts.

WISE — Finding 'Little' Brown Dwarfs

By definition, a brown dwarf need only be larger than the planet Jupiter. Yet, the brown dwarfs we're presently discovering with other space telescopes are several times as large as that. If Planet X is a 'little' brown dwarf just barely larger than Jupiter, then it makes sense to find other similar sized objects in distant solar systems so that we can observe their behaviors.

This makes the **W**ide-field **I**nfrared **S**urvey **E**xplorer or WISE spacecraft the perfect 'little' brown dwarf hunter. Due for launch in 2009, it will survey the entire sky in the infrared spectrum, just like IRAS did in 1983 except that it will be up to 1000 times as sensitive as IRAS. This will enable it to detect previously unseen brown dwarf stars that are too small to be detected with current observation assets.

Spitzer — the Ultimate Brown Dwarf Hunter

The Spitzer telescope is the largest infrared telescope ever launched into space. While the Hubble was large already at 2.4 m (8 ft.), Spitzer tops that with 4.45 m (nearly 15 ft.). Launched in August of 2003 for a 2.5-year mission, it is considered one of NASA's "Big Four" space telescopes. The others are Hubble, Chandra X-Ray and the Compton Gamma Ray.

The Spitzer mission is to image distant objects by their emission of infrared radiation. Many areas of space are filled with dense clouds of gas and dust. Infrared light penetrates these clouds, which enables us to look into the center of these clouds, into galaxies and into newly forming planetary systems.

In September of 2006, the Spitzer telescope directly imaged a brown dwarf orbiting a larger and brighter star. About 50 times the size of Jupiter, it orbits its parent star at ten times the distance between the Sun and Pluto.

Another recent Spitzer observation of keen interest was that of a brown dwarf in an unstable death orbit around its massive parent sun. This proved that brown dwarfs can and do spiral into their parents as they destabilize the orbits of other planets in the system. The proof gave us an urgent reason to find and colonize new Earths elsewhere in the galaxy.

The Search for New Earths

Assuming that Planet X is a brown dwarf in an unstable orbit nearly perpendicular to the ecliptic, this could be the last survivable flyby. A role of great importance to humanity therefore becomes the search for extrasolar Earths in the distant systems within our galaxy. And the clock is ticking...

Nostradamus predicted what could likely be the end of the world in 3797 CE. This date could very well represent the final death plunge of Planet X into our Sun. Along the way, it would likewise cause Earth and the other planets in our system to spiral into the Sun or to fly out outwards into the cold depths of space. Another possibility is that Planet X simply spirals into the Sun in 3797, thereby causing a massive solar eruption that burns our planet into a lifeless, rocky cinder.

Hubble — New Life for an Old Telescope

Launched in 1990, the Hubble Space Telescope has surveyed the sky with unprecedented accuracy. After an initial focal error nearly killed its mission, NASA fitted Hubble with a correcting adaptation to its optics. Since then, it has provided some of the most spectacular pictures ever taken. Its best-known pictures are those of galaxies and nebulae that are billions of light years away.

Hubble has allowed astronomers to see the birth of stars and find valuable clues on the origin of our own star and planets, and it is powerful enough to find brown dwarf stars and exoplanets around stars light years away. These objects emit hardly any light and are far more difficult to find than the parent stars they orbit.

Several manned missions using the Space Shuttle have prolonged its mission life several times, and until recently, NASA scheduled its decommissioning for 2010. However, they scheduled a new service mission for 2008 that will extend Hubble's mission life to 2013.

Thanks to this new mission, Hubble will continue to give us invaluable insights into the behaviors of brown dwarfs as it also helps us to find possible new Earths in distant galaxies. For example, in September 2006, Hubble imaged an object 12 times the size of Jupiter. It might be a brown dwarf or a massive planet.

COROT — A Powerful New Extrasolar Earth Hunter

In December 2006, ESA launched COROT (**CO**nvection **RO**tation and Planetary Transits). This satellite will search for planets and new Earths that orbit distant stars. To do this, it will employ a transit method that will enable it to detect the small changes in the brightness of distant stars that occur as their planets orbit (transit) in front of them.

Other space-based and ground-based observatories are good at finding large extrasolar gas giants like Jupiter and Saturn, but if this observatory performs as hoped, it will be our most powerful extrasolar Earth hunter, capable of detecting rocky worlds, such as our own. For this reason, the COROT observatory will play a vital role in finding prospective, habitable planets around distant stars and will without doubt be the first of many such satellites.

Survival of the Species

In a June 2006 radio interview, world-renowned physicist and author of *A Brief History of Time,* Stephen Hawking stated his belief that the risk for total annihilation of humankind on Earth is growing day by day. Consequently, he has turned the survival of our species through off-world colonization into a personal crusade.

In the process, he is often mocked by less visionary scientists, who believe we need to get things right here on Earth before we colonize other worlds. These self-righteous debunkers assume we have the luxury of time to do this, but Stephen Hawking and those who share his views know otherwise.

We do not have the luxury of time, and colonizing Mars by 2046, as Hawking predicts, is merely a temporary stepping-stone. Colonizing other bodies in our solar system will give us a relatively convenient backyard laboratory to learn what works and what hurts. Once we've created this badly needed expertise, we'll be more capable of successfully pushing beyond the boundaries of our own solar system towards new extrasolar Earths. Unlike Noah's ark, which took a matter of years to construct, this future off-world migration will take form in stages.

First, we'll need to locate prospective Earths and then send robotic missions to these far planets to determine their habitability. This will take centuries. After which, we will begin to build massive space arks as we genetically enhance ourselves to endure the special rigors of extended space travel.

One day, our descendants will watch our beautiful, blue green home world recede from view as they take with them all of the hopes and prayers of those many generations who've come before them. We will survive!

10

Arks for the Chosen

When we hear or read the word "ark," we think of Noah's Ark, a large boat built by Noah and his family. The great wooden vessel they built to save themselves, along with one pair of every kind of creature during the Flood, as described in Genesis 6 – 9.

However, in a modern sense, an ark is much more than a big wooden vessel. Rather, an ark becomes any place of protection or security that offers refuge or asylum. Consequently, planetary arks can be diverse in size and nature. The biggest difference between them will be those who build them and those who are chosen to inhabit them during the worst of the flyby.

Those left behind by the world's power elites to survive on their own will need to find safety in natural caves or dig bunkers with at least 6 ft (1.8 m) of top soil. Those whom the power brokers choose to save will take refuge in man-made oceanic, subterranean and undersea arks. Amongst these, the odds of survival will vary, and there are no safe bets.

No Ark will be Absolutely Safe

Anticipating what kinds of arks are needed for a 2012 flyby of Planet X is tricky, as there is no way to be certain of the severity of the catastrophic consequences.

Despite all our massive astronomical and computing resources, we're still dealing with the three basic rules of real estate success: location, location and location. When translated to orbital mechanics, this becomes objects, objects and objects.

Ascertaining where Planet X will go and how fast it will get there requires something called an orbital solution. The more objects you inject into these solutions, the more complex they become.

- **Two-Object Solution:** Assuming that the Sun and Planet X were the only two substantial objects in our solar system, a good calculator and a bit of time is all that would be needed to calculate a solution.

- **Three-Object Solution:** Assuming that the Sun, Planet X and the Earth were the only three substantial objects in our solar system requires a lot more time and computing power than a two-object solution, but it's doable, mathematically.

- **Twelve-Object Solution:** In order to arrive at a final solution for the orbit of Planet X, the influences of 12 major objects must be factored into the calculations. Even if all the computers in the world were linked together to solve this orbit, they are unlikely to conclude it accurately to the last decimal. They can only "come close" mathematically. Or in other words, it is far easier to determine how many angels can fit on the head of a pin.

The whole point of this is that, despite all of our scientific prowess, knowing exactly what will happen during the Planet X flyby, and how best to survive it, has been and will likely remain a well-informed guesstimate at best.

While it is common knowledge that our leadership maintains underground bunkers to ensure Continuity of Government (COG), these arks are enough to save a government, but not a nation, let alone a species.

For this reason, our visible and invisible governments are not following one simple strategy. Rather, they're covering all their bets with several different types of arks in different places.

Most of this activity is hidden from view; however, the most visible types of Planet X – 2012 survival arks appear on television most every night. We call them cruise ships, and they are the best-kept 2012 secrets on television. In the turbulent years ahead, these modern day Noah's arks could save as many as 150 million lives.

Oceanic Arks

In order to be a true ark, a refuge must offer a habitation complete with living accommodations, food service, waste management, medical facilities, communications and so forth. In this context, ocean liners and cruise ships can be adapted to serve as arks.

Unlike ocean liners, which are designed primarily for port-to-port transportation, modern cruise ships are more like a Las Vegas casino and hotel with a bow and a stern. Consequently, cruise ships operate roundabout courses that usually return them to the same ports of call time-and-again.

Ocean liners, on the other hand, usually do not visit the same ports of call for many years. Itineraries and luxuries aside, the biggest difference is speed. Ocean liners are built to go faster than cruise ships.

As arks, there is no difference between the two types, except that modern day cruise ships are better suited as futuristic arks. A quick comparison of three well-known ships will help put this into perspective.

Modern Cruise Ships as Arks

In 1977, the American sitcom, "The Love Boat" featured light-hearted romantic comedies aboard the cruise ship *Pacific Princess*. An all-new *Pacific Princess* is now in service, and the original Love Boat has changed hands and names several times. It was refurbished in 2003, and it now cruises between Eastern European ports as the *MV Discovery*.

Compared to the *RMS Queen Mary*, which is now a floating museum in Long Beach, California, USA, and the cruise ship *Freedom of the Seas*, which just made its maiden voyage in 2006, the original Love Boat fame is a sluggish love dingy.

	Queen Mary	The Love Boat	Freedom of the Seas
Entered Service	1936	1972	2006
Vessel Type	Ocean Liner	Cruise Ship	Cruise Ship
Length	1,019.4 ft (311 m)	554 ft (168.8m)	1,112 ft (339 m)
Beam (Width)	118.5 ft (36.1 m)	81 ft (24.7 m)	184 ft (56 m)
Displacement	81,961 tons	20,636 tons	160,000 tons
Cruising Speed	29.5 knots	18.0 knots	21.6 knots
Passengers	2,139	650	4,370
Crew	1,101	305	1,360

In the cruise travel industry, the number of passengers is typically expressed in terms of berthing capacity. This varies, as each ship is configured differently with large multi-room staterooms, double occupancy cabins and so forth. The same holds true when we travel on trains. We can book private compartments with double bunk beds or single berths in a sleeper car.

Berthing can also be changed. For example, when The Love Boat first saw service in 1972, it was configured to carry 780 passengers. However, during its refit in 2001-2003, its berthing was reconfigured to carry 650 passengers with more spacious berthing arrangements.

Likewise, cruise ships and ocean liners can be used as floating hotels, nursing homes and apartment complexes. A good example was the 2004 Summer Olympics. Due to a severe shortage of hotel accommodations, several cruise ships were moored in Athens to provide additional tourist accommodations. In 2005, FEMA moored three cruise ships in New Orleans to provide local housing for displaced Hurricane Katrina victims.

The point here is that any ocean liner or cruise ship can be reconfigured for different applications and with different berthing arrangements. This in turn will affect their ability to carry more or fewer passengers, and this presents us with three simple questions:

1. How many cruise ships are operating in the world right now?

2. How many will come into service between now and 2012?

3. What is the total berthing capacity of these ships?

At first glance, it would seem that this information could be easily found on the Internet. Go and try it. After a while, you'll come to the same conclusion as the Lighthouse Foundation for the Seas and Oceans did. "There is a paucity of studies and little academic literature on cruise ship tourism despite it being the fastest growing sector in the tourism industry." That pretty much hits the nail on the head.

However, if you have $1900.00 to spend, you can buy a 2005 report with these figures from the Bharat Book Bureau. Short of that, here is a summary of what you'll eventually learn through considerable effort on the Internet.

Cruise Industry Growth

The big growth in cruising began in the late 1980's, and by 1991, there were approximately 100,000 berths available for cruises centered on the Caribbean, Alaska and Mexico areas.

At that time, a huge building boom began as European shipyards began growing the international fleet by approximately 8% each year, and by 2000, the number of available berths rose from 100,000 to 1 million.

As of 2004, the world's cruise lines now operated hundreds of modern cruise ships all around the globe. As with the Freedom of the Seas, these ships are becoming increasingly larger. Shipyards are now building cruise ships that are designed to carry over 3,000 passengers and measuring over 100,000 gross tons as fast as they can.

At the present rate of construction, the global cruise ship fleet will grow to 20 million berths by 2012! That is, berths for vacationers, who like to sleep in comfort, gamble and eat tons of ice cream each week.

Assuming the world's governments refit all operational cruise ships in time for 2012, how can 20 million berths designed for ice cream eating tourists be re-purposed for Planet X flyby refugees? People who'll be willing to sleep in small cots and live on bland rations in much the same way American soldiers did as they crossed the Atlantic to England aboard the *RMS Queen Mary* during WWII.

Turning Cruise Ships into 2012 Oceanic Arks

During WWII, moving war fighters and materials across the Atlantic meant running a gauntlet of Nazi U-boats. The workhorse of the U-boat fleet was the Type VII.

On the surface, the Type VII could reach a sustained speed of 17.7knots (20.50 mph, 33km/h) and half that while submerged. While these gray wolves of the sea could easily catch most merchant vessels, one ship, *RMS Queen Mary*, could easily outrun them.

Spacious, luxurious and magnificent to behold, she could sustain a maximum speed of 32.6 knots (37.28 mph, 60 km/h) and she held all the speed records for modern ocean liners from 1936 to 1952. This made her the perfect vessel for carrying America's most precious resource past Hitler's U-boats lurking in the Atlantic — our war fighters.

Originally, she was designed to carry 2,139 passengers and a crew of 1,101 during peacetime. She underwent a major refit following the outbreak of WWII, and she was converted into an Allied troop ship with high-concentration berthing. During one trans-Atlantic crossing, she safely transported over 17,000 American war fighters to England.

If all the cruise ships in the world in 2012 are likewise converted, we will have the capacity to berth well over 150 million refugees with a global fleet of Noah's arks, supported by an auxiliary flotilla of oil tankers, grain carriers, cargo ships, fishing trawlers, floating dry docks and so forth.

Designed for sailing anywhere in the world, today's modern cruise ships can be positioned over the deepest regions of our oceans, where they can handily deal with tsunami waves passing under their beams. Even though these waves can be monstrous when they make landfall, most will pass unnoticed by cruise ships at sea; they are as a passing "hump" in the ocean.

The most severe threats to these ships will be storms, radiation and the shock waves caused by asteroid impacts. In a best-case scenario, most of these oceanic arks will survive the worst of it and serve as badly needed temporary housing as humanity begins to rebuild port cities that have been laid to waste.

While oceanic arks will certainly offer refuge for the greatest numbers of people, most would not survive a worst-case scenario. The loss of life would be catastrophic, and those ships that remain afloat will be floating wrecks. After the flyby, they will be more valuable as sources of scrap steel than as moored accommodations.

In contrast to the oceanic arks, man-made subterranean and undersea arks will offer refuge for considerably fewer numbers, but give them better odds of survival.

Invisible to the world, these secretive arks will handily survive a best-case scenario, and a substantial number of them will likely survive a worst-case scenario.

The Invisible Arks

For the sake of argument, imagine you're running a government dark program, and you have access, legally or illegally, to limitless sums of money.

You learn that Planet X will arrive in 2012, and top scientists warn it could cause an extinction level event of cataclysmic proportions. You're then told that others will be responsible for COG (Continuity of Government) and that you're responsible for:

- Designing a global network of interconnected subterranean and submarine arks to ensure the continuation of the human species.

- Building highly survivable Planet X-hardened arks with sufficient stockpiles to last a decade.

- Creating a fear and family separation management program to exert initial control over distraught survivors chosen to inhabit the arks.

- Populating the arks on command, with pre-selected healthy, educated and mentally stable men and women of breeding age.

- Rebuilding an infrastructure essential to a recovering world after Planet X passes.

If you were such a person, the fruits of your labors would likely resemble a secret network of present-day arks described by government whistleblower, Philip Schneider.

Schneider Reveals Global Network of Arks

In the mid-90's, an American geologist, general engineer and structural engineer by the name of Philip Schneider, who allegedly quit his job building secret military bases for the US government, gave over 30 lectures in 1995.

He suffered a highly suspicious death in January 1996, and his story is presented in this book to illustrate a very realistic view of what shelters could exist today.

Before delving into his alleged description of a globally interconnected system of subterranean and submarine arks in existence today, let's first become acquainted with the late Philip Schneider.

About Philip Schneider

As a geologist and engineer, he had top government clearances. Consequently, he visited many foreign countries and briefed their government leaders during his 17-year tenure with the US government. For 11 of those years, he worked at Groom Lake in the Nellis Air Force Base area of the US state of Nevada, North of Las Vegas.

He co-invented shape-charge blasting and rock deflagration technologies and was the son of a former Nazi U-boat commander. After WWII, his father helped to build the Nautilus, the world's first nuclear-powered submarine.

The maser/laser rock deflagration devices Schneider invented are used to create underground tunnels and complexes by melting and agatizing rock. Used in tunnel boring systems, they can bore a 28 foot (8.53 m) wide x 28 foot (8.53 m) tall shaft at a rate of 7 miles (11.27 km) per day.

To clear the tunnel of haulage that the device didn't agatize, workers would bore vertical holes to one side of the lateral shaft and use hoists. This would reduce the chance of rock dust getting into the machinery or the laborers' lungs or masks. Also, they would bore ventilation holes for fresh air. By working together, machines could accomplish the 7-mile rate, while minimizing pollution.

Schneider's Credibility Issues

Those in the minority, who reject the notion that our governments are in secret contact with alien races altogether, will find everything Schneider says as lunacy. They will point to his statements in his lectures that the USA, along with possibly many other nations, is in contact with 11 alien races, of which two are benign. The other 9 races are exploiters who ruthlessly covet our planet, its resources and life forms.

On the other hand, the majority who believe in the existence of extraterrestrial races will find a strong correlation between what he was saying back in 1995 and current globalization trends that are creating larger under-classes, while transferring more wealth and power into the hands of just a few.

Schneider warned us that a New World Order has been steadily dismantling national governments and merging them into the United Nations, which will eventually morph into a one-world government.

Those who serve this secretive cabal are told they're working towards the noble purpose of putting an end to war. After 17 years of faithful service, Schneider resigned after reaching the belief that a much darker purpose is at hand and that it is controlled by off-world races that routinely violate their agreements.

This very behavior caused the 1979 Alien-Human War of Dulce, New Mexico, which happened purely by accident. According to Schneider, 66 US service agents and Special Forces members died during this unplanned and short-lived battle, and he was one of the three who survived it.

The battle occurred while Schneider's engineering team was drilling 4 cross-holes to start a new underground complex. One of the holes began emitting foul odors and breaking drill bits as fast as they could lower them down the hole. Because of this, he led a group of investigators down through a small elevator shaft to examine the hole. Garbed in an environment suit with a utility belt adorned with geology tools and collection containers, he began taking samples.

This is when he encountered two tall gray aliens, and having been trained for such encounters, he immediately drew his semi-automatic pistol and shot both of them dead. A third alien then appeared and shot him with a beam weapon that burned out one of his lungs and two fingers from his hand. He also claims he was saved by a green beret, who subsequently lost his own life during the engagement.

Afterwards, he underwent over 400 days of radiation therapy. The other 2 survivors languished away in Canadian nursing homes. This specific aspect of his account raises questions, given that the alien beam weapon was used in an attack and that the 400 days of therapy he cited for his radiation therapy is highly irregular. There are other concerns as well.

During his last lecture, he stated that the small pistol he used to kill the two tall gray aliens was a "Walther PPK pistol with a 9-round clip." This is a clear misstatement, because Carl Walther GmbH Sportwaffen never made a PPK model with a 9-round clip. The PPK models of that time were chambered for the .380 round and came with a 7-round clip. Otherwise, they were chambered for the .32 ACP round and came with an 8-round clip.

Granted, the PPK chambered for the .32 ACP round could have 8 rounds in the clip, plus 1 in the chamber, for 9 rounds. However, during his last lecture, Schneider said he had to load the pistol before he fired, which indicates that he did not carry the pistol with one round already in the chamber. Rather, he had to load the pistol by pulling the slide firmly to the rear and releasing it so it could go forward, while stripping a round from the clip and chambering it.

Therefore, a 9-shot clip is a clear misstatement of precise fact from Schneider's own lips during a recorded lecture, which can be independently vetted using unimpeachable sources. Yet, his 1995 warnings about globalization have begun to ring true in most unsettling ways. That same could be said for his 1996 death.

The Manner of Schneider's Death Conveys Credibility

The manner of Schneider's apparent suicide in January 1996 is highly suspicious, and according to his ex-wife, Cynthia Drayer, his partially decomposed body was discovered in his apartment in Wilsonville, Oregon.

The examining coroner determined his death as a suicide, because they found him with a rubber catheter hose wrapped three times around his neck and half-knotted in front. This was odd, given that the man was missing two fingers from his hand and had a medicine cabinet filled with powerful prescription painkillers for his many ailments.

According to Drayer, her ex-husband's body fluids were drawn, but never tested, and investigators never found a suicide note. Additionally, Schneider's personal library of government black operation research materials was taken, while considerable amounts of cash and valuables were left untouched.

During his 1995 lectures, Schneider told audiences that 13 attempts had already been made on his life. His ex-wife, Cynthia Drayer, further adds that he continually told his friends and relatives that if he ever "committed suicide," they would know he'd been murdered.

At face value, this paints a picture of a man who was finally silenced on the 14th attempt. Given the suspicious nature of his demise, his following statements on government black operations and underground / undersea bases arguably offer us a deathbed statement level of credibility.

Schneider's Subterranean and Submarine Arks

According to Schneider, as of December 1995, there were 131 underground bases worldwide. The subterranean variants are known in the black operations community as Deep Underground Military Bases (DUMBs). The submarine versions, which exist beyond the continental shelf, are designated DUMB2 bases. Schneider focused his lectures on the subterranean DUMB variant and offered the following facts:

- **USA Subterranean Locations:** DUMBs are typically located on government owned land. For example, 9 DUMBS are situated under Nellis Air Force base, North of Las Vegas.

- **Average Size and Cost:** 4.5 cubic miles (18.76 cubic km) at a cost of $17 to $31 Billion Dollars (US) each.

- **Largest Base Size and Cost:** Located in Sweden, it is 30 cubic miles (125.04 cubic km) at a cost of $2 trillion dollars US. It took 5 years to build and was wholly underwritten by the United Nations.

- **Range of Depths:** Depths range from 500 ft. for older storage bases to just over 10,560 feet for military installations (152.4 m to just over 3,218.69 m), which is almost as deep as the East Rand mine in South Africa. That mine goes to a depth of over 11,761.81 ft (3,585 m).

- **Average Depth:** During earthquakes, it is safer to be deep underground than on the surface, which is why most DUMBs are at a depth of 5,700 ft (737.36 m). This is an optimal depth in terms of survivability, without the need to engineer for heat and pressures associated with deeper depths.

- **Types of Subterranean DUMBs:** Older DUMBs, dating back some 40 years, are located at the shallowest depths and are primarily used for storage. The newer, deeper DUMBs are either fully self-sufficient, multi-level military installations or prisons.

- **Number of Subterranean DUMBs:** In 1995, the active number was 131. At present, an average of 2 new DUMBs is being completed each year, while several older sites at shallower depths are being removed from service. The current number of active DUMBs is unknown.

- **Construction Labor:** Each DUMB requires anywhere from 1,800 to 10,000 skilled workers to construct with wages of $4,000 to $40,000 per month, depending on position and tenure. All workers are bound by very tight non-disclosure security agreements.

- **US Distribution:** On average, there are 3 DUMBs per state, of which approximately 1/4 are prison camps. Most are located in the lower 48 States.

- **Transportation Networks**: Two different types of tunnel networks join all the DUMBs. One is a simple network of narrow 2-lane tunnels. The other is a sophisticated maglev train system with electrically driven trains capable of traveling at twice the speed of sound. Amongst these are trains designated as United Nations prisoner-transfer cars, each with 143 shackle placements for prisoners.

- **Power Sources:** Grid-bed nuclear motors the size of small refrigerators are used. Reverse-engineered from captured alien craft, each of these motors is powerful enough to power three aircraft carriers.

- **Funding Sources:** Some of the funding comes from taxes, but most of the funding comes through clandestine operations, including the drug trade. The combined annual funding is over US $500 billion.

According to Schneider, he worked on 13 DUMBs during his 17-year tenure, during which time, he witnessed a considerable, ongoing reverse-engineering effort to blend captured alien technologies with advanced human designs.

By today's standards, where the periodic table taught in our schools contains 117 confirmed elements, the periodic table used in black operations contains 140 elements, and that was as of 1995. Examples he cited included Mirrinite. Mirrinite, a new substance composed of rare earth minerals, clays and alien elements from crashed alien ships, is now used to coat stealth planes and black helicopters.

He also mentioned Niobium - Titanium - Uranium - Copper - Oxide in scalenohedral crystals (crystals with no sides of equivalent size). These are used to coat stealth ships or to seal the titanium hulls of Phoenix-class submarines, so they can operate at extremely deep depths for months at a time.

This in part is how Schneider explains the mind-boggling proliferation of the DUMB network and its transportation infrastructure. During his lectures, he expressed the belief that military technology is more than 1,000 years in advance of public technology. He added that this disparity in favor of the military is growing by 45 years for each year in the public sector.

All of this, in the context of the reason that Schneider gives for his defection, raises the red flags of questions that can never be answered. Nonetheless, in the context of a species seeking to save itself from an impending global natural cataclysm, it all clicks together like a box of Legos™.

Therefore, if we back away from the daunting concept of hybrid alien technologies being used to build an immense network of well-hidden subterranean and submarine arks, is there a more conventional example to study?

Yes, there is, and this source is unimpeachable. Robert Hopper and the Bunker Hill Mine.

The Bunker Hill Mine in Kellogg, Idaho

Thirty miles East of Coeur d'Alene, Idaho is the small mining community of Kellogg and the Bunker Hill Mine, the industrial anchor of the Coeur d'Alene Mining District and its current owner, Robert Hopper.

According to the Environmental Protection Agency (EPA), the Bunker Hill Mine is the largest underground lead-zinc-silver mine in the nation. Early in the Clinton administration, the EPA began the first of its many outright attempts to steal the mine from Hopper. Yet, Hopper claims he has not broken nor is suspected of violating any applicable State, Federal or mining laws that would allow them to legally do so.

This battle is of keen interest to the Planet X and 2012 debate, because Hopper fought the EPA to a standstill. He continues to fight despite their abusive use of extrajudicial powers to confiscate the mine without paying Hopper for his property.

A Mine the Size of 25 Cities

The site that would become the Bunker Hill Mine. First discovered in 1887 by prospector Noah Kellogg, it operated continuously until its closure by Gulf Resources in 1982. During this time, it produced 6,094 US tons (5,528 metric tons) of silver, 3.156 million US tons (2,863 million metric tons) of lead and various other metals. At one time, it employed up to 600 workers.

In April 2004, Hopper appeared on the Cut to the Chase Internet radio program with Marshall Masters (yowusa.com/radio). During the interview, Hopper offered the following description of the Bunker Hill Mine:

- **Levels:** The EPA describes the mine as "25 cities stacked on top of each other." Each level is fully developed, with water and electrical runs, compressed air, rail transport and work areas.

- **Horizontal Workings:** 150 miles of 10 ft (3.05 m) wide workings that are 10 ft (3.05 m) or 12 ft (3.66 m) high. These are horizontal passageways big enough to drive a pickup truck through.

- **Vertical Shafts:** Navigating vertically through the 25 levels of the mine is done through 6 miles (9.66 km) of shafts. These shafts are used much like the elevators found in modern high-rise buildings.

◢ **Ore Reserves:** According to Hopper, the mine still has 40 million tons (36.29 million metric tons) of combined lead-zinc-silver ore with a reserve value of $2 billion.

◢ **Potable Water:** The mine sits adjacent to a vast underground supply of natural water. In recent years, the bottom levels of the mine have become completely flooded with pure artesian water.

◢ **Ground Transport Access:** The main entrance of the mine is about 1,000 ft (304.8 m) from the town's main street and Interstate 90.

◢ **Air Transport Access:** The main entrance of the mine is approximately 2 miles (3.22 km) by freeway to the Kellogg City Airport, which has a 6,000 ft (1,828.8 m) runway. An easy fit for America's newest Jet transport, the C-17 Globemaster III that can land on runways as small as 3,500 ft (1,064 m).

In its present state, Hopper estimates that the mine could easily accommodate 1,000 refugees in the event of a prolonged natural emergency. With improvements, it could shelter upwards of 10,000 refugees. This arguably is the reason why the EPA has ruthlessly wielded its extrajudicial powers to try to confiscate the mine.

EPA Extrajudicial Powers

The pretext for the confiscation of The Bunker Hill Mine was lead contamination. Under the guise of the superfund cleanup mandate, the EPA relied on the extraordinary legal powers granted it by President Richard Nixon in 1971.

The EPA's takeover plan started with an innocuously titled investigatory power called a Request for Information (RFI). An RFI immediately makes any law-abiding citizen a person of interest, subject to criminal charges, unless they provide the EPA with copies of every word they write, summaries of conversations they hold and the names of all their contacts – for the course of their natural lives!

Simply put, rapists and axe murderers have more rights than any honest US property owner who receives an RFI from the EPA. However, the most corrosive aspect of an RFI for a mine owner, such as Hopper, is that it closes off his access to credit. Even though he has never been named as a suspect or charged with a crime or any violation of law, he must nonetheless disclose the RFI served upon him by the EPA. To bankers, the RFI is the kiss of death.

The EPA's abuses were so onerous that 2 different congressional hearings were convened, and during the second, a national ombudsman was appointed by congress in 2001 to investigate the matter. The National Academy of Science also became involved, and top NASA scientists, one of whom worked on the Mars exploration projects, completely debunked the EPA's science. In response, the EPA surreptitiously closed the ombudsman's office and seized all of his files.

To his credit, Robert Hopper is still fighting the EPA with all he's got, but in the end, this is going to be about geology. Given enough time and pressure, the EPA will eventually acquire the mine, by one means or another. After that, they'll operate it through a front company and convert it to whatever purposes they wish.

If you have a golden Willy Wonka ticket that gets you into one of these DUMBs or a renovated Bunker Hill bunker, lucky you. What about the rest of us?

Building Your Own Ark

Those of us who will be left to fend for ourselves on the surface will need to build survival bunkers or find natural caves for the worst parts of the Planet X flyby. We're not going to have tunnel-boring machines that use lasers to carve out 7 miles (11.27 km) of tunnels each day.

Rather, we're going to have the same sophisticated equipment the Vietcong used to dig their extensive wartime tunnel network in South Vietnam. Spades, picks, shovels, buckets and wheelbarrows.

In our present day material world, hobnobbing with lawyers, accountants, life insurance salesmen and advertising gurus at the local Rotary Club lunches is a shrewd use of time. On the other hand, if you do not have a golden Wonka ticket that gets you into a DUMB, you might want to spend time with the kind of folks who will increase your odds of survival.

A grandmother with a green thumb in the garden is worth 10x her weight in pencil pushing accountants. Likewise, an undocumented worker who left his corn farm in Mexico to sneak across the border into America will be worth more than an army of lawyers.

That's right, today's hard-working illegal aliens could very well make the difference between whether you live or die in the years ahead. This is because, when we get hungry in a highly industrialized country, all we know how to do is to get into our air-conditioned cars and drive to the local supermarket.

When it comes time to scratch a few meager calories from the Earth, will we have enough time to learn the basics of farming passed down from one generation of campesinos (small farmer or farm worker in Spanish) to another? How many of us can honestly afford to starve our way through a heuristic trial-and-error process to relearn old survival skills?

If that question insults you into countering that argument by pointing out that we do not need these campesinos when we have our own small farmers, you need to come up to speed on what's really happening.

In 1935, America was blessed with 6.8 million small family farms. Since then, government subsidized corporations and large family operations whittled that down to 2.1 million by 2002.

Today, the average age of small family farm operators is 50-something, and over 40% work a second job to get by. Meanwhile, their children and grandchildren have all but disappeared into the cities to become office and factory workers.

This is why NAFTA (the North American Free Trade Area) could very well be viewed by future generations as a true survival blessing to all those Americans left behind by their government to fend for themselves.

American farm corporations have been enjoying windfall profits as their subsidized corn enters the Mexican markets, forcing the deaths of entire farming communities there. Desperate to care for their own families, many of these campesinos have come to America to wash dishes and dig ditches, along with their marvelous farming skills.

When it comes time to build shelters with spades, picks, shovels, buckets and wheelbarrows, they'll do what they're already doing. They'll get their hands dirty and do what needs to be done without whining about their good old days at the Rotary Club lunches. For now, keep this in mind, because there is an even darker, but necessary, aspect of how the government arks of 2012 will be filled.

The Shackle Placements Revisited

During his lectures, Philip Schneider told audiences that a sophisticated tunnel network with a maglev train system connected all the DUMBs. Amongst these, certain trains are designated as "United Nations prisoner transfer cars" with 143 shackle placements for prisoners per car.

To him, these shackle placements represented the brutal establishment of a one-world government and a tragic loss of human rights. One that would turn a nation state like America into mythical Atlantis, along with its constitution.

Given the time in which he worked on these projects, that makes sense. However, in light of the hellish environment Earth's surface will become at some point in the flyby of Planet X, there could be a more logical explanation.

Assuming the planet's surface is going to become a nightmarish place, why bother transporting prisoners to safe places, where you'll have to secure, feed, clothe and care for them. Think about it. Would you go to all the effort just to unleash unmanageable undesirables upon a ravaged post-2012 world? More to the point, are these humans worth spending countless trillions of dollars to save to ensure the continuity of the species? Only in Hollywood!

It's time to face a brutal reality. Regardless of what the motivation is for governments and dark operations groups to prepare the various arks discussed in this chapter, there is but one common goal. They want our species to survive.

How we get there may not be noble, but if it works – it works. We must accept it and hope for the best. If for just one brief moment, we dare consider the pronouncement of Philip Schneider, what could that mean in some future time?

The Gathering

At some point in the years ahead, a trigger point will be reached, and then the gathering shall begin. Candidates for the DUMBs will have already been chosen without their knowledge.

There could never be enough room or supplies for everyone, so those chosen will be of childbearing age, healthy, educated, highly skilled and well adjusted.

As the gathering unfolds, any cul-de-sac in America's neighborhoods could be turned into a ready-made landing pad for a transport helicopter, such as a Huey or Blackhawk. The result will be that families become forcefully separated.

For those watching their loved ones going to safety, there will be gratitude and sorrow. For those chosen, there will be the horror of knowing that they will be looking at everyone they love most, possibly for the last time.

Those on the surface will take comfort from knowing that someone they love is more than a mile down, ensconced in the safety of a DUMB. Yet, those torn from their families will surely feel a deep, tormenting sense of loss.

As with all momentous events in life, we each take them in our way. Most will glumly accept the situation and grieve in their own way. Others will certainly become hysterical with irreconcilable grief. For their own safety and that of others, they will be treated as prisoners until they adjust to their loss — or worse.

This is why the shackle placements in the maglev trains will eventually serve a brutal, but necessary purpose: the survival of our species.

After the worst has come and gone, we'll still be here, and those from below will rise up out of the ground to share a more enlightened future with those, who thanks to the grace of their own spiritual strength, will have managed to endure.

Part 4 – Fending for Yourself

"It is better to eat beans from your own bowl, than steak from another man's hand."

—*Marshall Masters*

After 2012, two kinds of humans will emerge based on the decisions being made today. Those chosen for survival and those who chose to survive as equals.

In the years following 2012, they will emerge together as the children of the future, and our world be the better for it.

11

Be a 2012 Rambo

When the prospect of what is about to happen really begins to sink in, we tend to feel a serious "every man for himself" consumer itch to do or buy something — now! To illustrate the point, let's assume that you've decided to turn a large room in your basement into a survival shelter. The first thing you do is to swear your family to secrecy. Your wife thinks you're a lunatic, but she'll humor you. The kids are easy. You bribe them with theme park season passes.

In the evenings, you haunt the Web for all the right construction methods and materials you'll need, and you start placing orders. Not all at once, though. You do not want to become a sudden drop-off site for parcel delivery services, so you stretch the process out while you stockpile products found locally.

Assuming that you'll need to remain in your shelter for as long as a year, you buy prepackaged survival food kits for yourself, your wife and your two children for an entire year, with a 10% reserve thrown in for good measure.

Eventually, the shelter has been completed and stocked, and nobody is the wiser for it. For the benefit of those neighbors who happen to tromp down into your basement, there is a tarp over the steel plate door with a sign that says, "Beware of sewage backups." After commiserating with neighbors about crooked plumbers, your basement becomes a dead topic. Next, you purchase an assault rifle with the red dot scope and pistols. During the weekends, you hone your skills at a local shooting range.

Everything is going along great until the annual family reunion comes along. After mass quantities of BBQ and beer, your wife accidentally blurts outs your secret preparations to her brother. A 35-year-old loser who continues to live at home, because he finds it hard to hold a job.

Once he learns that your sewage problem is actually a survival bunker, he begins poking at you without mercy. You're furious with your wife for exposing you to his ridicule, but she tells you to lump it and go on. He's her little brother, after all.

A year later, the worst happens, and you're in the bunker with your family. Well-provisioned, safe and snug. That is, until a few weeks later, when little brother shows up with two new acquaintances in tow. They both look like they just got out of prison, and he's told them about your bunker. Now, all three feel you should do the right thing for them by taking them in and giving each of them an equal share.

Aside from the threat posed by taking strange undesirables into your home, the math looks pretty bad. Feeding three grown men will cut your family's chance of survival in half. This is unacceptable, so you give them a three-day supply of canned food and politely send them on their way. Little brother complains bitterly to your wife, but this time, she stands by you. She's done the math, too.

Now, time begins to move at a crawl as you wonder if little brother and friends will move on or return with a vengeance. The answer is not long in coming. They've traded some of the food you gave them for whiskey. This, and a long night of partying, have helped them come to the conclusion that you're a bad fellow. Little brother's friends assure him that nothing will happen to his sister or her children, but your number is up. After all, hardhearted bastards like you do not deserve to live.

The next morning, they assault the house with sledge hammers, axes, bats and a few old revolvers. You've anticipated an attack like this, and you're ready for them. It's all over in a few minutes.

Dispatching the strangers was easy, but little brother is wounded. You just couldn't find it in you to take the kill shot. Rather, you aimed for a flesh wound so as to give him a second chance. Mistaking your compassion for bad marksmanship, he swears he'll kill you, and a voice deep down inside you says enough is enough. You put the next round between his eyes.

As you drag the bodies to a small pit in your backyard, your wife steps out of the shelter. She sees the weapons and the bodies, and begins to cry. Angry, she marches up to you, slaps your face and screams, "you bastard, you killed my little brother! I hate you!"

You're stunned into silence. Partly by her rage and partly by the realization that you're going to spend the next year cooped up in a closed-in space with a hateful woman and two very distraught children. Over the course of the coming year, you'll agonize over that second shot. Dumb luck, that.

The most notable mistake was the naïve notion that you could buy your way out of 2012. Had you invested the time and effort to network with like-minded individuals to form the nucleus of a survival community instead, little brother and his friends would have encountered a tightly knit survival group.

Most likely, he and his friends would have taken the food and gone on down the road to find an easier target to plunder. Or perhaps before they could do that, other hooligans would have killed them on sight, just to steal the food you've given them.

Nonetheless, had they attacked instead, the group would have responded in force and without mercy. At that point, little brother's death would not have generated an irrational outrage aimed at you. Rather, it would have been about the threat he presented to the group. Ergo, the secret to surviving 2012 is not consumerism.

Consumerism is not a 2012 Survival Method

A line, attributed to the popular cartoon character Ziggy, best captures the ever-present marketing message of our modern consumer societies. "If it itches, scratch it." As consumers, we're inundated with hundreds of messages each day telling us that when we itch, we need to buy something.

We're so hopelessly inundated by this cacophony of capitalism that, once we desire or fear something, we instinctively go shopping. Admit it. (Group hug; you're not alone.) Just like Pavlov's Dog, this is what we've been trained to do since we first set eyes on a television. When we get the itch for something to fill our tummies, we go to McDonalds. The only complex part of the process is wondering if we'll have the willpower to ignore the itch to supersize our McScratcher meal.

So what? Isn't that how it's always been done? No. For millennia, our hunter-gather ancestors went to the Earth to find fresh carrion and edible fruits, vegetables, grains and tubers. Perhaps their diet was woefully short of secret sauce, but they nonetheless survived numerous global cataclysms. News flash. This is something we modern-day consumers have yet to do, unlike our primitive ancestors. A simple fact that can make you wonder if we're a dark horse running in the evolution derby of life and death.

Imagine it. Centuries after 2012, future archeologists will marvel at the majesty of the Great Pyramid of Giza during the day. In the evenings, they'll sit around the campfire and speculate as to whether the magical golden arches of the fabled consumer angels actually did exist.

Then, one of them will mention the recent discovery of a time capsule with a perfectly intact copy of a revered ancient historical cinematic folklore called *Rambo: First Blood*.

> **NOTE:** To achieve the maximum benefit of this chapter, obtain a copy of *Rambo: First Blood* (1982), the very first Rambo film starring Sylvester Stallone. Before reading further in this chapter, watch the movie on an entertainment level. Then, continue on.

Rambo's Moral Compass

Understanding what it means to be a 2012 Rambo is not about seeing the character of John Rambo in the context of present day beliefs or the thought of you enduring all odds with your trusty Rambo combat knife in hand. Rather, it is about focusing on what endeared him to America.

Tormented by his memories of his several tours in Vietnam as a member of an elite U.S. Army unit designated as "Team Delta (Delta Force)," the Rambo character's most endearing virtue is his ethical sense of right and wrong. It is Rambo's inner moral compass that binds the character through all four films in the series, which gives him an admirably human appeal.

Stouthearted, Rambo always speaks the truth, fights injustice and willingly puts his life at risk to protect the innocent and the vulnerable from exploitation and abuse. To understand the strength of this virtue, one must go back to the times of the first film.

When the first Rambo film was released in 1982, it capitalized on a growing mainstream regret that Vietnam veterans had been unjustly cast as barbarous and inhuman. With a miserable war behind them and prosperity ahead, many Americans could not forget how a proud nation had turned against its own. Now, there was a deep desire amongst many to set things right.

This is why the first Rambo film was such a phenomenal success. It came out when people still remembered seeing news accounts of young girls running up to soldiers in airport terminals – not to hand them flowers – but to spit upon their uniforms.

Today, one can only wonder how many of these righteous girls later watched their own sons or grandsons march off to war, wondering if they too would be similarly dishonored upon their return, or if they would return at all. Regrets are like ghosts. They follow you forever.

In the years ahead, you will face tribulations that will likely be more severe than those depicted in the Rambo films, but you must remain firm like a Rambo and keep a true moral compass. Those who live in service-to-others, as does the Rambo character in this popular film series, will prevail. The ancients have told us this:

The Kolbrin Bible: 21st Century Master Edition

◢ **Manuscripts 3:09** "Then men will be ill at ease in their hearts, they will seek they know not what, and uncertainty and doubt will trouble them. They will possess great riches but be poor in spirit. Then will the Heavens tremble and the Earth move, men will quake in fear and while terror walks with them the Heralds of Doom will appear. They will come softly, as thieves to the tombs, men will not know them for what they are, men will be deceived, the hour of the Destroyer is at hand."

◢ **Manuscripts 3:10** "In those days, men will have the Great Book before them, wisdom will be revealed, the few will be gathered for the stand, it is the hour of trial.

THE DAUNTLESS ONES WILL SURVIVE, THE STOUTHEARTED WILL NOT GO DOWN TO DESTRUCTION."

If you lose your true moral compass and exploit the innocent for self-gain, you will become a lost and angry soul, shaped by your own service to self.

So then, what about those service-to-self types, the ones who always manage to survive momentary cataclysms at the expense of others? Will they fare as well in the catastrophic years ahead? Although they will endure for as long as they can find others to exploit, that supply is not inexhaustible. Eventually, it will run out, and they will begin to feed upon themselves.

They will know about the elusive 2012 Rambo types, but they will have neither the strength nor the will to confront them. This is because a 2012 Rambo is a master of situational awareness (SA).

Hit the Ground Running

We often hear the old axiom, "hit the ground running." First coined in the 20th century, it is used to explain how some people always manage to find themselves in new situations and then instinctively get off to a successful start. For example, hobos jumping from freight trains to explore new towns and airborne troops being dropped by parachute into hostile territory.

Whether you're a hobo who learns through painful trial-and-error, or you're trained by the military, as the Rambo character was, the first step in hitting the ground running is a survival concept called situational awareness (SA).

Rambo: First Blood Situational Awareness Scene

An excellent example of SA occurs in the film after Sheriff Will Teasle wrongfully arrests Rambo for vagrancy and brings him back to the jail to have him booked and detained.

Falling back on his military training, Rambo remains quiet during the booking process. He ignores the disrespectful way the deputies manhandle him and scans the office, searching for possible escape routes. He also makes special note of the desk, upon which his survival knife was casually tossed.

Take note of what happened when the booking officer threatened Rambo that he'll "break his face." The booking officer was too self-absorbed with his own power over Rambo to notice that he has shifted into survival mode. Director Ted Kotcheff makes excellent use of his highly knowledgeable production consultants by directing Stallone to assume a telltale hyper-attentive expression (eyes wide open with jaw set) during the scene.

SA is Not About Assigning Blame

In essence, SA is a 3-step process, by which you quickly assess whatever situation you find yourself in so that you can respond accordingly:

1. What is happening, and why?

2. What will happen next?

3. What are my options?

Therefore, SA is not about finding someone to blame in a survival situation. On the contrary, if you react by saying things like "FEMA should be here! Where are they?" or "This is the governor's fault!" then nature will cull you out of the herd, should that be your fate.

If FEMA does eventually show up or the governor stops acting like a deer caught in the headlights, that's great. In the meantime, you've got a situation to deal with. Be objective enough to see it exactly for what it is through SA, and trust your intuition.

Trust Your Intuition

Being creatures of purported free will, we prefer rational thinking to an intuition-based approach. With rational thinking, we're in control of a process that relies mostly on logic and quantitative analysis. This approach yields a sense of control as we evaluate the various options relative to expected outcomes, importance, utility value, risk and so forth. At the end of the process, we select an option with the best chance of success — or not. Either way, we're in control up to a point.

When you have the luxury of time to formulate a plan, rational thinking offers a great way to avoid a dire fate that Alexander Pope warned about when he said, "Fools rush in where wise men fear to tread." Furthermore, rational thinking enables you to reap rewards others would normally overlook because, as Louis Pasteur best put it, "chance favors the prepared mind." However, when we DO NOT have the luxury of time for rational thinking, a more intuitive approach can easily mean the difference between life and death.

We all have this inner voice, and we use many different names to define it, such as subconscious, spirit guide, Yahweh and so forth. For the purpose of this discussion, let's call it good old-fashioned intuition, or gut instinct, if you will.

Bookstores are stocked with a robust number of books that teach us how to capitalize on our intuition, and they show us how to make better business deals and to effectively handle spontaneous life situations. The key to making it work effectively is that you must be willing to trust your instincts enough to forego the sense of control that comes with rational thinking.

The Benefits of Trusting Your Intuition

In terms of surviving 2012 catastrophes, relying on an intuitive mode of thinking during a fast moving crisis will give you three very powerful benefits:

Symbiotic Processing

An intuitive approach allows us to fully utilize the full processing power of our minds.

With rational analysis, our conscious mind virtually excludes our subconscious mind. Conversely, while intuitive thinking is dominated by our subconscious mind, it links to our conscious mind with a powerful symbiotic balance.

Holistic Perception

An intuitive approach allows us to turn on the powerful human survival computer within us.

Rational analysis is a process that somewhat resembles the old 1960's-era punch-card processing machines. Problems were solved using tall stacks of sequentially punched cards. While this rational, but very rigid, process is well adapted to handling record-keeping tasks, it has never been well adapted to systems that resemble human thought.

Humans view situations holistically, where different fragments of the same picture emerge in parallel. A well-honed skill that nature has perfected since our ancestors first walked the Earth.

Emotional Connection

An intuitive approach increases the likelihood that we'll choose the right option in a fast-paced moment of crisis.

With rational analysis, we try to distance ourselves from our emotions, and in many situations, this is the best thing to do. Hence, we count to ten before saying something we'll later regret, or we decide to sleep on the matter to avoid making a hasty decision.

However, when the circumstances you're in are moving faster than you can process them or are difficult to discern, connect with you true emotions. Know the difference between emotions that are driven by a wounded ego, greed or pride, and set them aside. Focus solely on those emotions that stem from pure instinct.

For example, if you have to make a fast decision, and one option that looks right to a rational mind does not feel right, go with what feels right. More often than not, it will be the right choice, because in the absence of clear logic, any option must be considered illusory at the rational level.

An easy example for most to visualize is the scene from the film *Star Wars IV: A New Hope* (1977), towards the end of the movie. Luke Skywalker is flying his X-wing fighter through the Death Star's equatorial trench, aiming for the exhaust vent to the Death Star's main reactor with Darth Vader and his two henchmen in hot pursuit.

The rational thing to do is to lock onto the Death Star's exhaust port with his targeting computer, but as he begins to set up his attack, we hear the voice of his mentor, Obi-Wan Kenobi saying, "Use the Force, Luke. Trust your feelings!" To the astonishment of the Rebel leaders, Luke switches off his targeting computer and presses home a successful attack, using his intuition alone. While this is a good example, the Rambo film offers a better example, because it applies more closely to the main point of this discussion.

Rambo: First Blood Intuition Scene

Rambo has fled to an abandoned mine, and National Guardsmen have laid siege to the entrance. After a volley of fire, they shoot a shoulder-fired rocket into the mine, which collapses it. Without hesitation, Rambo fashions a torch made from strips of his poncho wrapped around a stick. He lights it and starts searching the depths of the mine for another exit. Along the way, he finds a little bit of gasoline in a can and uses it to soak more strips for more light.

After traversing a flooded section of the mine, where he uses the torch to fend off a rat attack, he notices the flame of the torch shifting in response to wind coming through a back entrance to the mine. It leads him safely out of the mine without detection.

Rambo uses his intuition, instinct and his ingrained military training to get himself through a life-threatening situation. By responding to his instincts, he exits the mine undetected by the sheriff and state police. Relying on rational thought, they have concluded that he is dead and called off the search. Why? They feared Rambo because he had the courage and the ability to run to the roar.

Run to the Roar

In the years to come, we shall come to know fear that is as yet unknown to those of us in the present. However, the ancients experienced it during the last flyby of Planet X during the Exodus.

The Kolbrin Bible: 21st Century Master Edition

- **Manuscripts 3:04** "When blood drops upon the Earth, the Destroyer will appear, and mountains will open up and belch forth fire and ashes. Trees will be destroyed and all living things engulfed. Waters will be swallowed up by the land, and seas will boil."

- **Manuscripts 3:05** "The Heavens will burn brightly and redly; there will be a copper hue over the face of the land, 'followed by a day of darkness. A new moon will appear and break up and fall.'"

- **Manuscripts 3:06** "The people will scatter in madness. They will hear the trumpet and battlecry of the Destroyer and will seek refuge within dens in the Earth. Terror will eat away their hearts, and their courage will flow from them like water from a broken pitcher. They will be eaten up in the flames of wrath and consumed by the breath of the Destroyer."

In other passages, we're told that women grew so fearful they could no longer conceive and that men became impotent — all this on a global scale.

Fortunately for us, our science will help us prepare better and to anticipate the staggered contractions of this evolutionary event. Yet with all that, we will face the same beast, and we will feel our courage flow from us, as well. In these moments, consider a manner, in which certain prides of African lions have been known to hunt.

The pride knows that a healthy gazelle can easily dodge around and outrun an old lioness, so they split up. The younger, faster lions that can bring down a gazelle silently crawl on their bellies through the tall grasses until they're in a good position downwind of the game.

When the moment is right, the older lions move upwind of the game and begin roaring for all they're worth. When the gazelles hear and smell the old lions, they react fearfully by running away from the roar. Consequently, they leap right into the waiting jaws of the younger, faster lions waiting for them in the tall grasses.

The point here is that, if the gazelles had the sense to run towards the older ions, or in this case to run to the roar, they could dodge past them to safety. Hence the expression, "run to the roar," in a very human sense, means that you must face your worst fear head-on.

This does not mean you should feel compelled to fight your way through 2012, as the Rambo character did through the film. On one hand, had Rambo been sensible, he would have walked or hitchhiked another 30 miles down the road, instead of challenging Sheriff Will Teasle at the outset of the film. On the other, there would have been no movie, had he been sensible. In 2012, you'll have to be more sensible.

The Essence of Rambo

In 2012, there will be no theaters with thrilled moviegoers watching the big screen as they dig hot buttered popcorn out of a paper bucket. The point here is that while the film contains a tremendous amount of realism that lends credibility to the action, it is nonetheless a fictional account.

Nor will there be hospitals stocked with antibiotics, painkillers and the other marvels of science we've become accustomed to. Rather, we'll be living in a world where people die of simple infections, if they do not starve to death first.

While vengeance and high noon antics are stupid ways to get killed, there will be situations where conflict it unavoidable. If that happens, get mad-dog mean; hit hard; hit fast, and then melt away. Otherwise, always want to avoid conflict wherever and whenever possible.

The combat theatrics of the Rambo films should be seen as entertainment and nothing more. When you set them aside, you can appreciate the following three lessons of the Rambo character:

- If you cannot trust your intuition, you'll be lost.

- If you lose your ability to feel compassion for the needy and vulnerable, you'll be lost.

- If you lose your ability to love and to be loved, you'll be lost.

No matter how much pain and suffering you endure, never, never, never, lose your inner moral compass!

12

Coping with a Violent Sun

In "Chapter 8 — Solar Storm Monitoring," we examined the Herculean effort currently underway by America, Europe and Japan, to put a large fleet of solar observatories into space by 2008. Even the mission life of the venerable SOHO solar observatory, which has been operational since 1995, was extended to 2009.

The goal is obvious. Our governments are monitoring the Sun so as to forecast probable solar storms before they happen and then track those that do erupt and present a threat to Earth. Why? Because a perfect solar storm, one that is massively violent and directly in line with the Earth, could be devastating to human life and our industrialized societies.

In fact, a perfect solar storm could so badly damage a space shuttle or even the International Space Station (ISS) that we could see them in an uncontrolled re-entry leading to a fiery encounter with our atmosphere.

Could this happen? According to Hopi folklore, it will happen; we shall know it as a harbinger of a time of woe, and this would be a double horror. First would be the tragic loss of brave crews, and the second, the realization that those who remain on the surface of our planet will suffer terribly, as well.

Solar Storm Overview

Scientists will be looking at many aspects of our Sun's behavior with this new fleet of solar observatories. The two types of storm behavior will be of keen interest: solar flares and coronal mass ejections (CME).

Both are caused by rapid, large-scale changes in the Sun's magnetic field and most often occur together like a one-two punch. However, they can also occur independently of each other. Or, one initiates a solar storm and then triggers the other.

Coronal Mass Ejection (CME)

A CME is violent hiccup in the Sun's lower atmosphere, an area called the corona. It is essentially a giant cloud of heated, electrified gas, called plasma, that can take as long as 48 hours to reach Earth.

For the most part, CME's are primarily a threat to satellites, spacecraft and astronauts and can disrupt communications on Earth. In a worst case scenario, a CME could be powerful enough to defeat's Earth's magnetic shield, thereby causing violent weather and radiation storms.

In the years ahead, we could bear witness to powerful CME's interacting with the magnetic field surrounding the Earth. The result will be powerful auroras. Appearing like the aurora borealis (Northern Lights), they'll extend down to the middle latitudes and reach cities like Seattle, Chicago and New York.

Similar effects could also be seen in the Southern hemisphere with the aurora australis (Southern Lights.) This is when we'll pray for our magnetic fields to hold.

Earth's magnetic fields protect us from the worst that these CME plasma storms can dish out, somewhat like the shields on the Starship Enterprise of Star Trek fame. Likewise, when Enterprise's shields are weakened, it starts taking brutal hits. A similar event happened to Earth back in the mid-19th century.

In September 1859, a massive solar storm slammed into the Earth. This was a fast moving CME of immense scale, and the magnetic fields contained within it were not only powerful, they were also aligned in direct opposition with Earth's own magnetic fields. Consequently, it overwhelmed Earth's own magnetic field, allowing charged particles to penetrate into Earth's upper atmosphere. This shorted-circuited telegraph lines all throughout the US and Europe and caused several fires.

Imagine that happening today. What would be left of our Internet, power grids and the computers in our cars, homes, offices, radios, televisions and so forth? Not much. Yet, the same CME events will likely begin to happen once we cross the threshold into 2012. This is because Earth's magnetic fields are weakening in preparation for a change in polarity, as the solar activity will be escalating to its highest point in recorded history.

What will happen to us if Earth's shield, its magnetic fields, are weakened just as a massive Earth-directed CME hits while our North and South poles are in the process of reversing polarity? The consequences could be grim, to say the least. However, a more immediate and less speculative threat comes from solar flares.

Solar Flares

In terms of human risks, solar flares are the Sun's most deadly jabs. The radiation from solar flares reaches us at the speed of light, which makes it much faster than the slower moving plasma of a CME. A secondary threat also comes from the charged particles that follow right behind the initial solar flare radiation at nearly the speed of light.

This means Earth is pounded by the one-two punch from a solar flare much faster than the slower moving plasma of CME, which can take up to four days to reach us. Or, it could arrive here in less than a day, which could be especially devastating if it happens to be a Y-class event.

Y-class Solar Flares

During the 20th century, solar flares were classified with the severity categories: A, B, C, M, and X. The X category was reserved for the most violent storms and within this X class, a solar flare could be ranked from X1 to X20.

On April 2, 2001, a solar flare blew past the X20 end of the scale. It was the largest in recorded history, and some placed it at X22, while others ranked it at X40! This breakthrough in the classification scale resulted in the creation of the new Y-class mega flare classification.

Lucky for us, the 2001 Y-class solar flare was pointed away from Earth. Had it been otherwise, 2001 could have seen humanity thrown backwards into another pre-industrial, agrarian age.

Earth-directed Solar Storms

Regardless of whether a solar storm is an X or Y class flare with or without a CME, the three rules of valuable real estate will shape the outcome. Those rules are: location, location and location.

Imagine that the Earth is looking down the business end of a shotgun, and that the Sun is the shooter. If you're looking straight down the barrel, you're in the absolute worst place to be. If you're standing a little to either side of that, then you'll catch a few pellets, because you're in the vicinity of the blast, but it will be survivable. Obviously, the third location, behind the shooter, is by far the best.

In terms of solar storms, most solar flares and CME's burst out in a direction that is nowhere near the Earth. Those pointed in the vicinity of Earth and of great strength become problematic. If a severe X-class or Y-class solar storm erupts with Earth in the crosshairs, then we're looking down the barrel of an Earth-directed cosmos of hurt coming our way.

Solar Storm Nasties

Nasty is the only world that describes X-Rays, UV Radiation, Gamma Rays, EMP and Magnetic storms spewed out by solar storms. In terms of the human race and the electrically powered infrastructure that shapes our daily lives, there is no positive message here. That is why you need to become familiar with the following solar storm nasties:

- **Gamma Radiation:** Generated during a solar storm, it is a lethal combination of a short wavelength and a high-energy content. Like X-rays on steroids, gamma radiation causes serious damage when absorbed by living cells.

- **X-Ray Radiation:** The actual term applies to man-made radiation, but is used in science to describe radiation that occurs naturally within this same bandwidth. X-rays are one form of ionizing radiation, which can be destructive to any biological organisms and cause DNA damage and mutations.

- **Ultraviolet (UV) Radiation:** The most dangerous high-energy variant of ultraviolet light. Prolonged exposure can result in acute and chronic health effects on the skin, eyes and immune system.

- **Electromagnetic pulse (EMP):** A short fierce pulse of electromagnetic energy that occurs across several bandwidths. With specific bandwidths, longer durations produce more severe results. However, with an EMP, the opposite holds true. The shorter the pulse, the more severe it becomes. While devastating to electronic devices, it passes harmlessly through living cells.

- **Magnetic Storm:** Caused when the charged particles from a CME impact upon the outer part of the Earth's magnetic field and create a worldwide magnetic disturbance.

Solar flares and CME's each have their own witches' brew of solar storm nasties, and some have a very short time to Earth of just minutes. Others take hours. Use the table below to see what is going to hit you, when and how hard.

Effect	Risk	Solar Flare Class	CME	Time to Earth	Event Duration
X-Rays		**A to Y**	**Severe**	**8.3 Minutes**	**1 - 3 Hours**
	Human *Cancer & Cataracts*	The primary concern is the carcinogenic effect. The organs most vulnerable are the thyroid and reproductive organs. (Testicular cancers for men and ovarian cancers for women.) A secondary concern is loss of sight due to cataracts and bone cancer resulting from prolonged exposure.			
	Electronics	Normally no effects. Levels deadly to life can cause electronics to fail.			
UV Radiation		**A to Y**	**No**	**8 - 15 Minutes**	**1 - 3 Hours**
	Human *Burns & Blindness*	High doses can result in severe burns (1st, 2nd and 3rd degree), especially with longer duration. Lower doses can cause blindness and skin cancer.			
	Electronics	Reduced lifespan and diminished functionality with open exposure.			
Gamma Rays		**A to Y**	**No**	**8 - 15 Minutes**	**1 - 3 Hours**
	Human *Kiss of Death*	The effects are similar to X-Rays, but Gamma rays are far more deadly. The primary concern includes all primary and secondary concerns for X-Rays. The secondary concern applies only to those who rely upon medical devices. It could impair the operability of hearing aids and surgically implanted electronic devices such as pace makers.			
	Electronics	Normally no effects. Levels deadly to life can cause electronics to fail.			
EMP		**X and Y**	**No**	**8 - 15 Minutes**	**<1 Minute**
	Human *Bad for Patients*	Expect surgically implanted electronic devices, such as pace makers, to fail. Hearing aids will fail. Hardest hit will be patients undergoing treatment. Hospitals and clinics use vast amounts of electronic medical devices and many will fail. Physicians and staff members will then be overwhelmed with an onset of code red emergencies, while simultaneously having to fall back on legacy manual systems.			
	Electronics	Kiss of Death. Transformers, solid state and printed circuits short-circuit and melt.			

Effect	Risk	Solar Flare Class	CME	Time to Earth	Event Duration
Magnetic Storm		**None**	**Yes**	**17.5 - 48 Hours**	**24 - 48 Hours**
	Human	Can temporarily impair operability of medical devices, such as hearing aids and surgically implanted electronic devices, such as pacemakers.			
	Electronics	Will diminish or disable any communication device throughout the entire event duration. Expect Radio, TV and cellular reception to be filled with static.			

Shielding yourself from these solar storm nasties requires the same level of preparation we already use when expecting tornadoes or severe storms. We look for a safe place where there is enough mass between us and what is trying to kill us to make a real difference. Some places are optimal, and others are better than nothing at all.

If you're lucky enough to hear a public defense siren or news broadcast warning of an imminent solar storm, start looking at the world around you with something called a half-value thickness in mind. In particular, you want something that will reduce your exposure to the most dangerous solar storm nasty there is. Gamma radiation.

The table below shows the half-value thickness of common construction materials you need to reduce incoming gamma radiation strength by half. Memorize it!

MATERIAL	Half-value Thickness (HV)	50% Less Minimal 1 x HV	75% Less Fair 2 x HV	87.5% Less Good 3 x HV	99% Less Excellent 7 x HV
Iron or steel	0.7" (18 mm)	0.7" (18 mm)	1.4" (36 mm)	2.1" (54 mm)	4.9" (126 mm)
Brick	2.0" (51 mm)	2.0" (51 mm)	4.0" (102 mm)	6.0" (153 mm)	14.0" (357 mm)
Concrete	2.2" (56 mm)	2.2" (56 mm)	4.4" (112 mm)	6.6" (168 mm)	15.4" (392 mm)
Dirt	3.3" (84 mm)	3.3" (84 mm)	6.6" (168 mm)	9.9" (252 mm)	23.1" (588 mm)
Ice	6.8" (173 mm)	6.8" (173 mm)	13.6" (346 mm)	20.4" (519 mm)	47.6" (1211 mm)
Soft Wood	8.8" (224 mm)	8.8" (224 mm)	17.6" (448 mm)	26.4" (672 mm)	61.6" (1568 mm)
Snow	20.3" (516 mm)	20.3" (516 mm)	40.6" (1032 mm)	60.9" (1548 mm)	142.1" (3612 mm)

When looking for solar storm shelter, use the gamma ray half-values in the table above and the following three rules:

1. **GET TO SHELTER FAST:** The instant you know you're in a deadly solar storm, stop talking, focus all your attention on finding the best available shielding option and get there — fast!

2. **THICKER IS BETTER:** The thicker the material, the better the protection. While standing under 0.7" (18 mm) of iron will cut your exposure in half, that is still better than standing out in the open like the proverbial poodle in the microwave oven.

3. **PROTECT FROM ABOVE:** Unlike hurricanes, tsunamis and tornadoes that come at you from the side, solar storm nasties all move in a straight line down from the Sun to you.

To help you further ensure your ability to avoid personal harm and the destruction of your valuable electronic devices, we've created a simple solar storm survival plan.

The 8-18 Solar Storm SA Survival Plan

The goal of the 8-18 Solar Storm SA Survival Plan presented in this book is to help you prepare for the worst-case scenario. A perfect solar storm: an Earth-directed, Y-class flare with CME. In the event of a perfect solar storm, you'll need to cope with it wherever you happen to be, so always remember this 15th century axiom: "Wherever you go, there you are." Make it your 2012 mantra.

In "Chapter 11 — Be a 2012 Rambo," you saw how situational awareness (SA) can significantly increase your ability to survive natural and man-made catastrophes. That is why SA is key part of this plan.

Eight minutes after the perfect solar storm erupts, gamma radiation from the solar flare begins penetrating your body like nuclear shotgun pellets. This deadly shower can last up to three hours. Then 18 hours later, CME plasma starts to slam into Earth's magnetic fields.

If the polarity of a severe CME is opposite to that of the Earth (Southward from the Sun Sun vs. Earth's Northward) it can disrupt our planet's magnetic field defenses, push into our outer atmosphere and reach the atmosphere with deadly consequences.

After Planet X crosses the ecliptic, our governments will be on guard for the first perfect solar storm. When the sirens sound (if they do), secret service agents to will scoop up our leaders and hand-carry them to safety.

Before most ordinary citizens comprehend what is happening, our leaders will already be safe, deep underground. Their shelters will be well hardened against solar storm dangers, with equally survivable electronic, communication and environmental systems.

What about the rest of us? When the sirens sound, there will be no secret service agents to scoop us up and carry us to safety. Therefore, we not only need to take care of ourselves. We also must try to protect our electronics, as well. Without them, we'll be making wooden ox carts by hand, just like our 3rd world cousins.

Therefore, the first step in the 8-18 Solar Storm SA Survival Plan is to find go-to-ground safety zones.

Go-to-Ground Safety Zones

Huddling in bunkers and basements for months and years on end is a sure way to go off the deep end. Rather, life goes on and so we take care of families, work at jobs, go shopping and do all the other normal activities of everyday life. That's why you need to find multiple solar storm survival zones within your everyday travel patterns.

Finding Protection at Home

- Safe rooms
- Storm shelters

- Root cellars

- Basements

Finding Protection in Cities

- Underground parking garages

- Auto and pedestrian tunnels

- Underground subway systems

- Tall buildings with deep basements

- Banks with open vaults

- Catacombs (underground burial crypts)

- Sewage systems

- Storm drain systems

Finding Protection in the Country

- Any cave

- Any mine

- Any tunnel

- Road culverts

- Cliff overhangs

- Natural stone arches

Charged particles from solar flares can begin slamming through your body in just 8 minutes following the eruption, so you need to begin locating these safety zones as soon as possible.

Remember the 2012 mantra. "Wherever you go, there you are." Start looking for the safety zones in your world today to hone this skill with practice. In time you'll be able to recognize them instinctively. You can even use your cell phone to help you find less obvious safety zones.

Using Cell Phones to Find Safety Zones

Thanks to modern cellular technology, most of us already possess an easy and effective way to find possible safety zones with our cell phones in much the same way Star Trek characters used their trusty little tricorders to find all kinds of things.

The best way to determine radiation safety zones is with expensive testing equipment and the training required to scientifically interpret the results. However, a less precise, but significantly helpful alternative is to monitor the signal strength bars on your cell phone when exploring buildings, caves, tunnels and so forth.

> **The Rule of Reception:** Areas with perfect reception (all bars) should not be considered as solar storm survival zones. Rather, the opposite is true. They are death zones, because they do not provide any electromagnetic (EM) shielding!

Always remember that areas located within a cellular footprint and which offer lower levels of reception are likely sources of EM shielding. Obviously, if you're standing in a store in the mall and you're getting five bars of reception on your cell phone, this is not the best place to sit out a solar storm.

On the other hand, the very same mall will usually have a multi-level parking garage. As you walk through the garage, you find a level where your cell phone shows no bars at all. Bingo. That's the place you're looking for.

When searching for go-to-ground solar storm safety zones with your cell phone, here are the five things you can do to get the best possible results:

1. **Minimize cell phone interference:** When you're looking for safe zones, go on foot, as cars can distort cell phone readings. If you normally carry other electronics, such as a PDA or a laptop computer, make sure they're completely turned off and not in a low-power hibernation state.

2. **Establish an Outside Reception Baseline:** Line-of-sight reception with the nearest cell site can affect signal strength readings. Especially when the building is located in an area where there is little or no overlapping cell site coverage. Begin by walking completely around the building or structure, and note any differences in high reception values.

3. **Search Inside for Low Reception Areas:** Walk throughout the building's lower levels, and continually check for reception. Be sure to test the stairwells, as well. Remember, the radiation will be coming straight down from above, so lower is better. Exterior walls are not a key determining factor for human survival.

4. **Do Not Call Attention to Yourself:** If someone asks you what you're doing, simply tell them what you're doing. Finding a cell signal. Since this is a ubiquitous aspect of modern life, they'll lose interest and go their own way. In some cases, they might voluntarily tell you about the worst cell reception spots in the building. This kind of information is pure gold. When it comes your way, take note of it and thank them.

5. **Compare Interior Readings with Outside Baselines:** Say for example, the North side of a building has the highest number of signal strength bars, and you find an area inside the North end of the building with absolutely no cellular reception. This tells you that you've located the optimal safety zone within that structure.

This cell phone procedure may or may not lead you to the most optimal safety zone in your everyday path through your life, but it is better than running around like a headless chicken. Now, let's talk about where you live.

Home-based Safety Zones

To paraphrase our 2012 mantra, "wherever you live, there you are," so when looking for a home-based safety zone, the only factor that matters is what kind of material is between you and the Sun above and how much of it is there.

In the half-value table above, several common materials are shown, including snow. When assessing the relative protection of your home, keep these half-values closely in mind, because what may appear to be an excellent solar storm shelter at first glance may later prove to be disappointing.

For example, rural dwellers in tornado prone areas often have an old root cellar near the house that also serves as a storm shelter. Since all it takes is two feet of dirt overhead to yield excellent gamma ray shielding, most of these shelters will already fit the bill. However, modern pre-built tornado shelters may prove to be death traps during a severe solar storm.

Modern storm shelters are often situated partly below ground for easy access. To help keep construction costs down, they will usually have concrete ceilings that are about 5 inches (127 mm) thick. While the thickness of this construction certainly gives them the strength to survive a tornado, it only offers a fair level of gamma radiation shielding at best.

Again, the only factor that matters is the material between you and the Sun above and how much of it is there. If you want to buy a pre-made shelter, do not trust the salesmen when it comes to overhead shielding. Do your own math, and make it count. Then, count the number of heads that will be under it.

Shelters for City Dwellers

We all watch the tragic scenes in movies about sinking ocean liners and cringe as overloaded lifeboats capsize, throwing frantic people into the sea with heartbreaking consequences. And in the overcrowded lifeboats that do not capsize, there always seems to be a shortage of food and water that begets all sorts of dog-eat-dog behaviors.

This may be great entertainment for Hollywood, but when the day comes that you'll be sitting out a bad solar storm, that will be real life. As you plan a solar storm shelter for your family, keep crowding in mind. The following table offers a minimal occupant guide for your designated solar storm shelter.

# of Adults	Sample Dimensions US	Sample Dimensions Metric
1 - 4	4' wide x 6' long	1.22 m x 1.83 m
5 - 7	5' wide x 6' long	1.52 m x 1.83 m
8 - 11	6' wide x 8' long	1.83 m x 2.44 m
12 - 15	6' wide x 12' long	1.83 m x 3.66 m
16 - 20	8' wide x 12' long	2.44 m x 3.66 m
21 - 25	8' wide x 16' long	2.44 m x 4.88 m
26 -30	8' wide x 20' long	2.44 m x 6.10 m

When designing your solar shelter, begin with assets you already have or can easily access. For example, if you live in a high-rise condominium, you're already in a structure with tremendous amounts of concrete and steel. If you live on a lower floor, you could already be living in a solar storm proof home. You're set. Be happy. If you live on one of the top floors, you'll have neighbors below, so get acquainted. Inviting a neighbor over for coffee and bundt cake today, can save your life tomorrow.

Alternatively, if your building has a basement, it should provide you with excellent protection against gamma radiation. Some high-rise buildings offers residents the use of basement storage lockers. These temporary living areas can be outfitted as comfy solar storm safety zones. If not, you'll need to build a shelter.

There are countless ways to find a free shelter, or to build an inexpensive one. Here are a few ideas to help self-reliant homeowners. If they do not apply directly to your situation, they'll still help you visualize the key concepts.

Urban Shelters for Freestanding Homes

Many of us own freestanding frame houses, which offer very little solar storm protection. However, adding on an effective solar storm shelter for these homes can be done for a modest amount and in a single weekend.

Homes in the East, as well as older European buildings, typically have a basement. If your home has a basement, clear a corner to make room for your shelter. Conversely, homes in drier climates, such as those in the American Southwest, seldom have a basement.

In this case, you can outfit a durable outdoor storage shed for use as a shelter. Even if you live in a patio home with a backyard that's not much wider than a sidewalk, you can find a sturdy, but attractive outdoor shed that complements your home's exterior.

Once you've decided on the dimensions for your shelter, check your local lumberyards to see if they carry bulk rack shelving. This type of high-strength steel shelving is designed for industrial storage areas where heavy goods are handled manually. These storage units can easily be assembled to meet your needs. Make sure the top rack is sheet steel, and get the heaviest grade possible.

Sides and floor are not necessary, unless a member of your family has a surgically implanted medical device, such as a pacemaker. In this case, you can cover the sides and floor of the shelter with heavy gauge expanded steel sheeting. Make sure that the ceilings, sides and floor, if needed, are solidly connected with enough conductive material to create a solid shelter.

After you've assembled your bulk rack structure, you're ready to add the shielding. Thankfully, this is easy and inexpensive. Find a local quarry, construction or masonry and landscape business that sells sand and sandbags. Give them the dimensions of your shelter, and tell them you want them to fill enough sandbags to give you a full layer of sandbags that is approximately 2 feet (0.61 m) thick from edge to edge.

Tell them you want your bags filled with washed sand. Washed sand is screened and washed to remove silt and clay. It is odorless and typically a light buff color, or almost off-white. Once they've calculated what you need, pay them to sack it and deliver it to your home.

While you're waiting for your sandbags to arrive, crisscross the top of your shelter with several sheets of tin foil, and seal the edges with duct tape to remove air space between the contact surfaces of the foil. When it comes to solar storms, think of foil are as your must-have, universal solar putty.

After the sand bags have been delivered and the top of your shelter is neatly covered with foil, gently stack the bags tightly together. Be sure to crisscross the layers so that any particles can only get past a few bags. Three or four layers of sandbags will be required.

As a final touch, stock your solar storm shelter with basic survival supplies such as food, water and a portable potty. Even a resealable paint bucket will do. Another container you might want to keep handy is a small, resealable tin with a tight lid for your cell phone or hearing aid.

Protecting Electronics

We live in a world of gadgets. We rely upon computer to work, learn and surf the Web. More of us each day rely on GPS navigation systems in our cars with panic buttons that let us call for help. Grandparents can now see a grandchild take his or her first step via a live Web-cam or digital video recording, and many of them also have surgically implanted medical devices, such as pacemakers and drug dispensers. No doubt, many teenagers would love to have their cell phones surgically implanted for no other reason than convenient text messaging.

All these devices have become such a ubiquitous part of our daily lives that we cannot imagine our world without them. Yet, all it will take to silence our colorful, noisy electronic world is one perfect solar storm. The EMP of a Y-class solar flare or the magnetic storm brought on by an Earth-directed CME will be the end of it.

It is an odd juxtaposition that what affects us most affects our electronics least, and vice-versa. While our body suffers most from radiation, our electrical and electronic devices suffer most from magnetic field disturbances.

For this reason, the electronic equipment we must protect will be small emergency and short-wave radios, wearable medical devices, such as hearing aids, cell phones and other communication devices, such as CB radios. You can do this in two ways: breaking the loop and shield caging.

Breaking the Loop

Every antenna and power cord connected to your wall-powered electronics such as radios, TV's and so forth is a solar storm EMP lightning rod, because they form closed current loops.

If we're lucky, our solar observatories will give us just enough warning time to take action. Once the first alert is sounded, here is what you do, assuming you have enough time to do this and then reach shelter:

- Remove the batteries from flashlights, cell phones, emergency radios, PDA's and laptops. If you have a hearing aid, remove the battery.

- Find the breaker box in your home or office, and throw every breaker switch to the off position. This includes the main breaker that connects your house to the power grid.

- Pull the power plugs from the walls on every home electronic device you value. For those with antennas, disconnect them, if possible.

While the computers in your car are susceptible to EMP, they are more survivable than home electronics, because they are designed to survive the harsh electromagnetic environment on existing roadways. However, that does not mean they're invulnerable. Rather, they'll probably be amongst the last types of consumer electronics to be disabled by a solar storm.

Aircraft have even stronger electromagnetic shielding than cars and should hopefully be able to land safely during a severe solar storm. That is, if they're still flying by then.

Nonetheless, if you're on the ground, the best bet is to go on foot. If you do not have much time, cell phones, small emergency radios and hearing aids are your first priority. As for the rest, if you have to halt your flight to save a laptop, is it really worth getting so irradiated you develop prostate cancer or cataracts? Think about it.

Shield Caging

As was pointed out earlier, think of aluminum foil as your universal solar putty. Keep a large square of it folded up in your wallet or purse in case a solar storm should hit when you away from home.

After you break the loop with your cell phone by removing the battery, you can use your sheet of aluminum foil to give it added protection by shield caging it. Simply remove your foil from your purse or wallet, unfold it and then tightly wrap your cell phone and cell phone battery, other hand-held electronics, their batteries and your credit cards with it. Sure, this is not the highest level of protection, but it is better than nothing — and that can make all the difference.

Once the solar storm has abated, and cellular service resumes, you should be able to call your loved ones to make sure they're OK. That is, assuming they've taken similar precautions.

The thing to remember about aluminum foil is that it can be used to create a simple and relatively effective form of something physicists and electronic experts call a Faraday cage. As any geek will tell you, there are more elaborate ways to create an even better Faraday cage for your electronics, and you'd be surprised at how simple they are to make.

Simple Faraday Cages for the Home

Every holiday season, we buy sealed tins of tasty caramel corn and shortbread, and for those who think they already have everything; a fruit cake is always the perfect gift. After the holidays, we throw these tins away (after feeding the fruit cake to the neighbor's dog), and that's a real shame.

These tins are fabulous home Faraday cages, because what makes them perfect for perishable food products also makes them useful for small electronics, provide they have the following two attributes:

- **Conductive Metal:** The container has to be made of metal that conducts, such as iron, copper, tin or nickel. Plastic or aluminum containers will not work for this purpose.

- **Tightly Sealed Lids:** In order to keep the cookies fresh, the caramel corn crisp and the fruit cake moist, the two parts of a resealable container must fit together close enough to be airtight. Because they're designed to keep out the air, they also keep out the EMP.

Next holiday season; tell all your co-workers you simply adore tinned fruit cake. By early December, you'll have a small Faraday cage for every room in the house. Then, use all the money you've saved to line the interiors of your fruit cake tins with tin foil for added protection.

If you want to protect larger electronics such as a home stereo or a small TV, a metal trash can is good, provided it is new and undamaged. Line the lip of the can with lots of tin foil to make sure there is a solid contact between the lid and the can.

If you're super-serious about shielding your electronics against a magnetic storm, you can build a Faraday cage with thick sheets of conducting metal. This is how the military builds Faraday cages so they can withstand the EMP generated by a nuclear detonation. Consequently, they're virtually impenetrable to almost any electromagnetic field.

If you want to build your own military-strength Faraday cage you must use a conducting metal such as iron, nickel or copper, and the cage must form a fully enclosed space.

On a smaller scale, your grandmother's metal cookie jar with tight closing lid will work much better than a surplus Army ammo can. An ammo can usually has a soft seal to keep water and moisture out. This soft seal breaks the contact between the lid and the can, thereby rendering it useless as a small-scale Faraday cage. Alternatively, you can replace the soft seal with tin foil. Same goes with your silver coffee carafe. If you're desperate for time, throw your cell phone in the carafe, and stuff tin foil in the spout.

In the years ahead, the three things you must remember if you want to preserve your electronics are:

- **Break the Circuits:** Pull the wall plugs, flip the breakers, remove all batteries, and disconnect antennas and cables.

- **Use Shield Caging:** With Faraday cages of any kind, you want conductive metals and tight seals to ensure reliable shield caging.

- **Seal All Gaps:** Tin foil is the universal solar putty for shield caging. Keep a good supply of it on hand.

Also remember that there are no absolutes. Our Sun is so powerful that it has the ability to generate solar storms capable of overpowering even the most hardened, military-strength Faraday cage. Do not use that as an excuse. Allowing yourself to become the proverbial poodle in the microwave oven is a very unpleasant way to die.

13

Coping with Economic Contractions

As 2012 approaches, we will all be faced with an increasing pattern of natural and man-made catastrophes. Many will perish, be injured and made homeless, but the majority of us will continue in much the same manner as we are now until the first of the major economic contractions are felt. Worse yet, the principal cause shall be the result of a one-of-a-kind oil epoch that started some 150 years ago.

Regardless of how we pray, and to whom, the world's economic god is oil, and it sent us forth to multiply in the 1950's with the petroleum-driven Green Revolution. In the boom years following WWII, the world's population was over 2.2 billion. Thanks to the Green Revolution, it is 6.5 billion and growing.

As much as we believe in our science and ourselves, the simple fact is that, without oil, our Green Revolution will die. At that point, our planet can only sustain 1.5 to 2 billion humans, assuming the biosphere remains in a stable condition, which it will not.

In terms of a worst case, this means the worst loss of life on our planet could happen before major cataclysms of 2012 occur, due to starvation, dehydration, war and disease.

Except for government leaders and the wealthy, industrialized nations will suffer less. Nonetheless, those in the mainstream will be hard hit. Of this group, those taken by surprise will suffer the most.

Therefore, the goal of this chapter is to show you key failure points in our economy that will most likely affect those of us in the mainstream. Thus informed, you'll be able to see the opportunities available to you today, which will help you to better survive these painful future economic contractions.

The key to these opportunities is to see them for what they are, so that you can exploit them to your advantage. To illustrate the point, we need to think back to 1999 and the impending sense of dread so many of us felt about Y2K.

In Chaos is Opportunity

It is easy to view our modern economies as being durable; yet losing a job is almost as stressful as losing a loved one. That's why we have a difficult time seeing our future's more fragile aspects. In fact, we often reject the very idea that our future is fragile at all, as was the case with the Y2K scare.

Y2K was a Titanic that sailed, but never sank, though history would remember otherwise. Therefore, in terms of managing the difficult years ahead, an understanding of the real catastrophic threat posed by Y2K offers substantial 2012 advantages.

Y2K Profiteers

For the public, Y2K was all about fear. We were stampeded into thinking that many of the world's computers and software programs would crash the moment they had to change over from the 20th century to the 21st century. Thankfully, that did not happen, and Y2K was wrongly labeled a non-event. It was in fact a genuine threat. The disaster was the deluge of self-serving hype.

Y2K was hyped up by media pundits, who kept our thumbs off the TV remotes with apocryphal doomsday scenarios about nuclear reactors going berserk and airliners falling from the skies. Afterwards, they pointed their fingers at the government, saying "off with their heads" for creating the very reason they used sell huge amounts of advertising.

Likewise, gold brokers drummed up public fears to line their pockets. They supercharged the media frenzy with Internet articles and junk mailers that painted Y2K in the most frightening ways. All designed to create the impression that anyone who possessed large quantities of gold would come through it unscathed and make a handsome profit, as well. It was a perfect one-two punch of fear and greed. Afterwards, they counted their windfall profits and went back to business as usual.

After all was said and done, who made the most money? The people who prevented Y2K from becoming a political and economic catastrophe, and they made their profits the old-fashioned way. They earned them by rendering a valuable service.

Thanks to their effort, the global economy rolled happily into the 21st century. Nobody saw airliners fall from the sky or Chernobyl-style nuclear meltdowns, except in television docudramas. So what was the real threat?

The Real Y2K Threat

While media pundits and gold brokers were cashing in on a public panic, information systems managers and their bosses were spending enough money on Y2K to fund a good-sized war in the Middle East.

In fact, industry publications reported that upwards of 18% of all information system budgets in America were devoted to preventing a possible Y2K crisis. This by people who are so conservative, they wear belts and suspenders to work! To believe the media pundits could stampede people such as these requires lots of naïve hubris.

After considerable research, these technologists understood that Y2K could not be left to chance. This is because Y2K posed the very real possibility of a catastrophic disruption in the global automated supply chain management network.

Whoa, that's a mouthful. Let's break that geek-speak down into something simple enough to read on the back of a box of corn flakes.

Corn Flakes and Y2K

Let's assume you have a hankering for a good old bowl of corn flakes, and you hop in the car and drive down to the local supermarket for a box of your favorite brand and a carton of milk. When you go into the store, you go straight to the aisle with all the cereals, and there, at eye-level, is your favorite brand.

Come wind, rain or snow, you've come to know that a box of your favorite brand of corn flakes can always be found in the same place. That's because the manufacturer has worked hard to get that good eye-level shelf placement, and keeping it means keeping the supermarket supplied with your favorite brand of corn flakes on a permanent basis.

Maintaining this permanent shelf real estate means keeping the store supplied with enough boxes of corn flakes so that it never runs out. This is an expensive proposition, as between the manufacturer and the shelf in your supermarket is a vast interstate network of jobbers, distributors, wholesalers and so forth. Each of which is like a link in a chain, and as the old saying goes, "A chain is only as strong as its weakest link."

In the days before computers, inefficient manual systems made it necessary for the corn flake manufacturer to keep a 90-day supply in the supply chain, so that it would work more like a Slinky (child's walking-spring toy) than a chain. No matter how many human mistakes were made, there would always be enough corn flakes in the supply chain to keep that coveted bit of real estate in your supermarket locked down.

Then along came computers, and a whole new world of cost-saving possibilities opened up, especially after June 1974. That's when the first U.P.C. scanner was installed at a Marsh's supermarket in Troy, Ohio.

This landmark event spawned a concept called automated supply chain management. Over the years, it evolved into a national (or global) system that combines dissimilar computers and software into a magnificent Information Age Tower of Babel that really does work! Messaging systems are truly the hottest thing since sliced bread.

Between the time it takes for the supermarket clerk to scan the bar code symbol printed on your box of corn flakes and for you to take it home and enjoy your first spoonful, an amazing sequence takes place.

The scanner sends a message about your purchase to the computer in the cash register, which sends a message to the computer in the store's back office. From there, it is relayed and tallied by the computers maintained by every wholesaler, distributor and jobber in the supply chain, until it finally arrives at the manufacturer's computer.

By the time you sit down to watch TV and happily munch your flakes, the manufacturer has already adjusted the production schedule to replace the product you just bought. All of this happens without one human being involved in the process, other than the supermarket clerk who scanned your purchase! Try outsourcing that kind of productivity to India!

If you think that is amazing, consider this. All of this takes place using vastly different brands and models of computers and software that all work smoothly together for one integrated purpose. That is to sell corn flakes, or whatever else we have a hankering for.

All of this would not be possible without something called messaging systems. Like the universal translators of Star Trek fame, they translate messages in real-time between different people speaking different languages. Except in this case, it is different computers running different kinds of software.

Herein was the Achilles Heel of Y2K that troubled corporate executives and managers.

The Achilles Heel of Y2K

What information managers feared was that, if enough older computers and programs maintained throughout the supply chain were catastrophically affected by the date changeover, their failures would spread through the system like malignant cancer cells.

Other systems, even though they would be wholly unaffected by the Y2K changeover, would literally be cut off from the supply system network by those that were. It would then take weeks to restart the global network. In the meantime, the distribution of food and products in the country would be paralyzed, as companies scrambled to dust off ancient manual handling procedure guides.

Given the assumption that there is a 90-day supply of product in the supply chain, why worry? You need to worry, because this assumption is false.

The whole point of creating a global automated supply chain management system in the first place was to eliminate the expense and waste of a keeping a 90-day supply of product in the supply chain. This it did, and remarkably well.

Our stores look as though they're stocked to the brim with an endless supply of goods to satisfy demand. Like beauty, this perception is skin deep. The 90-day supply of product that once stood behind store shelves was reduced to a 90-hour supply thanks to computerization.

Had Y2K really happened, our grocery stores would have looked like Soviet-era markets in no time at all. Barren shelves everywhere, and bread on Tuesdays – maybe.

Had it not been for the courage of a few government officials and the forward thinking information technology decision makers who listened to them, Y2K could have very certainly been an economic and political disaster.

Yet, their only reward was to be publicly scorned and humiliated by the media for sounding the alarm. This foolish and greedy behavior of the media at large will no doubt have long-term ramifications when the ghosts of Y2K come back to haunt us once again.

The Ghosts of Y2K and Planet X

As Planet X interacts with our Sun, we can expect a rash of solar flares to bombard the Earth. If we're not prepared for them, they'll literally cook our computers in their own juices, which is precisely why America, Europe and Japan are rushing a sizable fleet of solar observatories into space.

In orbit about the Sun, they'll spot the early signs of massive solar flares long before the Sun's nose even begins to twitch. This capability will help us to prevent what could have happened on Y2K, had we not been prepared.

However, there is another weak link in the supply chain besides the messaging systems we use to help dissimilar computers and software programs talk to share information. It is our transportation system.

Without a well-fueled system, even our modest 90-hour supply of foodstuffs in the system could wind up wasting away on abandoned railway sidings until hungry looters learn of their locations.

In other words, the supply chain between the corn flake manufacturer and supermarket shelf in our previous example is not only dependent on messaging systems; it is even dependent on a vastly larger system — the petroleum industry.

Our Global Dependence on Oil

Oil is the next best thing to free energy. One barrel of this black gold is equal to the annual work output of 12 people, and we use it for most everything.

From each barrel, 70% is used for fuel. The rest is used for plastics, medicines, fertilizers, paving asphalt and much more. Consequently:

- **Oil Moves Us:** 98% of all transportation energy comes from oil. Fuels, such as gas, jet fuel, truck diesel and marine diesel.

- **Oil Feeds Us:** For every one calorie of food we consume in the Western world, 10 calories of petroleum energy were used to produce it. (Remember that the next time you supersize that order of fries.)

- **Oil Populates Us:** Just after WWII, there were approximately 2.2 billion people in the world. Then came the "Green Revolution," where farm productivity was increased fivefold by petroleum based fertilizers and insecticides. This fed a growing world population to the point where we're now 6.5 billion and counting.

Back in the days when whales were nearly hunted to extinction in order to keep our lamps lit, we could have said the same three things about wheat. That is, with one notable difference. Oil is not wheat, which we can easily renew with another planting season.

Rather, the bulk of the world's oil reserves was created during two periods of extreme global warming, 90 and 150 years ago. Ergo, the supply is finite, and what there is of it is becoming more difficult to locate and extract.

The USA and Oil

For nearly a hundred years, the US produced more oil than any other nation on Earth. Believing it would never run out of this wonderful energy goo, America was the Saudi Arabia of the world and acted like it.

When they threatened to stop exporting oil to Japan in 1941, the consequences of that threat were every bit as severe then as they would be today, should Saudi Arabia do the same. The results were the attack on Pearl Harbor and the US' declaration of war upon Japan, along with Nazi Germany's declaration of war upon the US.

While the US entered the war short on weapons and trained troops, they had an unlimited supply of oil and the manufacturing capacity needed to fight a world war on two fronts. The US didn't win WWII with war bonds; they won with the oil that fueled the creation of the military-industrial complex former President Dwight D. Eisenhower warned about in 1961.

After WWII, weary GI's came home and made families. To keep up with demand, American started the "Green Revolution," which is the single most important cause of the world's current population growth to 6.5 billion and beyond. They started using oil for everything, and farms became five times more productive, thanks to petroleum-based fertilizers and insecticides. It also created a whole myriad of other products and uses.

Between winning WWII and starting the Green Revolution, America's reign as the world's Saudi Arabia ended in the 1950's, and in December 1970, the output of American oil finally peaked. Then in 1973, the US received a nasty petroleum wake up call.

In the 1973 Yom Kippur War, an Arab coalition launched a massive 2-front surprise attack on Israel, during its most holy day of the year. They were inflicting heavy damages and casualties and ignoring a U.N. ceasefire, when President Richard Nixon came to Israel's support with intelligence information and a massive airlift of badly needed war materials. Nixon's support turned the tide for Israel, and in retaliation, Arab states embargoed oil exports to America, to punish the US for denying them their Jewish genocide. That was a wake up call for the world.

In WWI and WWII, oil reserves had been the spoils of war. Now, OPEC had turned them into weapons, and the political dynamics of energy were completely remapped. Proof of that would come decades later with Iraq's invasion of Kuwait in 1991 to steal their oil fields.

The embargo of 1973 created a windfall for domestic oil exploration in states like Texas and Louisiana. However, the rest of the nation was forced to slog through the economic consequences of the Arab-led oil embargo.

Houston, Texas, the oil capital of the world, enjoyed boom times such as it had never seen, but ultimately could not deliver. This happened despite a fourfold increase in drilling, and American petroleum production continued to decline.

The result is that today, the US possesses 2% of the world's known reserves and consume 25% of all the oil produced worldwide. Now, Americans are not only vulnerable to the whims of fascist and fundamentalist dictators, they've also got nature working against them.

Oil and Natural Disasters

Oil is an incredibly cheap source of energy. It costs about $1.00 to pump a barrel of oil out of the vast reserves of the Middle East. After that, the process of transporting it, refining it, storing and delivering it to consumers is broad, intensive and highly vulnerable to man-made and natural disasters.

When these fragile networks are disrupted, the effects are immediate and deeply troubling. Case in point is what America experienced in 2005 after Hurricane Katrina ploughed through the Gulf Coast. Not only did it cause flooding in New Orleans, it also crippled 95% of America's Gulf coast oil production.

In its wake, Katrina left behind a useless, twisted jigsaw of rigs, refineries and pipelines. Given the fact that the storm interrupted 95% of Gulf oil production and 88% of the outer continental shelf's natural gas production, the financial impact at the gas pump was virtually immediate. Prices shot up as speculators elbowed their way into the financial troughs of panic buying, and the pickings were good.

Months after Katrina, the oil companies announced a record level of embarrassing profits. Citing the free market mantra, they were shocked by the notion that anyone would dare begrudge them such a righteous windfall. We can wring our hands all day, but this is what they do. You want the gas? Lump it, and pump it. That's life as they say, but not for much longer.

Planet X and Peak Oil

The whole issue of peak oil is hotly debated. Naysayers point to China's recent discovery of an offshore oil field with estimated reserves of 2.2 billion barrels as evidence that we'll never run out of oil. All we need to do is to dig a little deeper and squeeze a little harder. On one hand, this is a simplistic, but comforting proposition. On the other hand, concerned industry experts see China's recent oil find in a very different light.

It took the Chinese 15 years of exploration to find it, and assuming they can pump out every drop of the estimated reserves, the field can only supply China with 2 years of oil. That is, assuming its present rate of consumption remains flat, which is impossible.

China has become an economic powerhouse, and its citizens, who now make televisions and air conditioners for the US, want them too – and the energy guzzling cars, washing machines, etc., we take for granted, as well. Consequently, it will soon outpace the US as the leading contributor of greenhouse gases. When it comes to finding new petroleum sources, China has become the most aggressive bidder in the world. They have to be.

With an economy spurred on by the rampant outsourcing of America's middle class jobs, India is close on China's heels in terms of growing oil demands. The result of all these rising demands, are new global political frictions.

Why Oil Has Become a War Magnet

The hottest friction point in global politics is oil, and one could say that the world has arrived at this point because we've picked off most of the low hanging fruit. What's left of that is still in the Middle East, but how much do they really have?

In order to double the amount of oil OPEC allows them to pump, countries like Venezuela, Kuwait and Saudi Arabia used a few pen strokes to double their stated reserves instantly. No matter how much they pump, the reserve figures never change. Who cares if the numbers are totally bogus? We want the oil, and they want to pump it. As American consumers like to say, "that works for me."

But what happens if one day we come to learn that Saudi Arabia's production has peaked? We'll be in serious poo-doo, because we're already fighting over the sparse leavings on the top branches of the tree, so to speak. That's why we're digging deeper wells, processing oil shale and employing more elaborate extraction technologies to suck up what's left at the bottoms of old wells.

It is also why the poor of Darfur are suffering under a horrible genocide conducted by Arab militiamen. They're sitting atop a huge, newly discovered reserve of oil, and the ethnically intolerant government in the North of the country wants it all.

Likewise, America is desperately trying to shore up its supply of Middle East oil by democratizing the region vis-à-vis its war in Iraq. This neoconservative concept makes about as much sense as marrying the same person for the third time.

The hope is that with Saddam out of the way, Iraq would not be selling oil to everyone in the world except the US, which is what the new democratic government in Iraq has announced that it will do.

In the midst of all this insanity, Planet X approaches, and the natural disasters it will cause will compound our own human foibles in ways we could never before imagine.

The Looming Crisis

As more Katrina-scale events begin to happen in multiples, and in concert with disruptive man made events, we'll see a return of lines at the pump as we did in 1973, when we could only buy 10 gallons (38 liters) at a time. Except this time, the prices will decimate our family budgets as the nation's drilling, pumping, refining and distribution infrastructure becomes progressively diminished.

As before, the bad news will come in spasms. How much bad news can our economy absorb - $5 per gallon (€0.91 per liter), $10 per gallon (€1.82 per liter) or more? How long will it take for those who routinely commute 30-50 miles (48 – 80 km) a day from their suburban homes and satellite communities to see their gravy days coming to an end?

When that happens, homeowners will find themselves in an economic vice. On one side, fuel costs will soar, which means driving their cars, buying groceries, heating and cooling will spell an end to discretionary income. On the other side, taxes will shoot up as governments labor under the same escalating fuel costs, and ARM mortgage payments will ratchet up as the markets respond to the bad news with higher interest rates.

After gas jumps past the $15 per gallon (€2.73 per liter) mark, industrialized countries like America will see a rising flood of layoffs, bankruptcies and foreclosures. Families in America will have to move from their suburban areas to overcrowded cities, as their once green and livable suburban neighborhoods become as desolate as the abandoned neighborhoods of Detroit. Europeans will be forced to do the same. And that's only round one. Worse yet, only one in fifty at most can actually imagine this happening.

For those who can imagine it happening, there is a ray of hope. And believe it or not, it will come from national box store chains like Wal-Mart and Home Depot.

Box Stores to the Rescue

If Wal-Mart were a country, it would be the world's 8th largest importer of Chinese goods. The official reason for this phenomenal success is that Wal-Mart has refined its network of automated supply chain systems (like those discussed earlier) into a perfect retail science. The result is that they have mapped human buying habits like no other company in the history of the world. Again, that's the official story.

The real story is that no matter how much savvy and buying power they have, box stores like Wal-Mart and Home Depot could never possibly get by without cheap petroleum energy. This is because it takes cheap energy to:

- **Manufacture** the goods overseas using sweatshop labor. The cost of powering the machines is about the same. The only difference is that taxes are lower, and labor is dirt-cheap.

- **Transport** the goods in massive container ships across the Pacific, the biggest ocean in the world. Such ships burn 30 to 50 tons of marine diesel fuel each day.

- **Distribute** the goods through Wal-Mart's distribution network of warehouses.

- **Stock** the goods in large Wal-Mart stores with an average floor space of 185,000 sq. ft. (17,187 sq. m.)

- **Power** the store registers and computers, light the store, and cool and heat the air.

To help put this retail energy demand in perspective, the Empire State Building in New York City sits on a site area that is 83,860 sq. ft. (7,790 sq. m.)

You could literally fit two such buildings inside the same area used by the typical Wal-Mart store. No wonder Wal-Mart is widely considered to be the second largest purchaser of total energy in America, second only to the US government.

Well aware of its own energy footprint, Wal-Mart has been experimenting with building more energy-efficient stores, maximizing the fuel efficiency of its fleet of trucks and so forth.

All this makes great PR for the environmentally concerned, but they are really half-measures designed to counter a looming threat. A global oil crisis will paralyze Wal-Mart's empire and throw it into bankruptcy. They'll have to respond.

A Moment of Hope for Box Stores

As natural and man made problems cause contractions in the global oil supply, large retailers like Wal-Mart will come under ever-increasing levels of stress on their ability to operate and make a profit.

Stores with lower energy demands are a halfway measure. At some point, they'll have to come to grips with the threat of being put out of business because of faltering oil supplies.

Will these retailers take this lying down because their business models were built on cheap energy? No.

While energy is not the raison d'être of their businesses, it is a product, and in this regard, they have a good deal of experience to leverage. They already sell energy products such as the batteries we use to power our cars, radios, toys, hearing aids and much more. Adding new energy products that make our cars and appliances use less fuel is a natural response. This is when we'll enjoy the temporary relief of passing through the eye of an economic storm.

National retailers will scramble to will find readily available, alternative energy solutions. Solar panels that are too expensive to manufacture in Europe or America will be manufactured in the third world on a massive scale.

Soon, cars will be pulling out of US Home Depot parking lots with boxes of affordable solar panels lashed to their roofs with ropes and bungee cords. This will be a time when we'll feel a sense of renewed hope, that maybe; just maybe, we'll save our way of life. That will pass. This is why you must become an early adopter.

As an early adopter, you must purchase these new alternative energy products without hesitation. As you do, mainstream buyers will watch you, because they typically hold back on purchasing new products and technologies. They watch the early adopters to see how things work out, and wait for the prices to go down. In an ideal world with plentiful choices, that makes sense. In a world of economic contractions tied to oil shortages, it means plenty of nothing.

When these new alternative energy devices come on the market, focus in on the standalone technologies that do not require an interface to the national power grid. Then mortgage the farm, sell a kidney or do whatever else it takes to buy as many of these alternative energy products as you can. Some will work, and some will not, but if you act like a mainstream adopter, the next economic contraction will leave you with preciously little that does work.

The Next Contraction

As we move closer to 2012, our Sun will become progressively violent. This will lead to more storms, earthquakes, tsunamis and volcanic eruptions. The large retailers will struggle to cope with these market perturbations, but over time, we'll see significant changes.

The vast amounts of wood and petrochemical resources needed to create the colorful product packaging Wal-Mart uses to great effect will become far too expensive to sustain. The result is that we'll see fewer and fewer goods on the shelves, and many will be packaged very simply or have no packaging at all.

Other factors will also affect every link in the supply chain between the manufacturers and the stores as natural disasters begin to take their toll. Unlike the fluid and speedy transport system of today, moving goods to the stores will become increasingly difficult.

> ◢ Tornadoes will rip up entire sections of the nation's roadways.

> ◢ Earthquakes will block the roads with rockslides, collapse bridges and overpasses, and split paved roads down the center, making them all impassable.

> ◢ Floods and tsunamis will wash away communities and roadways.

> ◢ Solar flares will disable the ignition systems in trucks.

As the petroleum-dependent transportation networks that big retailers depend upon fail, they will be forced to retreat from smaller towns and communities to larger cities. In the process, their tens of thousands of employees will join the ranks of the unemployed.

Only when things are at their darkest will the powerful grip of the oil interests be broken, and then, we'll see the emergence of several breakthrough technologies that have long been suppressed. No doubt revealed by the same energy and mining companies that have kept them locked up in their vaults for decades.

By this time, the enforcement of intellectual property rights in America (and the rest of the world, too) will become more like it is in China today, where only few hundred copies of Vista, Microsoft's latest operating system were sold.

As soon as these new alternative power technologies become available, people will buy them and find ways to make knock-offs for much less to sell locally to their friends and neighbors. Mostly likely, they'll be selling them from an inexpensive 10x10 stall in an old Wal-Mart store that was abandoned and then claimed by the city for back taxes. Likewise, their neighbors will also be running their own cottage shop survival business to help them get through the economic contractions.

The eBay Phenomenon

If there is one virtue of American culture that benefits us all, it is that Americans are an incredibly inventive and resourceful people. Only in America could you hear the expression, "When you get a lemon, make lemonade," and that's exactly what they do.

Case in point is what happened to many middleclass American workers. After devoting their lives and energies to the success of a manufacturing plant, they had to collect their last paycheck and then watch the machinery being shipped off to China.

This has been a struggle for many, and many go home and bury their sorrows in a bottle of bourbon. Meanwhile, others immediately bury themselves in their attics, scavenging for things to sell on eBay.

A few months later, after they've learned the tricks of the trade, they've replaced most or all of their previous income. Best of all, they're free to watch their kids playing soccer any time they choose, because they turned the lemon into lemonade.

This is why you need to start planning and stocking your own cottage industry survival business today.

Survival "R" Us

For years, politicians in the US have told their constituents that "a rising tide lifts all boats." A pithy insight employed by former President John F. Kennedy. He invented the expression to counter the criticism that his tax cuts would mostly benefit the rich, which they did.

Likewise, there is another saying. "What goes up must come down," and as this tide falls, the large ships of the wealthy will become grounded in the shallows and the little boats will own the day.

To carry this metaphor to the next logical step, that is exactly how Planet X and 2012 are going to affect our economy, so wondering what the big boats are going to do about it is pointless.

Your time will be much better spent building a small boat with a shallow draft that can carry lots of cargo. An MBA is not required, and anyone can do it! To help illustrate the point, the following examples show how three different women could start simple, but effective 2012 cottage shop survival businesses.

Survival Candles "R" Us

Are you an office worker who types 80 WPM from 9 to 5, but on the weekends, do you love to make decorator candles? You've got the making of a home cottage survival business.

Beeswax or paraffin, wicks and candle molds are still inexpensive and readily available, so start stocking up. Likewise, stock up on boxes of safety matches while they're still cheap, and haunt the thrift shops for a manual typewriter in good condition. Have it serviced, and then buy fabric ribbons. Seal them up for safekeeping, along with blank labels for your candles. Then, pack up everything you've gathered to start your survival candle business, and pack it all away somewhere safe and dry.

While you're at it, start learning how to make your own candles from scratch, using anything that could work as a replacement. Instead of decorating candles on the weekends, make them from scratch in every way possible; test them to see how well they perform. It is best to learn what works and what hurts while mistakes are still cheap.

Victory Gardens "R" Us

During WWII, Americans had to live with rationing because the war effort rightfully needed first dibs on everything. Resourceful as always, Americans compensated by growing Victory Gardens everywhere they could.

Many seniors can remember local grocery stores with canning rooms in the back where people could pickle and can whatever they grew in their gardens. Are you one such person? Now retired and living on a fixed income and enjoy gardening?

Congratulations! You've got the making of a home cottage survival business. Start haunting garage sales for bargains on gardening tools while they're still cheap and plentiful. Also, build a seed bank with species that will grow in a diverse range of temperatures and conditions.

The basics, such as cabbage, carrots, potatoes, peas, corn and herbs for flavoring, will always be in demand. So will flowers that can be used to brighten a windowsill and then steeped to make nourishing mugs of tea or herbal poultices. Even in 2012, we'll still want to gossip, and sharing a cup of tea with a dear friend is good food for the soul.

In the years following 2014, our Earth will abound with plant and animal species once again. Amongst them will be a wide variety of herbs, flowers and various other plants with medicinal properties. It is difficult to say which species will come back and where, however *The Kolbrin Bible* does offer a helpful list of those that have survived past cataclysms. See "Appendix E — Post-2014 Medicinal Herbs and Plants" for a detailed listing.

2012 Clothing "R" Us

In New York City, the fashionable know that men who cannot afford new suits wear bright new ties. That's because a bright new tie is an inexpensive way to draw attention away from a suit that is starting to get a little long in the tooth.

In the world of 2012, we're not going to worry about being fashionable. Rather, just keeping the fashion we've got on our backs will be more to the point. This is when a good tailor or seamstress is worth her weight in gold.

If you've got the latest Singer sewing machine with all the great stitching patterns, lucky you. Enjoy it while the electric grid is still working, because in the future, it will not. In 2012, your fancy electric sewing machine will likely be dead as a doorknob, because its microprocessor circuitry will have been toasted in a surprise solar storm. At that point, you're sewing everything by hand, and that is a hard way to make a survival living, but there's a better way.

Today, while they're still available and relatively cheap, buy an old turn-of-the-century Singer sewing machine in good condition. The kind powered by a foot treadle. In fact, there were several different brands with foot treadles, and all were made to last. Acquire two or perhaps three of them, and have them professionally serviced. Also, see if you can locate spare parts, and then pack them away for safe keeping.

While sewing supplies are still cheap, stock up on needles, threads, zippers, measuring tapes, etc.. Haunt the closeout sales on cloth. Today's out of fashion is tomorrow's go to town outfit. Besides, what you cannot sell, you can cut up and use for patches. Remember, mending clothes will be the biggest share of your business in the years to come.

Also, haunt the thrift shops for serviceable clothing. Not the colorful fashion statements. They'll only draw the wrong attention, and people will know that. Rather, they'll want durable clothes with the comfort of natural fibers and the reliability of strong fasteners.

Above all, make sure they have lots of pockets, as we'll be scavenging a lot more in the years to come.

Start Today

The three examples above were for women, but the same holds true for men. If you're a good mechanic, you can start finding old bicycle frames and matching them up with serviceable car alternators and to make foot powered electricity generators and so forth.

Likewise, if you load your own ammunition, stock up on surplus ammo, primers, powders, etc.. People will need reliable firearms and ammunition to protect their families, and feral dogs will be a big problem in the lean years ahead. A 3-year old that wanders off from a sleeping parent will be easy pickings for a starving pit bull.

This is part of the various disaster scenarios in this book. However, assuming the worst happens, is planning and stockpiling supplies a pointless exercise? Absolutely not! At this moment, you're not living in that dark future scenario and you have the luxury of time. Use it wisely.

14

Scoot Packs and Walkouts

In "Chapter 13 — Coping with Economic Contractions," we examined the practical things you can do to stockpile inexpensive survival provisions and supplies for your cottage shop survival business.

These are helpful things we can do today, but what happens to all our provisions and business supplies if a disaster makes our town or city uninhabitable? Likewise, how can we possibly transport all of these goods to another area when the roads are gridlocked with abandoned and derelict autos?

In the coming years, we'll all have to contend with the same kinds of catastrophes we experience now, but under very different circumstances. They'll happen with greater frequency, be more intense overall, and they'll begin to happen in completely new areas. The result is that the very nature of how we cope with these catastrophes will change.

One solution is to have a walkout plan and all it entails ready, so that when disaster strikes, you can lead your loved ones to a safe harbor. This new reality shall be very different from how we plan for disasters today. To understand that difference, we must begin by looking at how the entire populace views disaster management currently.

3-Day Disasters

When disasters strike today, we focus on protecting our loved ones and our homes through a relatively short period. Any TV pundit knows enough to tell viewers to set aside supplies for 3 days. It is a safe bet, because if they voluntarily propose more drastic measures, they'll be branded as doomsday nuts and lose their jobs.

Most Americans believe they have this down to a science. They assume that if they survive the worst, they'll have a soft landing in a government safety net. In areas that suffer frequent natural disasters, there is greater if not more practical awareness.

On the West coast, Californians are used to preparing for Earthquakes with a 3-day supply of bottled water, batteries and so forth, and they are upgrading old homes to withstand earthquake effects more easily.

They also teach their children to stand under a doorframe when they feel the ground start to tremble, and some even use museum wax to secure their favorite porcelain figurines, so they will not fall in a quake.

On the East coast, lumberyards in Florida stock up on plywood in advance of the hurricane season for customers who'll need to board up their homes before leaving town. To their credit, Floridians have become especially adept at working with their state government to get out of harm's way before a hurricane makes landfall.

People living in wind-storm prone areas around the world are building safe rooms to protect their families from deadly storms. Forecasters in wind-storm prone areas all over the world rely on an expanding network of Doppler radar sites to give their viewers the precious time they need to dive into basements, root cellars and safe rooms.

All of these are testaments to the fact that we've become far more proactive as a species in coping with these natural disasters, but we're still focused on short-term solutions. After the disasters have passed, those who bear the brunt of the damage are left to pray, bury the dead, pick up the pieces and argue with penny-pinching insurance companies. All in all, it is not perfect and certainly not pleasant, but we still manage to muddle through, nonetheless. As 2012 approaches, that will change.

The Worst Will be Worse Than Before

Those who've researched this topic for years have labored hard to predict which areas of which countries will be safe havens in the years to come and which will become uninhabitable or simply disappear altogether.

In the US, moving to safe areas such as the mountains of Appalachia and Sierra Nevada is reasonably good advice. Anywhere in mountainous regions near your home will be good. Nevertheless, picking up and moving away from home, your livelihood and your life is easier said than done. Consequently, we steel ourselves to the possibility that we may have to move at some future date, but that for the time being, life is good right where we are, and there it is.

One such place that's difficult to imagine leaving for the cold dry air of the Sierra Nevada mountains is San Francisco. Yet, if there ever was a city in the cross hairs of 2012, San Francisco is it. A chilling scenario is accurately painted in *Godschild Covenant: Return of Nibiru*, a fictional 2012 adventure novel based on science. Another city with similar prospects lies on the other edge of the Pacific Ring of Fire: Tokyo.

2012 and the San Francisco Tsunami

Coastal areas are where we find the highest population densities. In the coming years, these areas will be beaten by intense natural disasters, made even worse by man's own ingenuity as is aptly described in *Godschild Covenant*. Early on in the book, an offshore earthquake triggers a massive tsunami, similar to the 2004 Indian Ocean earthquake and tsunami that killed some 250,000 people.

The tsunami causes horrific devastation as it ploughs its way through the San Francisco Bay and Silicon Valley areas. In this brutally realistic scenario, the suffering is magnified by the destruction of the petrochemical plants dotting the East of the bay, along with the electronic manufacturing plants stocked with their molten heavy metals at the South end of the bay. The result is a deadly soup of petroleum and heavy metals that causes huge numbers of horrible, lingering deaths.

Overwhelmed with dead and dying, the government builds a triage center in the dry silt of an empty reservoir nestled in the Southern hills of the Los Gatos area. People from all over the Bay Area walk there or are transported in trucks for one reason: to see if they live or die, which in very simple terms explains the triage process.

Those who can be saved are treated with the limited resources available. Those beyond help are offered assisted suicide or are continuously medicated with Heroin until they die from natural causes.

As dramatic as this fictional scenario may sound, it offers a very realistic picture of what to expect in the years to come. Or as Oscar Wilde so aptly put it, "Life imitates art far more than art imitates life."

Should the area in which you live suffer a disaster such as this scenario in *Godschild Covenant*, you too will be faced with a similar decision. Will you develop a walkout plan that will get you and your loved ones to a safer place? Or, will you cross that bridge when you come to it, on the assumption that a government safety net will be waiting for you on the far side?

Governments Will be Overwhelmed

Compared with just 20 years ago, America's and Europe's current proactive management of natural disaster threats has come far. Consequently, fewer people are dying in events that would have previously taken many more lives.

Imagine what would have happened if there had only been a few minutes' warning before Katrina or Lothar made landfall? There would have been the same $81.2 billion dollars (or currently €107.19 billion respectively) in damages, but the death toll would have been worse than the 238 (150 or so respectively) that did perish. It could have easily reached into the tens of thousands!

To cope with hurricane disasters, the government of Florida instituted a brilliant evacuation system to help coastal dwellers motor away from approaching storms in a way that avoids deadly gridlocks. Yet, during the 2005 hurricane season, spotty gasoline shortages proved to be the Achilles Heel of this evacuation system.

As we approach 2012, we can depend on two things to happen. There will be more Katrina-like storms each year, and gasoline shortages will become commonplace. At first, many will adapt by hoarding emergency stores of gasoline in their homes or pay staggering sums to profiteers.

Meanwhile, governments will go all out to help citizens and to prevent anarchy. At some point, the carrying capability of local relief assets will give out, and the focus will be on directing refugee streams to relief areas beyond the disaster zone. At first, there will be hot meals, sleeping cots and medical care, but in time, those resources will be grossly overwhelmed. Then will come the triage centers, as described in *Godschild Covenant*, and it will not be a pretty sight. If you want to avoid this fate, you must start walking out today.

Creating a Walkout Plan

The very first thing you must do when creating a walkout plan is to decide where you're going to walk to. This destination must be an area that you feel with a comfortable level of confidence will survive the most likely catastrophes. For example, if you live in an area prone to flooding, find a nearby area that is well above the flood plain.

Because there are so many variations on these possibilities, you'll have to do some research on your own. If you live in an area where you know you will need a walkout plan, you must do it before you:

- Organize your cottage shop survival business;
- Stockpile safe haven supplies;
- Create your walkout plan;
- Purchase walkout gear and supplies.

In terms of getting through the years to come, 3-day disaster plans and ill-conceived survival shopping sprees will only put you in harm's way. This is because you must first decide on where your walkout haven will be. Once this where question is settled, the how and when become obvious.

Choosing Your Walkout Haven

If you know that you'll have to walkout at some future date, you will need to prepare your walkout haven long before that day ever comes. While things are still relatively stable, use this time to gather and transport your survival provisions and survival business stock to a safe haven.

Storing these invaluable provisions and supplies in an area that is likely to become uninhabitable is pointless. Therefore, the obvious immediate choice for a walkout haven is the home of a close friend or family member. Someone with whom you share a warm and trusting relationship.

Likewise, if you're a retired grandparent, finding such an area and moving there for the benefit of your children and grandchildren will be tough in the short term. In the short term, you'll leave a network of friends behind, as well as better medical care, in some cases. In the long term, the wisdom of your years will allow you to see your beloved ones alive and well in a world gone mad with disaster.

Another option is to pool your resources with responsible, like-minded people. For example, you could pull together and purchase a small rural farm in a safe area. You essentially create a commune, where everyone works together on a collective basis to stockpile provisions and business supplies. When you do, make sure someone is living on the property at all times. Think of it as your survival timeshare.

If you cannot create trustworthy relationships with others in your intended walkout haven, another option is to rent a locker in a secure facility, and store your things there. Share these locations with others on a need to know basis only.

Regardless of your safe haven arrangement, stock it with plenty of hand tools, such as picks and shovels. You'll not only need to begin growing your own food, you'll also need to prepare and maintain solar radiation shelters, as well.

Whether they are underground bunkers, abandoned mines or natural caves, you'll need a place to go to ground when the solar storms discussed in "Chapter 12 — Coping with a Violent Sun" begin to batter the Earth.

When the worst comes, you may be able to get part of the way to your safe haven in an auto or truck, but do not plan on it. Rather, expect to walk all the way on short notice. For this reason, you need to know how far you can walk in a day, and how many days you can stay on your feet, before reaching your safe haven.

Planning the Walkout Route

When disasters loom far off on the horizon, we often have enough time to gather our loved ones together so that we can hunker down or flee together. Other times, these disasters strike with little or no warning at all. When that happens, the first thought on most everyone's mind is to return home.

Home, or wherever your children happen to be, will be a natural rally point in any disaster. When loved ones are lost, finding them becomes a nightmare, especially when cellular networks fail.

For this reason, families and friends must develop sophisticated systems of rally points that incorporate various scenarios. They must not only include natural rally points like homes, schools and day care centers, but nearby walkout rally points as well.

When planning your one walkout route, remember one cardinal rule. Always have a Plan B — an alternate route you can use in case your first choice is impassable. Choosing your rally points depends on your circumstances and your primary and alternate walkout route choices.

If others in your walkout group are straggling behind because their feet are killing them, how long do you make everyone else wait until they catch up? You'll have to make these kinds of decisions when developing your walkout plan, so be sure to create a simple signal system for everyone to use.

Develop a Simple Signal System

Simple stick figures were used by the Hobos of the early 20th century to share valuable information between men who were continually on the move. These homeless drifters worked where they could, slept under the stars and stole rides on passing freight trains.

They were a loosely knit community, so they would leave commonly recognized symbolic messages for fellow Hobos. These simple stick figures let other Hobos know if a certain place was safe for camping, to beware of a bad dog, or to pass quickly through a certain area so as to avoid an unfriendly policeman.

Like the Hobos, design your own symbolic stick figures. If you have young children, let them design the figures. They'll be more likely to remember the symbols they create, especially if you rehearse them in games and other fun activities. Another benefit is that you'll involve them in the process in a constructive way.

Once you've decided your routes and rally points, designate rest points that offer potable water and shelter. This is especially important if your walkout will take two or more days. Take the time to travel this route and to inspect personally all of your rally points and rest points.

Be thorough. The more you know about your routes, such as nearby towns, medical facilities, police stations and military bases, the better. Also, take the family on these trips, and make it a constructive game for the kids. Such as offering them a quarter for every pond, water tank or well they spot alongside the road.

Once everything is organized into a complete walkout plan, make sure everyone has a copy with maps, contact information and so forth, in a sealed clear vinyl cover. That being accomplished, it is time to go shopping for walkout gear and supplies. The first thing you'll want to get is a backpack for each adult member of the family.

Scoot Packs for Adults

Daypacks and backpacks have become common sights at schools and colleges around the nation, as students comfortably lug around as much as thirty pounds of books, notepads, lunch bags, water bottles and so forth.

In a catastrophic setting, these versatile packs have one particular virtue. Unlike a large bulky hiker backpack with an aluminum frame to make it manageable over long distances, a backpack is ideal for anyone fleeing a catastrophe. Loaded with thirty pounds of provisions and gear, it can be dropped on a moment's notice, used as a shield for self defense or easily dragged through tight crawl spaces.

Your scoot pack could very be the most important piece of 2012 survival gear you'll ever own. This is why putting it together the right way requires careful attention to details. Always remember that the amount of gear you can lug on your back varies with your age and state of physical fitness.

Wherever possible, use multi-function items. When choosing between two items, lighter is better, as long as it is reliable. In a very real sense, less weight equals more comfort when creating your own custom scoot pack.

The following suggestions for the kind of backpack you need and other items are solely intended as a starting point. Use them as a jump-off point to build your own scoot bag ounce-by-ounce, while keeping your geography, seasons, types of threats and personal needs firmly in mind.

Selecting a Backpack

When it comes to buying a backpack, ignore the back-to-school sales bargains. Saving a few dollars this way will later come back to haunt you with debilitating aches and pains. Visit local sporting good stores like an REI store, and try several different packs on for size. Pay close attention to the parts that come into contact with your body.

The straps need to be wide, well padded and easy to slip on and off. S-style straps are best. Make sure they feel comfortable fit naturally on your shoulders. Backpacks also come with carry handles at the top center of the bag. Make sure it is strong and comfortable in your hand.

The back of the pack should be padded and comfortable to keep your back from becoming sweaty and bruised by the contents in the pack. Also, side web pockets for 32oz wide mouth water jugs are good things to have.

Ask a clerk if it is OK to stuff a few pounds in the pack and then walk around the store for ten minutes just to make sure it stays comfortable. While you're there, check to see if there are other handy lightweight survival items to consider.

Adult Scoot Pack – Non-food Items in Outdoor Stores

Here are a few extra things to look for in the outdoor sporting goods store if you do not already have them:

- **Compass:** As we approach 2012, the Earth's magnetic field will continue to weaken, and taking an accurate compass heading may become problematic. However, a compass will still be a must. A combination sighting and map compass is best, but a simple compass is just fine too.

- **Survival Knife:** A high quality 4" fixed carbon blade survival knife with a wood or rubber grip and a sheath is a safe bet. For those willing to pay more, the World War II era 7" Marine KA-BAR offers a time proven design. While knives are a very personal thing, make sure the knife you buy is made with high quality carbon steel by a reputable firm in the US or Europe.

  A folding knife is handy as a backup and for general use, but be aware that they can break when cutting through something hard. A Buck knife is one of many reliable brands, or consider a folding multi-tool, such as a Swiss Army Knife or Leatherman, instead.

- **Hiking Staff:** Hikers use staves to help them cross creeks, streams, rivers, and to traverse hillsides because they give you extra power and balance while easing wear and tear on the knees, hips and backs. In the future, you'll need them to help you navigate broken roads and debris and to keep hungry animals at bay.

  While there are all kinds of staves, here is one area where you want to spend a little extra and get a high-strength, anodized aluminum telescoping hiking staff with a cork knob handle and a steel spike. If you happen to own a spotting scope and want to use it instead of binoculars, choose a hiking staff with a camera mount under a screw-off knob.

- **Binoculars:** The world of 2012 will be filled with obstacles and nasties. The ability to see them at a distance can make all the difference. You can often find good general purpose or birding binoculars in the 8x30 range on sale or at garage sales. Sporting goods stores often run specials on 10x25 folding compact binoculars. Before you buy any binoculars, try them out. Be sure they are sharp, easy to focus, durable, etc..

◢ **Spare Reading Glasses or Magnifier:** Many of us wear prescription reading glasses, but sometimes, when we're in a hurry, they can be left behind. Keep a small, inexpensive pair of generic drug store readers in a hard case in your scoot pack. This way, you always can read a map, see a sliver under the skin or an irritating speck in someone's eye. If you do not need reading glasses, a small magnifier like the kind designed to fit like a credit card in your wallet can come in mighty handy.

◢ **Lens Cleaning Kit:** The lens cloths we get with prescription glasses are a must-have in what will become a windy 2012 environment filled with dust, pumice, ash, smoke, salts and other small particles. Additionally, you want small lens cleaning kits like the ones used by photographers. They come with a blower brush, cleaning tissues and optical cleaning fluid.

◢ **32oz Water Bottle:** Filling a wide mouth water bottle is faster and easier than most canteens. Make sure your backpack has a side web pocket for a 32oz wide mouth water bottle, and buy a new water bottle along with your pack. Some come with a built in compass, which is a nice 2-for-1.

Your water bottle or canteen will be your first line of defense against dehydration. Drink enough water to keep your urine relatively clear. Dark yellow means you're dehydrated and seriously impaired. When this happens, you need to make hydration your first order of business.

◢ **Flat Pack Water Tank:** The Israeli army once had a squad of men walk for days through hot desert terrain. They found that as long as you stay hydrated, you will be able to keep on the move for long periods without losing energy. All it takes is 5% dehydration, and you're on the slippery slide to trouble.

In 2012, potable water will become a scarce necessity, so keep a foldable water tank in your pack. Make sure it is durable with heavy seams and a comfortable handle. When dry, they weigh about 1 oz for every liter of capacity, so a 6-litre tank you can roll up for compact storage in your pack will weigh about 6 ounces or less.

◢ **Water Purification:** There are many different kinds of portable water filters to choose from, and those that can be screwed onto 32oz wide mouth water bottles are very handy. However, they are expensive. Another more inexpensive way to sanitize your water is with 2% tincture of iodine or 10% Betadine solution, with the added advantage that you can also use them for first aid.

Assuming you're using a 32oz wide mouth water jar, you can use 8 drops of 2% Tincture of Iodine or 4 drops of 10% Betadine to disinfect the water. Before you drink, allow 30 minutes for clear water and 60 minutes for cloudy water.

This is a time-tested way to treat water, but it is not 100% effective. The only surefire way to kill all the nasties in the water is with a pressure cooker or an autoclave.

⚐ **Hooded Poncho:** A hooded poncho not only provides excellent protection from the rain, you can sleep under it like a tarp or over it to protect yourself from ground moisture. If you are fleeing a volcanic eruption, it will also help you keep pumice from caking to your body and getting in your clothes.

⚐ **Space Blankets:** Maintaining a constant body temperature of 98.6 is vital. Designed by NASA for space exploration, they are ideal for compact emergency protection in all weather conditions.

A space blanket also offers protection from UV sunlight in the event of a solar storm. In the event of a nuclear attack, it will keep the nuclear fallout from falling directly on your body or inside your clothes or hair while you evacuate from the fallout area. Once used for this purpose, you must dispose of the blanket, so keep 2 or 3 space blankets in your backpack.

Dealing with Nuclear Threats During a Walkout

We face the threats of nuclear irradiation from several sources, such as nuclear missile attacks, terrorist "dirty bombs" and nuclear generating plants. Most of these plants are very safe and can withstand heavy blows and flooding. However, older plants along the coastlines may be more susceptible to earthquakes and tsunamis. Also, no nuclear plant is safe from a major asteroid impact.

In the event you see a mushroom cloud, remember that the initial detonation releases over 90% of the radiation immediately. Otherwise, the release will vary. Either way, if you hear a warning siren, get below ground or duck and cover as best you can. If this happens during a walkout, do the following:

⚐ **GET OUT OF HARM'S WAY.** Distance from the source is your only real protection. Wherever the radiation is or will be, you need to be elsewhere.

⚐ **STAY ON THE GO:** If you lay down to sleep before you get to safety, you'll sleep in a grave of your own making. *Keep on walking.* Use the caffeine tablets, hoodia tablets and chocolate covered coffee beans in your scoot pack to keep going.

⚐ **PROTECT YOURSELF FROM FALLOUT:** Fallout particles will settle in your hair or clothes. Without protection you would have to burn your clothes and shave all the hair off your body. Remember, once this radiation is in your body, it will never come out again. *Use your space blankets for protection from radioactive fallout,* and discard them when you're out of harm's way. This is why you want to carry two or more in your scoot pack.

⚐ **AVOID RADIOACTIVE POISONING:** In a fallout situation, *anything you pick up off the land is poisoned.* Ponds and other bodies of standing water are dangerous. Only use the bottled water and sealed food you're carrying with you. For added protection, take your Iodine tablets.

- **Signal Mirror:** Volcanic ash from volcanic eruptions will cause global dimming; the skies will become reddish and black streaked. While this will diminish the light reflected by a signal mirror, this handy device should still be in every scoot pack. They have a peep hole in the center for sighting your target.

- **High-decibel Whistle:** If you find yourself buried under rubble, and your mouth is so dry you cannot speak above a loud whisper, a loud whistle will help rescuers locate you more quickly. Make sure the whistle is durable and can be heard over most natural and man-made noises.

- **GI Can Opener:** Taking a few side trips during your walkout to forage for canned goods can net you some immediate sources of protein, and when you're hungry, Spam tastes truly fabulous. Likewise, canned corn packed in water offers energy boosting carbohydrates and flavored water for safe hydration.

  Beware, opening cans with a knife or crude implement is a good way to injure a hand. Better to carry the greatest little can opener ever invented. During WWII, the US Army issued small can openers called the P-38. They're a cheap and easy way to safely open any can. A larger model called the P-51 was issued to field cooks. It works the same and is ideal for anyone with arthritic hands.

- **GI Magnesium Firestarter:** In terms of a walkout, you only want to start a fire during the day for an emergency. At night, a fire offers safety and warmth. That's when you'll really appreciate these old Army issue magnesium block firestarters. Small enough to hang on a keychain, they work well in inclement weather and can be used to start hundreds of fires.

- **Renewable Energy Flashlight:** A Maglite is a great flashlight to have, provided you're willing to lug extra batteries. However, the new renewable energy flashlights are more practical for the years ahead, because they never need batteries or light bulbs. You energize them by shaking them, which moves a high-power, rare-earth magnet back and forth inside a wire coil. Three minutes of shaking can give you about 20 minutes of light.

- **Folding Camp Shovel:** For adults, a surplus army field shovel is cheap and sturdy. For those with a little more to spend, consider a lightweight, multi-function folding camp shovel. These new designs come with extra attachments such as a wood saw. For children, a gardener's hand spade is a small, but useful tool.

Taken together, all of these items weigh a few pounds / kilos at most and are available at Army Surplus stores, as well as on the Internet. Your next list is less expensive to fill, as you'll likely have much of this at home.

Scoot Pack Clothing You Can Buy at the Mall

Whatever shoes and clothing you'll need will vary, depending upon your own needs and plan, but always keep the following three suggestions in mind:

1. When you're outside, you're vulnerable to all forms of radiation, but you can mitigate the effects of UV radiation with the proper clothing

2. A walkout is never the right time to break in anything new. Whatever clothing you're going to set aside for your walkout plan, test it, refine it, and test it again.

3. Keep your walkout clothes clean and packed away in collapsible packaging, such as vacuum packed Space Bags.

Comfort is important, so if you lose or gain weight, check items of your clothing, as well as your gear. To check them, take everything out, inspect it, replace as needed and repack it. When the time comes, your memory of where things are will come in handy.

With this in mind, consider the following clothing items:

- **Boots:** No matter what else you do, this is where you've got to dig in, pull out the long green and buy Western. You want good fitting, high-top boots you can walk 8-10 miles a day in. Get them from a trusted brand so you know they're well stitched together with top grain leather that will protect your ankles from minor twists and snakebites.

  American and European boot makers stopped competing on the low end with the Chinese long ago, and if you buy a cheap pair of Chinese sweat shop boots made for the box stores, here is what will happen.

  During a long walkout, your feet will likely begin to hurt so bad that every step becomes an excruciating agony, and then you'll start moving in a fog of pain. This is when you'll become oblivious to such things as poisonous snakes, until you happen upon them. Then you'll learn how easy it is for a snake's fangs to pierce through soft, paper-thin Chinese leather or plastic.

  For those on a limited budget, you can usually find a pair of surplus mil-spec combat boots at gun shows and through the Internet. However, the best thing is to ask around, shop around and get the best boots you can afford. Then break them in by going on long hikes as you scout out various walkout routes, waypoints and havens.

- **Hat:** A good hat will be your most important piece of UV protection, so avoid breezy Panama hats and comfy baseball caps. You'll want a wide-brimmed hat with a solid fabric such as leather, heavy felt or canvas depending on your climate and preferences. Expect high winds in 2012, due to abnormal weather, so consider an Australian canvas snap-up or a cowboy hat with a chinstrap.

◢ **Goggles:** Losing your sight because of excessive UV radiation, ash or pumice in 2012 can be a death sentence. During low-wind periods, always wear a good pair of sport sunglasses with high-impact lenses and strong UV protection. If you wear prescription eyeglasses, you can also order sunglasses with strong UV protection.

For protection from high winds and small wind projectiles, a high-impact military goggle with polycarbonate; anti-fog lenses is best, but expensive. Alternatively, you can keep an inexpensive clear pair of swim goggles in your pack to protect your eyes from dust, smoke, volcanic pumice, ash and sand.

Regardless of the brand or design, swim goggles must offer shatter resistant, polycarbonate lenses with UV protection. Anti-fog is a nice feature, but the seal is the most important thing. A soft, hypoallergenic silicone seal will be more comfortable for long durations.

◢ **Cowboy Bandana:** This small bit of cowboy technology is a must-have. Bandanas help control body heat, provide a head cover, help keep flying pumice and dust out of the mouth or from slipping under the collar. Go for natural fabrics and bright colors that can be seen at a distance when waved over the head. Larger bandanas that are 40 inches x 40 inches (1 m x 1 m) can also be used as arm slings.

◢ **Clothes:** Be sure to wear a cotton or flannel long-sleeve shirt, along with blue jeans, military fatigue pants or khaki cargo pants. Your clothes need to be loose-fitting and comfortable. A uniform web belt is better than a leather belt, because it is more durable, and it can be easily adapted for other applications, such as tourniquet.

◢ **Leather Jacket or Vest:** Leather is best, because it acts like a second skin for your body, and it offers excellent protection from exposure, UV radiation and abrasion. A leather jacket with a liner or a separate vest is recommended for those in cooler climates. For warmer climates, consider a light vest. Forget the style statements, and go for the pockets and heavy stitching.

◢ **Change of Socks and Underpants:** Survival can be a scary business, and after standing in dirty water to pull someone out of debris, a dry pair of socks is a nice thing to have.

Store your socks and underwear in a self-sealing plastic bag and keep an extra bag inside that, so that you have a clean bag and a soiled bag. If you soil yourself because you got the runs from something you ate along the way, a fresh pair of underpants will help you feel somewhat normal again.

◢ **Leather Work Gloves:** In the years to come, medical care is going to become strained, and the supply of the antibiotics and painkillers we now take for granted will be problematic, to say the least. When you have to do something such as clearing brush or digging a fire pit, take a moment to put on a pair of sturdy work gloves. Remember, even a small cut can become a death sentence in 2012.

Adult Scoot Pack – Non-food Items In the Home

We have lots of non-food items in our homes we can use for survival.

- **Toilet Paper:** When you see a half-used roll of toilet paper, replace it with a full roll. Then, compress it and put it in a self-sealing bag. When life is miserable, it's the little things that help you hang on to your sanity. A moment in the bushes with a few sheets of quilted double-ply might remind you that you're still human.

- **Soap and Personal Grooming:** Ever brought home a few of those little boxes of soap home from a hotel? Seal a few in a plastic bag along with a small nail clipper, toothbrush and a comb.

- **Self-sealing Plastic Bags:** If you accidentally drop your scoot pack in a river, or it gets left out in the rain, anything that is not waterproof becomes dead weight. Put everything you can into self-sealing, heavy duty plastic bags, and save the bags.

- **#4 Coffee Filters:** Triangular shaped #4 coffee filters are a must-have in any scoot pack, because they can filter muddy water. They're also a great way to keep dust and pumice out of your lungs.

  Do you remember how the 9-11 collapse of the twin towers exploded large billows of choking dust into the air? Keep a #4 coffee filter in your purse or wallet in case the same happens to you. It will fit perfectly over your mouth and nose and block out the dust.

  Expect lots of volcanic eruptions in the years ahead, and when the pumice and ash begin to fall, two #4 filters can keep volcanic pumice from turning into a deadly, glassy cement in your lungs. A self-sealing bag with 20 or more #4 filters is light, and you'll have enough to share with others. Keep your filters at the top of the pack, where they are easy to find, or in a zippered pocket.

- **First Aid Kit:** While prepackaged home first aid kits are convenient, they're usually way too bulky for a scoot pack. While a chemical ice pack or hot pack is nice to have, lugging them is a weighty proposition. On the other hand, salt tablets and a sterile eyewash solution are a must-have in any 2012 first aid kit. This is why you need to make your own compact first aid kit based on your region, needs and circumstances.

  When choosing non-prescription items, favor light items that can keep you moving forward on your walkout. For example, pain medication such as aspirin and naproxen, anti-diarrhea tablets and activated charcoal tablets or capsules for poisoning. To save space, remove them from the bottles or boxes and place them into small, labeled zipper bags. Also, Sun block (or zinc oxide) and lip balm, such as Carmex, are good to have.

  Blisters and splinters will slow you down, as will menstrual cramps. Make a small kit with practical things like small scissors, needles, tweezers, bandages, antibiotic cream and matches. Include a few sutures, as well, to close serious wounds. You can use a Leatherman multi-tool as a crude needle driver.

⬚ **Iodine Tablets:** If you are downwind of a nuclear detonation, you can mitigate the effects of radioactive iodine on your thyroid gland by taking Potassium Iodide Anti-Radiation Pills. These pills essentially fill the thyroid to capacity with normal iodine, so that there is no physical ability for the thyroid to absorb radioactive iodine. Store one tablet for each expected walkout day in each scoot pack (and include a few extra to allow for unforeseen delays).

⬚ **Duct Tape:** A quick way to patch a tear in a hooded poncho, this ubiquitous product saves lives time-and-again. You can also use it to tape #4 coffee filters to your face to free your hands. Or, use it to restrain someone who has become mentally unstable. A small roll or a half-used roll from the work shop is good.

⬚ **Clothesline:** There will be hungry animals on the prowl, especially at night, and they'll smell the food in your packs. Before you go to sleep, throw your clothesline over a high tree limb and hoist your consumables into the air, beyond the reach of hungry critters. A 25-foot (7.62 m) bundle of clothesline will do.

You might want to consider a heavy duty web belt such as the kind used by construction workers or a surplus military pistol web belt. They offer a great way to distribute part of the load from your back to your hips with clip on pouches.

All of these non-food items will have long shelf lives, but they should be inspected periodically to make sure they are all in working order. The perishable food items you'll need to pack are another thing.

Adult Scoot Pack – Food Items In the Home

Waking up in the morning and making oatmeal is a cheery way to start a camp out day, because you have plenty of time to start a fire and prepare the oatmeal and water to make the oatmeal and to clean the pot and utensils.

When packing food for a walkout, keep in mind that you will be walking out — not camping out. Instead of spending lazy days camped next to a babbling brook, you will be grieving, and your mind will be filled with finding safety for yourself and your loved ones.

In a 2012 world, water will be scarce, and the smoke from a fire will give away your location. Therefore, you need finger foods with a fairly balanced ratio of protein, fats and carbohydrates that you can eat on the move, because you'll be walking from can-to-can't each day until you reach your safe haven. With this in mind, here are some simple things you can put in your pack to keep.

⬚ **Beef Jerky and Dried Fruit:** These are great, eat-on-the-go foods that store well. While you can buy them in bulk, a better idea is to buy a home food dehydrator and make your own. A great idea if you have several mouths to feed and a multi-day, walkout route to consider.

There are great jerky recipe books, so buy one and experiment, so that you have a mix of interesting flavors. Then, do the same with fruits, which as we approach 2012, will become increasingly scarce. For example, sweet Red Flame grapes make great raisins in your dehydrator.

⤸ **Peanut Butter and Crackers:** Nuts are a popular snack food, but they need special handling and storage to keep them from going rancid. Also, most contain pungent or bitter aromatic oils, and they ferment, which make them hard to digest. That is the last thing you need on a long walk.

Instead of nuts or trail mix, pack a small, unopened jar of any brand of creamy style peanut butter and some crackers. It is a rich source of easy-to-digest protein, especially for diabetics and those with dental issues. Avoid natural style peanut butter, as it separates in the jar. The stabilizers in commercial brands like Skippy will prevent that.

⤸ **Dark Chocolate:** Dark chocolate bars with a cocoa solids content of 70% or more are good to have. The best are made with pure cocoa butter and are very nutritious. Look for brands from France, Switzerland and Venezuela.

The caffeine in chocolate is a helpful pick-me-up and will help keep your spirits up. It is also similar to codeine for suppressing persistent coughs and helps reduce hunger.

⤸ **Chocolate Covered Coffee Beans:** If you're a heavy coffee drinker, the last thing you need on a walkout is to go through caffeine withdrawal. Keep a bag of dark-chocolate covered coffee beans in your pack, enough for a few mouthfuls each morning. They'll zip up your day and keep the withdrawal blues away.

⤸ **Hoodia Tablets:** A popular weight loss supplement, Hoodia was originally used by indigenous peoples for energy and to curb their appetite on long treks where meals were few and far between. This is a popular weight loss supplement, so beware. A lot of hoodia scammers are selling counterfeit products on the Internet. Your best bet is to buy it locally, from a reputable merchant.

Now that you have all these things organized, you're likely wondering if this is a good time to buy a gun, if you do not already own one.

Is it Time to Get a Gun?

If you do not already own a gun, keep in mind that as public tensions rise, the government will begin confiscating weapons. If your walkout route takes you through a checkpoint, you may very well find yourself surrendering your weapons to an impatient sergeant as one of his squad members trains a machine gun on you.

The sergeant will no doubt be as disgusted with this process as you will be, but it will be his job, and thanks to his job, his family enjoys base housing, free medical care and enough to eat. As they say in show business, "that's a tough act to follow." Or in other words, do not expect your constitution to survive the coming meat, bread and potatoes scarcities of 2012.

Given the erosion of liberties vis-à-vis the Patriot Act or similar laws throughout the world, that's not a far reach. The principal targets of gun confiscations will likely be semi-automatic and automatic weapons.

In the early stages, simpler weapons like bolt action hunting rifles, shotguns and revolvers, will be exempted, but that will likely change in subtle increments. A good example is what happened to war surplus ammo for the .303 British Lee Enfield bolt action rifle during the Clinton administration.

One Way or Another

The Enfield saw action in WWI, WWII and Korea, and it has long been popular with American hunters, because it is the easiest bolt action rifle to operate. Plus, the rate of fire with an Enfield is twice as fast as other WWII era military rifles, such as the German Mauser and the Russian Moison Nagant.

Unlike the 5 round capacities of the German and Russian rifles, the Enfield uses a ten round magazine that is much easier to reload. Since it requires relatively little physical strength to operate, it is a natural choice for women and boys.

Still the same, all three rifles are excellent survival weapon choices, especially for those on a limited budget. This is because surplus ammo they use costs pennies per round, compared with modern factory ammo costing more than ten times as much.

This is why President Clinton banned the sale of surplus ammo for the Enfield in America, even though it is still widely available elsewhere in the world. President Bush never repealed this ban. Why? Even though the design for this rifle is over a hundred years old, it is still the fastest shooting bolt action around. This is because it uses a large ammo clip and has a fast cycle design that is easy to handle for mom, dad and the kids. Still the same, it is a bolt action rifle!

The point here, is that by the time 2012 arrives, the Supreme Court will be interpreting the 2nd Amendment as having the right to bear sling shots, hammers, and not much else, so maybe buying the right kind of hammer could turn out to be your best bet, after all.

If I Had a Hammer

When we talk about hammers today, most of us think of those cheap little nail hammers we buy in the discount stores to fix loose steps and to hang paintings. Hammers like these are completely useless during a walkout, so leave them in the bottom drawer.

Nonetheless, the great thing about hammers is that certain designs make excellent weapons, and there are no laws on the books against carrying a hammer. With this in mind, what you want is an oversized claw hammer.

Used in framing carpentry, they feature a larger and heavier head to increase accuracy and to reduce the number of blows needed to drive the nail in. The also come closest in design to the medieval German war hammer.

This was a rather nasty hammer-like weapon that was used for centuries throughout the world. It was originally designed by the Germans to defeat the proliferation of plate armor that was spreading across Medieval Europe. Unlike swords, these crushing weapons could tear open a knight's armor plate and then be used to inflict devastating concussion blows.

The best way to pick out a good 2012 survival hammer is to visit your local hardware store. For comparison purposes, start with a top end model such as the 22 oz FatMax Xtreme AntiVibe rip claw framing hammer and heft it for feel. As you do, imagine yourself in the following situations where you are:

- ◢ Striking an animal that is attacking one of your children.
- ◢ Defending yourself against a knife-wielding thief.
- ◢ Clearing low hanging tree limbs and digging a fire pit.
- ◢ Prying loose siding from a collapsed house to make a shelter.
- ◢ Using the hammer to claw your way up an embankment.

Then ignore all the price tags and look for the following features:

- ◢ **1-Piece Design:** The hammer must have a double-forged steel head and handle. These designs are ideal for combat because they're stronger and more balanced. Plus, they offer more reliable leverage power, which comes in handy when freeing yourself or a victim from wreckage and debris.

  While you can economize on other items, you should not scrimp on this. Cheap hammers from places like India and China are a bargain until you need them. As with knives, quality hammers need to have been made by reputable firms in America or Europe.

- ◢ **Weight and Length:** A popular weight for most men is 22 oz. The heavier the hammer, the longer it is. Also, a heavier hammer will distribute impact energy through the swing and into contact because of its added length. German war hammers were commonly 21" long, which is considerably longer than today's rip claw hammers.

- **Head:** Checkered face design. This design helps to keep the hammer head from slipping off the nail head. The same holds true for everything else. No matter where you strike an attacking thug or animal, you will waste less energy from "glancing blows" and deliver it where it's needed.

- **Claw:** A rip claw hammer has a slightly curved claw, whereas a typical home nail hammer has a steeply curved claw. The straighter design of a rip claw hammer is still good for pulling nails. Something you'll need to do when stripping damaged buildings for materials to build a shelter.

  Avoid hammers with deeply wedged claws, for easier nail pulling. This design gives you a weaker claw for digging, clawing and cleaving. Look for thicker claw designs with a shallower wedge.

- **Handle:** A broad flat handle between the head and the grip with a thin leading edge is best. When defending yourself from an attack, this kind of handle will deliver a much more powerful blow than a rounder wood or fiberglass handle.

- **Anti-shock Grip:** Look for a design that reduces the effects of torque on wrists and elbows while it minimizes vibration and shock at impact. It will not only help you fight more effectively; it will make the hammer that much easier to use in general.

If you choose to buy such a hammer, you will also need a good utility web belt with a hammer holster that you can wear on either hip. The best placement is where you can quickly draw your hammer and swing your pack off your back to use as a makeshift shield. Also, have your name engraved on your hammer.

When facing a knife-wielding opponent, a hammer like this takes you off the easy-mark list real fast. This is because your opponent will have to thrust a 4" to 8" knife past your pack while you have three times the reach with your hammer. All you need is one good blow anywhere on your attacker's body, and you will paralyze him with bone-crushing pain. Ergo, just don't buy it and pack it away. Practice fighting with your hammer, and stay proficient!

Part 5 — An Enlightened Future

"When human beings are free of debt, insecurity and fear of their neighbors, they become much more amiable."

—*Jacque Fresco*

Future generations will understand that the key to survival for our species is to seek oneness with the cosmos. They'll look back upon these days and wonder how so many of us could have been blinded for so long by greed and stupidity.

Then they will say with one voice, "never again" and they shall know the full meaning of that, and they shall make it so.

15

2012 as an
Evolutionary Event

How we get through this impending cataclysm is important, but of greater importance is why. That, in a nutshell, is what the backside of 2012 is all about. It is also why the authors of this book often like to say: "catch you on the backside."

While many think of December 21, 2012 as an absolute date, it is actually a midpoint of an evolutionary event of staggering proportions. Once we cross this cusp, our species will bifurcate, just as it did when Cro-Magnon and Neanderthals began walking the Earth together.

In 2012, Planet X will become the "missing link" of a similar bifurcation. After it passes, Modern Man and Enlightened Man, a new breed of Homo Sapiens, shall emerge from the destruction. Together, they will rebuild the world.

The Modern-Man Homo Sapiens will largely come from those described in "Chapter 10 — Arks for The Chosen," who will be saved by the elites of the world to perpetuate their rule on the backside.

The Enlightened Man Homo Sapiens will be those left behind by the power elites to fend for themselves. From amongst them, shall come the one Jesus prophesied during his Sermon on the Mount when he said, "the meek shall inherit the Earth."

Used in this context, the word "meek" has long been an enigma. After all, how could people who are defined as being submissive, spiritless and docile, ever inherit the Earth? That's the modern definition of the word "meek." Conversely, the definition used in the time of Jesus described gentle and kind people.

In order for all this to happen, humanity must undergo a major evolutionary leap forward, and this is what Jesus, Buddha and most likely many other religious leaders tell us will happen: that the day of the Enlightened Man shall come. If you want to find those who are directly opposed to this enlightened vision of humanity's future, seek out those who perverted this ancient and beautiful word — meek. They are the dream killers.

This is a bold statement, and some may feel an impulsive need to reject it out-of-hand, with a great flurry of indignation. Not because they've fairly examined the logic of the argument, but rather, they're responding to their own Pavlovian conditioning.

Evolution and Indoctrination

From an early age, ruling power elites indoctrinate us with belief systems that complement their agendas. This is why there are so many competing political, theological and philosophical variants.

Many of us occasionally walk out to the edge of these belief systems for a look-see because we think we have free will. This is why we get the occasional urge to peek beyond the edge of our belief systems. But all too often, our free will is just a manufactured placebo, because once we are standing at the edge, an ingrained fear trigger kicks in and yanks us back to the center.

Troubled by what we've seen, we glue our backsides to the center and repeat the mantra, "oh my gosh, that was such a crazy thing for me to do!" This is why many fail to realize how deeply ingrained this fear-triggered obedience response is into the human psyche.

Nonetheless, we occasionally see too much for the center to be as comforting as it once was. Perhaps it is because a pesky little voice inside whispers the alarm, "Wake up. You've been had." The power elites know all about these inside whispers. God created us to hear the alarm, although only a few amongst us can resist the temptation to punch the snooze button time-and-again.

In the coming tribulations of 2012, our suffering will be so great there will be no snooze button to slap, and the alarm will be deafening. Then, we will either have the courage to confront and disassemble these artificial beliefs or resign ourselves to whatever fate befalls us.

In this respect, Planet X shall painfully push us towards the next step in the evolutionary ladder of our species. This ladder is crowded with contentious bullies, each trying to pry loose the other's hold on the ladder.

Evolution and Power

Evolution is one of the most, if not the most, polarizing topics in Western civilization. Consequently, pursuing the truth of who we are and how we got to this point is more about contention than continuum.

On all sides of this centuries-old debate, proponents of one idea or another are more interested in seeing their take on evolution trump the others than actually living long enough to see it come to pass. What they seem to miss with all this contention is that evolution is still nearly as much a mystery to us as cosmology.

Cosmologists will tell you that we barely know 1% of all there is to know about our universe. Assuming we know ten times that much about evolution, how are we to be absolutely certain about the evolution of the universe and our evolving role within it? Likewise, are we to believe that 90% of what we still do not know about evolution must be taken on blind faith alone?

Evolution and Power Elites

If scientists, scholars and theologians stop their incessant jostling and elbowing at the funding trough for a moment, they might happen upon a novel idea. They're all partly correct. Each of them brings a significant piece to this non-heterogeneous puzzle of ideas.

In the meantime, we onlookers hold our collective breath waiting for some kind of consensus to emerge from this cacophony. The real harm of this pointless waiting game is that we're not able to see the whole puzzle for ourselves. That would empower each and every one of us in ways that the ruling elites cannot allow. This is because our ignorance is the very foundation of their power.

A good example of the power of ignorance is what happened to Russian serfs (peasants) during the rule of Peter the Great.

The Power of Ignorance

During his reign as the czar, from 1682 to 1725, Peter rapidly transformed a backwards country into a Western-style empire. To achieve that, he used immense amounts of cheap conscription labor.

What enabled him was that the serfs of that time accepted their fate as chattels. Denied knowledge and ruled with a brutal hand, they accepted their low station in life as their true evolutionary fate as was taught to them by the Church. This fate bound them to the land they worked, and in turn, to whomever owned that land.

Ergo, the state and the church colluded to misuse Creationist theory as a way to demote the human rights of serfs to that of the livestock they tended. Evidence of this is St. Petersburg, Russia, a city literally invented by Peter the Great.

If you take a guided tour of St. Petersburg, Russia today, you'll be escorted from one impressive monument to Peter's ambitions to another. At each point in the itinerary, your guide will tell you how many serfs he conscripted at will to satisfy his bold ambitions. Then, you hear the death statistics.

After learning how many serfs died in brutal working and living conditions like expendable chattels, you begin to imagine blood oozing out from between the bricks and running down into great huge pools upon the ground.

All this happened because a core belief system was misused by the church and the state to cleverly deny Russian serfs their God-given right to explore their evolutionary heritage, in their own way. The result was a Godless state that is once again brewing trouble in the world. This is why understanding who we are and how we came to be is a personal responsibility.

Evolutionary Heritage is a Personal Endeavor

In 2012, we'll come face-to-face with our evolutionary heritage and the wisdom God gave us to understand it. That is, if we choose to accept it — no matter how alien it may seem to our present beliefs.

What if, because of the next Planet X flyby, we learn that we're a bio-engineered species? What if alien races created us to serve a utilitarian purpose, no differently than how we create genetically modified crops to increase harvest yields?

Are we prepared for the shock that would come from realizing an evolutionary heritage that both theologians and scientists have steadfastly rejected? Yet, we do think about it from time to time.

In a speech to a full session of the General Assembly of the United Nations on September 21, 1987, President Ronald Reagan said, "I occasionally think how quickly our differences worldwide would vanish if we were facing an alien threat from outside this world. And yet, I ask is not an alien force already among us?"

What Reagan stressed was not the danger of an alien threat. Rather, it is the threat of our own contentious behaviors and the manner in which we do battle over our own petty differences. With this in mind, let's put the differences aside, and see another picture of evolution in the light of 2012.

Merging Present Day Evolutionary Theories

For the purpose of this discussion of 2012 evolution, we'll focus on three well-known schools of thought on the topic of evolution: Creationism, Darwinism and Catastrophism.

- **Creationism:** God created the universe and everything in it in six days by thinking it into existence. Based on a literal interpretation of Genesis from the Torah (Old Testament), strict creationism places the creation of the universe somewhere between 5500 BCE and about 4000 BCE.

- **Darwinism:** A prodigious process of natural selection where species evolve in response to their environment. Based on the scientific philosophy of uniformitarianism, it is frequently summarized by the statement: "The present is the key to the past."

🖋 **Catastrophism:** Unlike Darwinism, which presumes a long, mercurial evolutionary cycle, catastrophists believe that major evolutionary leaps forward are the result of cataclysms such as the Chicxulub impact event some 65 million years ago that caused the extinction of the dinosaurs.

Politically speaking, these three schools of thought are worlds apart, so let's reintroduce them as three components of a new unified theory, which we'll call the Three Tests of Evolution.

The Three Tests of Evolution

Unlike Creationism, Darwinism and Catastrophism, which help explain why new species prosper, the Three Tests of Evolution tell us why old species fail.

Keep in mind that 99% of all species that have ever lived on our Planet are now extinct, and as the new kids on the block, we humans have yet to "make our bones" as they say in the mobster movies.

In this new unified theory, we presume that every living organism must pass the following three tests: Purpose, time and cataclysm.

Test #1 — Purpose (Creationism)

Genesis tells us that God created everything for a purpose by simply thinking it into existence. Given that the Heisenberg uncertainty principle tells us that we can alter a thing by the simple act of thinking about it, who is really taking their position on faith?

Creationists, who ask us to believe that we are the product of intelligent design?

Or, the Darwinists who essentially tell us that billions of years ago, a lightning strike accidentally jolted a few molecules into some kind of primordial soup. Then, fast-forward a few billion years, and voilà! The soup is reading Shakespeare!

The Darwinists poke fun at the Creationists for their devotion to blind belief, as though God faxed them the answer. In the same vein, how can Darwinists embrace their dumb luck take on evolution on blind faith as well?

Even those of us who wouldn't dare to be seen crossing the threshold of a church or synagogue do not want to spend the rest of our lives singing "is that all there is?"

This is because we sense that there is more. Much more. Consequently, the colloquial phrase "everything happens for a reason" has become a standard fixture in the modern *Zeitgeist* (German for "spirit of the times").

It tells us that in all things there is a purpose and a purpose to each life. This *Zeitgeist* concept was aptly described in the film, *The Matrix Reloaded*, in a scene where the character Neo is confronted by Agent Smith and his clones: "…without purpose, we would not exist. It is purpose that created us. Purpose that connects us. Purpose that pulls us. That guides us. That drives us. It is purpose that defines us."

However, the difference between the purpose spoken of in *The Matrix* and that of Genesis is enslavement vs. enlightenment. In *The Matrix*, we have a dark and sinister message that is consistent with all the other uninspiring negativity coming out of Hollywood these days.

Creationists, on the other hand, offer an enlightened vision that suggests our purpose in life is to evolve closer to our creator. Regrettably, their beautiful vision of purpose is marred by the *Matrix*-like hubris of those who believe God will punish the nonconformists, infidels, non-believers, etc. as a validation of their own faith.

In 2012, the test of purpose will decide the matter, and it does not play favorites.

Test #2 — Time (Darwinism)

The Darwinian view of evolution is often used to describe any process that slowly unfolds at a prodigious rate, over a long period of time. On the other hand, it really points out that, to be considered a successful species, you must survive the test of time.

An example of a species that has withstood the test of time are the Coast Redwood trees that grow within 5-47 miles (8-75 km) from the Pacific Ocean, along America's Northwestern coastline. These hardy survivors date back over 150 million years. There was a time when these sub-tropical conifers were the dominant species of the Northern Hemisphere.

They grow to heights of over 300 feet (91.44 m), and a mature Redwood will consume 500 gallons (1,893 liters) of water each day. When genetically compared with humans, Redwood trees are the clear winners.

Each human cell normally contains 23 pairs of chromosomes, one from each parent for a total of 46 chromosomes. Redwoods have 11 pairs of chromosomes from six different parents for a total of 66 chromosomes! The next best thing to a Las Vegas wedding chapel.

While few humans live to celebrate their 100th birthday, Redwoods can live to be 2,200 or more years old, and they reproduce in two ways. Like other conifers, the seeds in their cones propagate the species, but they can also sprout new trees from their own root systems in something called a cathedral.

Redwoods are different from most tree species, because each tree interconnects its roots with the other Redwoods around it and shares water and nourishment. You can even find Albino Redwoods, which are white and feed solely upon the nourishment freely given them through the root system by nearby Redwoods.

In fact, this root system connection is so strong that if you were standing in a grove of old-growth Redwoods during an earthquake, you'd experience a sensation somewhat akin to jumping up and down on a trampoline. This is why they've easily withstood the sways and jolts of nature's worst Earthquakes for over 150 million years.

Still the same, Redwoods do die. They are felled by storms, burned in fires or simply pass from old age. When they fall over, their broken trunks become nurse logs that feed a cathedral ring of new Redwood saplings, which in turn will spring up from the root system in a nearly perfect circle. There is no big hurry to grow, as the nurse log continuously feeds nutrients back into the soil over a period of roughly 4,000 years.

Redwoods were here at least 85 million years before the Chicxulub impact that wiped out the dinosaurs some 65 million years ago, which means they've survived every flyby of Planet X and all the various cataclysms caused by each of those flybys. In 2012, they'll do it again.

Therefore, instead of putting our faith in man-made evolutionary theories and theologies, let's endeavor to be more like Redwoods. A species that has handily survived the test of time through genetic diversity, self-sacrifice and community.

Test #3 — Cataclysm (Catastrophism):

Before Darwinism and uniformitarianism, catastrophism was the dominant belief of many cultures. It was used to explain the creation of the world and the evolution of species. In terms of modern science, three men stand out as critical proponents of catastrophism:

- **Georges Cuvier:** A French anatomist and paleontologist who first proposed *Catastrophe theory or Catastrophism* in the early 19th century. Cuvier's theory would later be drowned out by Darwin's theory of natural selection, even though Darwin's theory never underwent any credible form of peer review.

- **Immanuel Velikovsky:** Having languished for many years, catastrophism was thrown back into the limelight in 1950 with the publication of the bestseller, *Worlds in Collision* by Immanuel Velikovsky. A respected psychiatrist and psychoanalyst, he argued that Earth had suffered catastrophic close-contacts with other planets in ancient times. Many of his theories were problematic, and the academic community ridiculed him. Nonetheless, his effort reintroduced and reenergized catastrophism as an evolutionary concept.

- **Luis Alvarez:** In 1980, catastrophism returned with a bang when Luis Alvarez, a physicist of Spanish descent published a paper on a 65-million year old impact crater he located at Chicxulub in the Yucatán Peninsula of Mexico. An impact so massive in scale, that roughly 70% of all species on Earth, including the dinosaurs, went extinct. His findings were so profound that they earned him a Nobel Prize.

However, to put catastrophism into a truly useful context, ask astronomers who specialize in Near Earth Object (NEO) detection for their thoughts on the matter.

They'll immediately tell you how deep-time geological records show us a clear pattern. One in which the species of this planet have prospered through long periods of relatively benign quiescence, only to fail during a punctuated moment of extreme natural violence.

While humankind had yet to completely pass the test of time, or the test of purpose for that matter, we certainly have passed the test of cataclysm. The worst that Planet X can throw at us is a pole shift with a global deluge. We've been there, seen it, done it and bought all the tee shirts. We can and will do it again.

On the other hand, many of our own intellectual inventions have not passed this crucial test, including many of the world's major religions, capitalism, communism, socialism and so forth.

All these came into being with great hopes during this current period of quiescence, and none have escaped internal corruption. So who is to say which shall endure beyond the coming tribulation?

For those that do fail, evolution, and not the vengeance of God, shall be the one to pass final judgment upon them, and one thing is certain. The petty triumphalism of man's present day belief systems will perish in the cataclysm to come, if for no other reason than that of sheer weariness.

As we look towards 2012, we know that the coming flyby of Planet X will refashion our world in ways we cannot yet fully comprehend. And so we ask, what shall become of us?

Something wondrous.

What Shall Become of Us?

One can literally spend weeks, if not months or years, studying the evolution theories of new age books and Web sites on the Internet. Whether they are talking about relationship with Gaia (Mother Earth), extraterrestrial intervention, the emergence of a new enlightened global mindset or whatever, they all promise us that we'll become a nobler species.

When these new age authors close their eyes, they see a universe of possibilities. Others merely see the back of their eyelids, such as Hollywood producers. Their souls have been so scorched on the dog-eat-dog ladder to success that they would likely view the belief of a nobler future for humankind as naive gibberish.

That is unless they can use it in some way to advance their own agendas. When that happens, they produce movies and television programs that say the right things about a nobler future, but always seem to miss the point.

However, if something within you resonates and you do get the point, the question then becomes how we get from here to there. The answer is that the path that is now leading to the future was blazed long ago — in the past. All we need do is to ignore pointless distractions and to stay true to that path. We must!

In catastrophic circumstances, environments can change suddenly or disappear altogether. Coping with this change requires rapid adaptation. The key reason why Coast Redwoods have survived for over 150 million years. Buried within their genome are dormant or partially dormant genetic codes, the timeless keys to their survival as a species.

When a global cataclysm does occur, those species that possess the genetic traits to cope are far more likely to survive. Our species is no different.

Humanity's Cataclysm Survival Genes

In June 2000, the U.S. Human Genome Project released a working draft of the entire human genome sequence, and the implications were profound. The world was stunned by the announcement that all of the approximately 30,000 genes in human DNA had now been coded (identified). While 30,000 genes is an impressive number, it merely represents 1.5% to 5% of all known human DNA!

So what about non-coding DNA that makes up the other 95% to 98.5%. Does it have a role in making us sentient beings? Just a few years ago, this non-coding DNA was dubbed "Junk DNA" because it seemed to serve no useful purpose. Like the Kuiper Belt at the edge of our solar system, it was thought of as the leftover debris of our creation.

In the years since then, geneticists leaned that this non-coding "Junk DNA" does in fact exhibit significant regulatory roles, which directly influence the behaviors of coding DNA. How significant?

In this new age of commercial biotampering, we are literally threading our way through unforeseen hazards. What should happen if researchers combine normally benign foreign genes and accidentally trigger a monstrous, non-coding DNA-driven genetic mutation that escapes the lab? It could happen, or maybe it already has.

Perhaps Robert Burns said best, "The best-laid plans of mice and men often go awry." That being said, there is an even more powerful, and pervasive agent of genetic manipulation — our Sun!

Solar Radiation and Longevity

A recent American study on genetic longevity found that people born in December have a longevity advantage because they were conceived in March.

Embryos conceived in March receive lower levels of solar radiation in the womb, which can cause small mutations in their DNA when they are most susceptible to them. Therefore, this reduced exposure ensures greater longevity vis-à-vis fewer genetic mutations.

In the last trimester leading up to a December birth, the womb is exposed to the lower ultra violet radiation (UVR) levels of that time of year. This makes a real difference with longevity, because UVR is known to predispose people to certain conditions.

The point here is that there is an unequivocal relationship between heightened levels of solar radiation and genetic mutations in the womb.

Increased Solar Radiation

In 2003, German scientists from the Max Planck Institute in Germany, along with Finnish scientists from Oulu University, published their findings.

Having reconstructed sunspot activity for the last thousand years, they concluded that our Sun has been in a "frenzied" state since 1940.

This 20th century date is an essential key to revealing the link between 2012 and human evolution. This is because the humans of tomorrow are already alive in small numbers. We know them as Indigo Children.

The term "Indigo" describes the hue of the aura (life energy color) that surrounds an Indigo, but this is not the only measure. An Indigo will also possess a genius IQ, an indomitable sense-of-self and a strong psychic intuition. Born to a natural knowing of things, they quickly sense goodness, compassion, evil intent and crisis in others.

Within almost everyone are the non-coding seeds of the Indigos of tomorrow. By the end of this century, they will come forth in enough number to perhaps become the vanguard of the "meek," of whom Jesus spoke. For now, their numbers are relatively few, but significantly on the rise.

A Growing Indigo Population

Many Indigo researchers and writers claim that these special children only began to appear in the last 40 years or so. While these researchers and writers are kind and caring people, they themselves are not Indigos, or more specifically, Indigo Elders.

If they were, they would intuitively know that the Indigo genetic predisposition has always been with most of us, buried deep in our non-coding DNA, where it awaits a triggering event or alignment.

Since 1940, two powerful Indigo mutation-triggering events have now aligned for the first time in the history of our species; increased solar radiation and population growth.

As was pointed out earlier, there is a direct connection between solar radiation and genetic mutations in the womb, and our Sun has been "frenzied" since 1940.

With that half of the alignment established, let's now turn our attention to the other half. In the process, we'll essentially bolt together the two shears of what is a remarkably sharp genetic scissor.

Indigos and Global Population Growth

As of July 2007, over 6.6 billion humans are now walking the Earth each day, and this number will continue to grow to somewhere between 8-12 billion souls by the end of the 21st century, assuming nothing happens to reverse that trend. Simply put, more people are alive today than ever before.

This translates into a huge statistical push from the growing global population. This results in increasing minorities to a size that makes them visible to the general population.

Although Indigos are visible to psychics, due to their purplish auras, there is no practical way for those in the general mainstream to vet these subjective, paranormal findings. There is, however, an empirical way for us to ascertain the global Indigo population trends. It is through the core criteria for determining the Indigo trait: IQ.

If you feel that your child could be an Indigo, your first step is not to take the child to a psychic. Rather, it is to have the child take an IQ test, such as the ones offered by Mensa (mensa.org), an international organization for high-IQ individuals founded in England in 1946.

In order to qualify for membership in Mensa, you need proof of a valid IQ test (or take one administered by Mensa) and to achieve a score that places you in the top 2 percent of the population. (Note: All three authors of this book were tested by and admitted into Mensa.)

When Mensa was founded, the top 2 percent of the world's population equaled about 45 million people; nearly the entire population of present-day South Korea. Since then, the world's population has more than doubled, and this has created a huge statistical push for Indigos.

To put this into perspective, let's look at how many eligible Mensans there have been in the world from 1A.D. up to the 2003 announcement by the Max Planck Institute in Germany that our Sun is "frenzied."

Date C.E. (A.D.)	Global Population	Eligible Mensans
1	150 million	3 million
1350	300 million	6 million
1700	600 million	12 million
1800	900 million	18 million
1900	1.6 billion	32 million
1950	2.4 billion	48 million
1985	5.0 billion	100 million
2003	6.3 billion	126 million

Just to be on the conservative side, let's assume there are only 100 million Mensa-eligible people alive today. Let's also assume that just 2 percent of these eligible Mensans are Indigos, as well. The result is that, even by using the most conservative assumptions, there could be as many as 2 million Indigos alive in the world today.

In the decades following 2012, there will be an explosion of Indigo Child births. This begs the logical question: how? To answer that, we need to make a little popcorn.

Popcorn Population Phenomenon

We previously mentioned that most all of us carry the Indigo genetic code within our non-coding DNA. That mysterious 98.5% of who we are, which still baffles geneticists.

Likewise, we saw the relationship between solar activity and the mutation of genes in the womb. So for the sake of comparison, let's view our Sun as the great microwave oven of evolution and the genes of the unborn in their mother's wombs as kernels of DNA popcorn.

Time to press the start button:

- **Early Poppers:** As the radiation begins to warm our popcorn, those kernels with the highest predisposition pop first. Their presence is announced in hesitant, little pops that come between long and irregular pauses. When we're finished, they'll be easy to spot. They'll be the big, tender puffs.

- **Mainstream Poppers:** Over time, we hear a near-rhythmic increase in the number of early poppers until we finally hear a wonderful, huge crescendo of popping kernels. These are the typical puffs that make up 90% or more of the final results. Not as fluffy as the early poppers, but tasty, nonetheless.

- **Late Partial Poppers:** After the mainstream crescendo, comes the ever-dwindling staccato of reluctant kernels. They usually turn out to be the small ones with bits of unpopped kernels mixed in. If we really have the munchies, we'll go for them.

- **No-Show Poppers:** When we take the popcorn bag out of the microwave oven, we always find a few unpopped kernels. We can nuke them until they turn to carbon and the kitchen becomes irradiated, but they'll never pop. That's just the way it goes.

Now, let's apply this popcorn population phenomenon analogy to Indigos and human evolution.

- **Early Poppers:** These are the early Indigos. Those enlightened geniuses, who throughout history have appeared from time-to-time to the greater benefit of humankind. After our Sun began going into a "frenzy" in 1940, that, plus the population surge, caused more early poppers to begin turning up. That quick, gentle staccato, which precedes the mainstream crescendo, started after WWII.

▟ **Mainstream Poppers:** In the years following 2012, after the world returns to a peaceful quiescence, the people of the world will begin rebuilding and repopulating. Those of childbearing age who've been left to fend for themselves will have received higher doses of solar radiation than those who sat out the cataclysms, safe in the underground bunkers. However, even at those depths, they will have received enough radiation to trigger a smaller, but still significant number of Indigo births.

▟ **Late Partial Poppers:** Starvation will be a problem for women in particular. A real concern for female athletes, who train to reduce their body fat to just a few percentage points, is that their menstrual cycles often stop, and they become barren or experience more severe complications. Many of the women who survive the lean years ahead will experience similar problems after the flyby.

▟ **No-Show Poppers:** This will be a cruel fate for many couples. Their DNA will have been so badly damaged that they will either be unable to bear children or worse yet, children that will be deformed, retarded or badly diseased.

The tragedy of 2012 is that many parents will endure the hardships only to see their children perish along the way, and when the Earth begins to heal, they will be barren. Yet in those days, there will also be children who will have watched their own parents meet a similar fate. They will find each other, and there will be love, and there will be family — once again — because there really is something wonderful to live for.

The Coming Millennium of Peace

This coming time of human tribulation and evolution have long been foreseen and prophesied. It is going to be difficult, painful and unavoidable, so we have to grasp the fact that our coming evolution is not about choice.

None of us has a choice, including the wealthy elites of the world, who view anyone outside their families as expendable chattels. Even they cannot stop it, channel it, change it or own it.

After 2012, the financial systems used by these self-serving elites will no longer be of interest to a world with new horizons. Then, stripped of their real source of power and attraction, they'll finally know what it means to face one's enemies all alone. Therefore, why waste time and emotion railing against their conspiracies and cabals? They're already yesterday's news.

Rather, consider the glory of what is to become of our world after all this misery has come and gone, and it will be a wondrous time. What will it look like?

The essence of what is to come was eloquently stated by one of the most remarkable Indigo Elders the world has ever known.

"The old appeals to racial, sexual and religious chauvinism and to rabid nationalism are beginning not to work. A new consciousness is developing which sees the earth as a single organism and recognizes that an organism at war with itself is doomed. We are one planet."

When you meet an Indigo, these are the kinds of thoughts you will hear. They were the words of the noted astronomer, Carl Sagan. They appear in the final chapter of his best selling book, *Cosmos*.

He believed that we are the living children of dead stars and that we were born to a powerful destiny. No matter how difficult things get, always remember:

- *We will survive.*

- *We will evolve.*

- *We will be unstoppable.*

Catch you on the backside.

16

Building a Star Trek Future

According to the translations of the ancient Sumerian texts by Zecharia Sitchin, nature would always jumpstart the food chain after the previous flybys of Nibiru (their name for Planet X.) This is why they hailed the arrival of this celestial visitor, even as they knew it would bring disaster.

They knew that afterwards, things would start anew, with seas teeming with fish and bountiful harvests to nourish their bodies. They also knew these flybys would nourish their minds and souls with major technological and sociological advancements.

When we enter this new millennium, we'll start from humble beginnings, but we will rise as a Phoenix from the flames. Ancient historical accounts and folklore tell us as much, and those who survive the days to come will become the foundation of a whole new incarnation of human civilization. One that will bear a striking resemblance to Gene Roddenberry's view of the future, as expressed in his original Star Trek television program.

Roddenberry's Vision of the Future

What turned Star Trek viewers into ardent fans and spawned a vast franchise of movies and television series was Roddenberry's egalitarian vision of life in the 23rd Century. One that followed a hazy, post-apocalyptic period in the mid-21st century.

Those who've made Star Trek an important part of their lives are believers and turning the stage props of the series into the realities of today.

As for the rest, many would like to see some form of Roddenberry's view of the future eventually come to pass. A time centuries from now, when money and all the grief it causes has been eliminated by a unified, compassionate and peace-seeking species.

And how does that work, anyway — in a world without money? That's a hard concept for many to embrace. Could it be that Roddenberry was simply baying at the moon to woo idealistic fans? No. It was his purity of vision that drew us to his view of the future, even though the path between here and there was, at best, obscure.

Roddenberry's vision of the future was right for the times. This is why it tapped directly into the *Zeitgeist* of the ongoing evolutionary process and fueled the creation of the gargantuan Star Trek franchise. Conversely, its notable absence following his death in 1991 explains why it all slipped away.

Following his death, studio lawyers, MBA's and accountants substituted his vision of the future with spin-offs, more in lock step with the cynical realities of their own lives. Incapable of believing in an egalitarian view of the future, they churned out formula-driven plots with 20th century humans using 24th century wizardry to solve 19th century dilemmas.

While this seemed sensible to those who filled Roddenberry's shoes, it only proved to be Star Trek's undoing as a major franchise. While much of the magic of Star Trek is gone, Roddenberry's vision of the future remains.

All that's missing of that is a way to link the post-apocalyptic period he envisioned in the mid-21st century to his egalitarian view of an enlightened 23rd century.

Thanks to our understanding of 2012 and Planet X, we now possess the first half of that link between 2014 and the 23rd century. By 2014, the worst will be over, and we'll see a renewal of life, as Mother Nature jump-starts the food chain and endows us with a world rich in new resources.

Jump-starting the Food Chain in 2014

As Planet X departs the core of our system, the volcanic dust from the eruptions triggered by it will begin to settle. As it does, the black-streaked, reddish orange hues of the 2012 to 2014 skies will be slowly replaced by a less threatening sky.

Once the ash has finally settled upon the land and at the bottom of the seas, the waters begin to clear. This is when life begins anew, and it will happen with or without us. This is because it will begin with the phytoplankton at the bottom of our planet's food chain.

Phytoplankton is responsible for most of the regulation of the oxygen and carbon dioxide levels in our atmosphere, and the vast amounts of iron deposited in our oceans by the Planet X meteorite storms will heavily stimulate its growth.

As they grow, they will help the atmosphere to clean itself, and in time, we shall see fleecy, white clouds against a blue backdrop once more. As the sky clears, the species that live on phytoplankton, such as krill, shrimp and whales, will begin to flourish again.

The global warming caused by Planet X will also begin to abate. This is because the phytoplankton will convert the vast excess of carbon dioxide in our biosphere into oxygen, while storing carbon and converting it into sugar that nourishes life. This will cause surface temperatures to lower, which in turn, will stabilize global weather systems.

Without the pressure of 6.6 billion hungry humans to feed, and with a new abundance of phytoplankton at the base of the food chain, global fisheries will expand massively. In a few years, they will begin to give the survivors of 2012 a wondrous bounty of life-nourishing protein.

There will likewise be a wealth of food resources on the land. Here too, Mother Nature shall restart the food chain where the great cities of man once dominated the coastlines of our continents.

Their great architecture and roadways will have been ground away by numerous cataclysms, and the broken ground left behind will be littered with rotting corpses of man and beast. Amongst all this will be rotting remains of sea life after the oceans recede.

All these will decompose and release sizable quantities of nitrates and minerals into the soil, thereby fertilizing it. As they do, whatever sea salt remains on the land shall be washed back into the sea by the rainfall of newly stabilized weather systems.

In all this new abundance, we will encounter the second half of our link between 2014 and Gene Roddenberry's egalitarian vision of life in the 23rd Century. It will resemble the 21st century view of the near future espoused by another brilliant visionary by the name of Jacque Fresco.

Beyond Money, Poverty and War

Like Gene Roddenberry, world renowned futurist and the founder of the Venus project, Jacque Fresco also sees a technology-driven future, where we strive to live with each other in harmony and peace.

Throughout his adult life, Fresco has worked tirelessly to offer us visual and mental images of a more benign world. Images that have inspired the very animators who create believable futuristic images for Star Trek as well as numerous other sci-fi movies and television programs. He is literally the man who inspires those who inspire our own view of the future.

What propelled him into this role was the Great Depression, which started with the 1929 Stock Market crash. As a young man, he lived through it, but could never bring himself to understand why so many tolerated such terrible hardships when the country was so rich in resources.

We have only lately learned the real truth of how elite banking families caused and manipulated the Great Depression to amass even greater fortunes, as they gained an even tighter control over America's money supply.

The result is that America's Federal Reserve Bank is owned by a network of private American banks, which are in turn owned by banks in Britain. Consequently, Americans now hold worthless currency and a national debt that can never be repaid. Other countries are undoubtedly seeing a similar financial situation.

The overall goal of all of these powerful cabals has long been a one-world government owned and controlled by them. They assure those who do their bidding that their goal is noble. They want to free humanity from the scourge of war — the very kinds of wars they finance.

To achieve this, they plan on implanting a radio-frequency identification (RFID) device the size of a grain of rice into every human body on the planet. Once completed, their control will be absolute, and governments will become impotent and disappear.

When that happens, step out of line, and your life will stop working. Your car will not start, your bank account and credit cards will become inaccessible, and you will not be able to buy groceries, go to school, work and so forth. That is, until you "behave."

The industrialized nations of the world will surely be the first to see the onset of this Orwellian future, as their citizens feel the bite of needles signaling the implantation of an RFID device into their bodies.

Getting people to accept these devices will not be difficult. Growing hunger, oil shortages and the growing battle over ever-dwindling resources will be motivation enough.

Even those standing in line for a free bowl of soup will feel the needle's bite before they're allowed one spoonful. This is how it will be through the great dying to come. But that will pass, and after 2014, things will begin to change in very profound ways.

After 2014

In 2014, Mother Nature will jump-start life on this planet. It will be slow at first, but as it picks up, we'll begin to see an abundance of fisheries and nutrient-rich farm lands. There will be far fewer mouths to feed.

Most Planet X researchers envision a global loss of life of about 50%, and many see more drastic figures. The worst estimates are that humankind will reduce to a similar global population of 1 C.E. (A.D.), at just 150 million. As with most things, the final outcome will likely be somewhere in the middle.

Of those who do survive, they will face a new world with vast resources and new lands for a fresh start. This is when they will run their fingers over the RFID implants in their bodies. They will think of them in the same way as African slaves felt about the scars left on their bodies by shackles and whips and how those who survived the Nazi Holocaust feel about the serial numbers tattooed on their arms.

That is when they will say, "enough is enough," and humanity will diverge onto a completely new path.

Once the survivors of 2012 resolve themselves to be free of their RFID shackles, they will replace the failed economic models of the first industrial revolution, and their modern reliance on RFID implants, with next-generation, resource-based economies.

In essence, the RFID implants of our near future will later spur an unstoppable global will of 2012 survivors to finally be free of Machiavellian financiers and their debt-slavery mechanisms once and for all.

So what could this new freedom look like? Just look around at the harbingers that are already shaping our world.

A Peek at the Resource Based Economies of the Future

In "Chapter 15 — 2012 as an Evolutionary Event" we saw how the Indigo children of today are the harbingers of our evolution from modern man to enlightened man. The same can be said of the resource-based economies that will drive our post-2014 future.

To imagine what this post-2014 future will look like, one need not look any further than the Open Source phenomenon that has shaped the Internet.

Open Source grew out of a desire to be free of the self-serving monopolies of the computer software industry, such as Microsoft, and it spawned a new generation of software developers who believed that software is too important to humanity to be monopolized. It must be free!

The result is that few know of the Open Source heroes spawned by this movement, such as Richard Stallman of GNU and Linux inventor Linus Torvalds. Yet, we couldn't enjoy the Internet without them, as we do. This is because more than half of the Internet is served by computers running free software, contributed to the betterment of humanity.

In a very real sense, Stallman and Torvalds are the resource economy pioneers of today, and their ranks are growing well beyond the world of software.

Fair Trade vs. Free Trade

In recent years, coffee aficionados have begun seeing more fair trade coffee choices when visiting their favorite buzz bistro for an espresso whammy or a latte. What distinguishes fair trade coffee from free trade coffee is a respect for the dignity of life.

Free trade blends are not suffering-free. The farmers who grow and harvest coffee beans receive a bare subsistence pittance from middlemen. Their coffee helps us stay up late to prepare for a college exam, yet they will never be able to give their own children even a modest college education.

With fair trade arrangements, participating merchants travel to where the coffee is grown and make their deals directly with the farmers.

The farmers receive the going market rate for their coffee, but without middlemen taking the lion's share of the profits. The result is a fair trade windfall of hope for these poor families, replete with better diets, improved healthcare and yes, the chance to send a deserving child to college.

These fair trade merchants are proving that being a "have more" does not give you the right to callously exploit those who "have less." This egalitarian concept is pure Roddenberry, and there are even more examples.

We're Not All Blood-sucking Financiers

A non-profit Web Site called Kiva.org connects those living in affluent industrial societies with those living in 3rd-world economies in a uniquely human way. Interest free loans.

These are typically small loans of just a few hundred dollars to small entrepreneurs and businesses, such as money to start a fruit and vegetable stand, or to remodel and to buy merchandise for a small family store.

The point here is that we're not all blood-sucking financial magnates, intent on ruling the world for the benefit of their own families. Yes, we have a lot of blood-suckers of one form or another to contend with now, but when Planet X culls the herd, they'll pass quickly.

Those Most Likely to Survive

The kind of people most likely to endure the tribulations of Planet X and 2012 will be people like the open source developers, fair trade coffee merchants and interest-free lenders of today.

This is because their love for people and their abiding respect for the dignity of life will enable them to create the kind of survival communities needed to face the tribulations ahead.

Once the worst is over, and they emerge to behold Mother Nature restarting the food chain, they and the Indigo children they bear shall be the meek who inherit the Earth.

At that time, there will be more resources than we could imagine now. There will be no need for obtuse financial shell games to allocate scarce resources to the benefit of a few. Rather, we'll understand the need to manage those available to us as good stewards.

We're doing it now. Every time you see a sign on the road that says a certain group has taken responsibility for keeping it litter-free, you're seeing good stewards. Every time you see people showing up on a weekend to clean a beach, you're seeing good stewards.

To have hope that will carry you through the tribulations of 2012 and beyond, you only need to look about you. All about us, in ever growing numbers, are new people who "get it."

2012 is about being in it for the species. Hold dear to that, and you'll weather the worst that comes, for this one simple belief will nurture your life with boundless hope.

We are a wonderful species with a noble destiny that cannot be denied.

Catch you on the backside.

Appendices

"We live in a society exquisitely dependent on science and technology, in which hardly anyone knows anything about science and technology."

—*Carl Sagan (1934 – 1996)*

In the years following 2012, the Earth will be verdant and beautiful once more, and humanity will rebuild, but woe to us lest we forget the lessons of 2012. This is because the next flyby shall bring a complete destruction of the Earth and all life upon it.

As a sentient species, we must fully utilize this precious time to colonize new Earths throughout the galaxy. Should we grow lazy and squander this last chance opportunity, then we shall perish altogether, and rightfully so.

Appendix A — Harbinger Technical Analysis

As Planet X approaches the Solar system, more signs of this continue to become visible on all bodies within it. From the outside in, all of the planets, their moons and the Sun are being perturbed. Likewise, comets are breaking up, and other mysterious physical phenomena are being observed as well.

Taken altogether, these events tell us that something is influencing the entire Solar system from the outside in. All this can be traced back to a single causality, and the best candidate is an approaching body. One that is causing the following changes:

- Plasma anomalies, with strange plasma behavior
- Inordinate temperature change
- Solar flares and anomalous solar activity
- Orbital perturbations of objects in the Solar system
- Electromagnetic effects on and between bodies in the Solar system
- Atmospheric and brightness changes of bodies in the Solar system
- Clustering of comet orbits
- Missing Kuiper Belt Objects (KBO)
- Increases in earthquake strength on Earth

Plasma Anomalies

On August 19, 2002, a plasma stream emanating from the Sun was bent away. Reconstruction of the direction of the stream showed it was deflected towards a region of space between the constellations Cetus, Eridanus and Fornax, just below the Zodiac near Taurus.

In June 2000, comet 76P/West-Kohoutek-Ikemura passed closely by Mars. Deep Space 1, at the time on its way to its mission target, comet Borrelly, observed the encounter. The LASCO (Large Angle and Spectrometric Coronagraph) C3 camera on SOHO (Solar and Heliospheric Observatory) captured the encounter on the edge of its field of view.

A zoom-in on Mars and the comet on June 4, 2000 at 14:18 UT from a SOHO C3 camera image showed a blurred view of the planet. There was clearly some interaction between the two bodies.

In images from LASCO 25 hours later, Comet 76P seemed to re-emerge above Mars. More importantly: a horizontal line began to reappear around Mars like the one that appears around Venus.

Such lines in the camera images are known as "CCD wings." These are image artifacts that arise from saturation of the camera's CCD chip; the size of the wings depends on the intensity of the light source imaged.

The brighter and more intense the light source, the longer the CCD lines become. Venus is much brighter than Mars. Therefore, Venus has a line that extends much further, but Mars normally has one also. This line was gone at the time of the flyby of 76P, however. The comet flyby blurred the entire planet, decreasing its brightness by orders of magnitude.

One month prior to the 76P flyby past Mars, a rare planetary alignment took place on May 5 of 2000. It involved the 7 nearest bodies to Earth in the Solar System (Sun, Moon, Mercury, Venus, Mars, Jupiter and Saturn).

To the surprise of scientists, Venus' plasma tail had reached Earth; SOHO had detected it. A planetary plasma tail creates a path of preferred conduction for the solar wind if the Sun is active. This observation shows that the electrical interaction between Sun and planets is stronger than anticipated.

In 1997, comet Hale-Bopp passed through perihelion. As the comet moved out of the Solar system again, an image was taken in 1999 that showed the comet light up like a fiery spider. Its 'spider legs' were electrical sprites; a plasma discharge was in progress. This was clear evidence of electrical interaction of the comet with something near-by.

Temperature Changes

Radar images taken of Mercury have revealed the presence of ice. As temperatures reach upward of 450 degrees Celsius on the side of Mercury facing the Sun, the presence of ice anywhere on the planet is remarkable.

The temperature on the surface of the largest moon of Neptune, Triton, has risen by about 5%. In the mean time, Pluto's average surface temperature has risen by 2 degrees Celsius (3.6 degrees Fahrenheit). According to MIT scientists, this is not a subtle change that can be attributed to seasonal weather patterns.

Solar Flares

Since the beginning of the twentieth century, the Sun's activity has increased notably. The Sun has started to emit more energy on average. Researchers have found that the energy emitted by the Sun increased by a few tenths of a percent over a few decades. As a result, Earth receives an extra amount of power from the Sun equal to 200,000 times the 2001 power consumption of New York City.

Also, more solar flares and more intense sunspots have been observed since 1940 than in the last 1,000 years prior to that. According to scientists, the next solar cycle will be extremely big. How big?

Research now shows peaks in geomagnetic activity indicate the expected intensity of the upcoming solar cycle. Consequently, it is predicted to be one of the worst cycles on record since monitoring began nearly 400 years ago.

The next solar maximum will occur in 2012. With that thought in mind, consider the following facts on recent cycles and predictions:

- Statistical analysis has led to a prediction of 160 sunspots per day with a variation of 25, 30% stronger than the last cycle peaking in 2001-2002;

- 4 out of the 5 most intense solar cycles were recorded in the last 50 years;

- During the 2001/2002 Solar peak, on April 2, 2001, the Sun unleashed an X20+ flare [9], exceeding any previous solar flare on record;

- A solar flare on November 4 of 2003 literally went off the NASA intensity scale. NASA was unable to determine its exact strength, but it was estimated stronger than X40. To get an idea of the intensity of this solar flare: it was about 40,000 times as intense as normal Sun activity;

- Three Solar flares hit or brushed Earth's atmosphere soon after October 28, 2003: the flares exploded from the Sun about a week apart. The flare on November 4 was clearly not aimed at Earth. The first two flares, however burst out towards the same region of sky that the plasma streams from the Sun were deflected towards a year earlier. Seen from the Sun on October 28, 2003, Earth is in Taurus, directly above Cetus.

Planet Orbit Perturbations

Uranus was discovered in 1781 by William Herschel, based on the orbital perturbations of Saturn. The orbital perturbations of Uranus led to the discovery of Neptune in 1846 by Johann Galle.

Both Uranus and Neptune were predicted from the observation of orbit perturbations. Likewise, perturbations to the orbits of Neptune and Uranus further indicated that another body had to exist beyond them. The mysterious Planet X, with X meaning the unknown planet. Not the tenth planet.

In 1930, Clyde Tombaugh discovered Pluto in his search for Planet X. Smaller than our own moon, Pluto lacked the mass needed to cause the orbit perturbations of Uranus and Neptune. It has since been demoted to the status of a dwarf planet.

Since Pluto did not explain the orbit perturbations for Planet X, the explanations we hear most often for the perturbations are:

- **The Math Was Wrong:** The orbital calculations for Uranus and Neptune were wrong to begin with. If so, how could a monstrous calculation error remain undiscovered for the better part of two centuries? An unlikely debunking scenario.

- **Pluto Gets a Bad Rap:** Others maintain that Pluto does in fact have enough mass to account for the orbital perturbations of Uranus and Neptune. A fact overlooked by over 70 years of erroneous calculation. However, this explanation is physically impossible, as Pluto, which is significantly smaller than our own moon simply lacks the mass.

It may be difficult to believe the gravity of a body larger than Jupiter caused the orbit perturbations for Saturn, Uranus and Neptune almost two centuries ago. It would not have stayed undetected throughout the twentieth century with everybody looking out for it. But something must be responsible for the orbit perturbations that led to the discovery of Pluto.

There are many clues to indicate that something big has to be out there in one particular direction, as we can see when we look at the planet orbits. Looking from the Sun, the probable position of Planet X, according to the orbit parameters presented in "Chapter 2 — Planet X Forecast through 2014," is the region between the constellations Cetus, Eridanus and Fornax.

On July 1, 1846, Uranus was located almost directly above this region of sky. Saturn and Neptune were at that time in the constellation of Aquarius. Neptune was quite near the region of sky between Cetus, Eridanus and Fornax at the time of its discovery; it reached this region about 25 years later, in 1871. Pluto in the mean time was nearing the lowest point of its orbit, which lies in the constellation of Cetus.

The inclination of the orbits of both Uranus and Neptune with regard to the ecliptic plane is almost in the same direction as the inclination of Pluto's orbit. The wider orbits seem to have a stronger inclination. Neptune dives below the ecliptic plane in Capricorn and comes above it again in Cancer. The lowest point of the orbit of Neptune lies near Aries. Uranus dives below the ecliptic in Scorpio/Sagittarius and comes back up in Taurus/Gemini. The lowest point of the orbit of Uranus lies in Pisces, also above the region of the three constellations.

The CRC Handbook [1] gives orbit inclination angles in degrees:

- 17.15 (Pluto),

- 1.77 (Neptune),

- 0.77 (Uranus),

- 2.49 (Saturn),

- 1.31 (Jupiter), all inclinations in nearly the same direction.

Mass is not the main factor in orbit inclination: Neptune is 17% heavier than Uranus, but Neptune is more inclined than Uranus. Saturn and Jupiter have an inclination in the same general direction. Their orbits are inclined more strongly again than Uranus.

A planet or failed star with a mass of a few times the mass of Jupiter approaching periodically from the region in between Cetus, Eridanus and Fornax would provide a common cause for the orbit inclinations of five planets, dependent only on their time of exposure to its influence. The tug of a heavy body passing by relatively slowly and relatively closely with regular intervals will gently incline the orbital plane on multiple passages.

The inner four planets have inclination angles in different directions. A more random effect is influencing them, possibly due to the fact that, while Planet X is within their orbit distance around the Sun, they complete one or more orbits around the Sun, so the tug on them is not as constant.

Electromagnetic Effects

A variety of electromagnetic phenomena has been found and studied throughout the Solar system over the last century. The last decade has shown an increase in these effects and their strength, and some of these new phenomena are puzzling scientists. Consequently, they're at a loss to explain them. Below, a few of them are listed that still await an explanation that makes some sense.

The exterior magnetic field of the Sun has more than tripled since 1900. This increase was reported widely back in 2000. Dr. Judith Lean of the Naval Research Lab lectured on this topic at the 2000 General Assembly of the IAU, the International Astronomical Union. So far, no explanation has been found for the increase that fits it into 'regular periodic' activity.

An intriguing feature on Mars is its Valles Marineris. This canyon dwarfs the Grand Canyon on Earth. It is 4,000 km long, up to 600 km wide and as deep as 10 km in some places. Seen from space, it appears as if a huge electrical spark hitting the surface of Mars carved it out of the planet surface.

An anomaly occurred in the Kp magnetic field index on November 25, 2002. The Kp index is a measure for the level of disturbance of the Earth's magnetosphere by external forces. This index went off the scale on that date. A strong peak in solar activity should have accompanied it, indicating M- or even X-class solar flares. It didn't; the graph seemed to point at a system glitch.

One day later, on November 26, 2002, the ELFRAD (Extremely Low Frequency Research And Development) group published a graph that had been recorded on November 24. The graph showed what looks like some sort of gravity wave hit Earth. The wave has a wavelength of approximately 4.38 AU; its origin remains unknown. It did coincide, however, to within hours, with the Kp index peak registered at NOAA.

Atmospheric and Brightness Changes

All planets seem to be showing an increase in brightness, as well as experiencing changes in their atmosphere that defy explanation within the theories currently at our disposal. Below is a list of a few highlights throughout the Solar system; most of them go unexplained.

The amount of sulfur found in the atmosphere of Venus has dropped 'dramatically' between 1978 and 1983. At the moment, a giant volcanic eruption is held responsible for the initial high level of sulfur; it is supposed to have taken place just before the first measurements in 1978.

The night-side 'air glow' on Venus increased by several orders of magnitude between 1975 and 2001. It contains high levels of oxygen. These levels of oxygen in Venus' atmosphere had not been found before.

In the summer of 2001, a violent storm burst out on Mars. Mars has regular dust storm activity, but it has rarely been so violent and large as it was in 2001. At its peak, the storm enveloped the entire planet, and it lasted for several months, non-stop. In August of 2003 NASA reported that the polar ice on Mars was melting at an increasing pace. NASA reported this as a seasonal effect. However, some independent researchers doubt the report.

On Jupiter, the large Red Spot, a super-hurricane structure larger than the Earth is quickly shrinking. At the current rate, the Red Spot will no longer exist in half a century. Aside from the aurora and Red Spot, Jupiter's atmosphere is also changing rapidly.

White ovals at middle latitudes on Jupiter are fast disappearing, and strong X-ray emissions are occurring at Jupiter's geographic poles. In August of 2003, a hot spot near Jupiter's North Pole was reported. This hot spot was emitting X-rays. It looked most like an aurora releasing tremendous amounts of energy. So far, no definite answer has been given to what is producing this phenomenon.

The single biggest volcanic eruption on record anywhere in the Solar System occurred on Jupiter's moon Io in February of 2001. It took NASA until November of 2002 to complete the data analysis of the event.

The cause for the volcanic activity on Io is difficult to establish. There is a good possibility it resulted from the double peak of the 2001 solar maximum affecting Jupiter. Jupiter affects Io via its strong electromagnetic field. Meanwhile, aurora activity on Ganymede, another moon, has more than doubled.

Both Jupiter and Saturn emit roughly 90 Megawatts of X-ray power. Jupiter has aurora rings in combination with a polar hot spot. Saturn only has the aurora rings. Some attribute the emissions from both planets to reflection of Solar X-ray radiation, since the spectrum of the X-rays is very similar to that of the Sun.

It is not possible the radiation from both is entirely reflection, because Jupiter orbits at 'only' 5.2 AU from the Sun, where Saturn orbits at more than 9.5 AU distance from the Sun. In addition, Jupiter is considerably larger than Saturn, 143,000 km vs. 120,000 km across. Because of this, Jupiter's visible surface from the Sun is 1.4 times as large as Saturn at equal distance, but Saturn is orbiting almost twice as far away from the Sun.

Therefore, the effective surface of Jupiter reflecting incoming radiation seen from the Sun is more than double the size of that of Saturn. Because the amount of solar radiation through a solid angle is constant, the power reflected by Jupiter should be at least twice as high as that by Saturn. Or, Saturn would have to be 50 times as reflective with X-rays as the Moon is to account for the amount of radiation it sends back at us. It would have to resemble a polished metal sphere to surpass the reflectivity of X-rays the Moon has. So a factor of 50 times more reflective for X-rays is impossible. There must be another source of X-ray radiation besides reflection.

In 1986, Voyager 2 passed by Uranus and saw no significant features on the planet surface. In 1996, Hubble Space Telescope imaged large cloud formations that were not there a decade earlier. At first, these cloud formations were attributed to seasonal changes. One season on Uranus lasts about 21 Earth years.

There is however not enough energy present in the atmosphere of Uranus to form this kind of cloud formation this quickly. In 2000 the brightest clouds ever were seen on Uranus. The change since 1996 has been too fast to be part of a normal weather pattern, according to researchers. Some additional source of energy has to be responsible for providing the extra energy.

The increase in brightness of Neptune is even stronger than the increase of brightness seen on Uranus. A strong increase in brightness occurred on Neptune in only 6 years, between 1996 and 2002. Neptune's blue light emission grew by more than 3%, red light by more than 5%, and near infrared by up to 40%.

Bottom line: Neptune is heating up at an even faster rate than Uranus, while Neptune is 11 AU further away from the Sun than Uranus is. The Sun is therefore probably not the main cause for Neptune's strong global warming. This implies an additional, unknown source for the heat supplied to Neptune.

Neptune once showed a great dark spot that marked a hurricane in its dense gas atmosphere. Hubble images of Neptune after Voyager 2 in 1989 showed the disappearance of the great dark spot and the emergence of another one in a completely different location on the planet.

The disappearance of one storm since 1989 and the emergence of another are not likely seasonal changes. One season on Neptune lasts for 41 Earth years. On a side note, the atmospheric pressure on Neptune's moon Triton more than doubled between 1989 and 1998.

Between 1979 and 1999, Pluto was closer to the Sun than Neptune and reached perihelion in 1989. Since then, its atmospheric pressure has increased by over 300%. According to scientists, this too is too great an increase to be attributable to seasonal changes alone.

Comet orbit perturbations

Not only are the planets of the Solar system subject to increasing change. The other bodies that inhabit or wander through our system are also evidencing anomalous behaviors, as well.

In June 2000, comet 76P/West-Kohoutek-Ikemura or 76P flew past Mars and disappeared afterwards. No reliable images have been taken of comet 76P after the June 2000 flyby past Mars.

As a matter of fact, no new images have been published at all of comet 76P or the moons of Mars since that flyby. Instead, old images of Mars and its moons were republished several times. The publishers claimed that they were new material, but these images were conclusively proven to have been published before the 76P flyby past Mars.

Another comet passage occurred in 2000. In July 2000, comet C/1999 S4 disintegrated upon passage through the ecliptic plane. Consequently, research into comets has led to claims that a heavy object has to be orbiting the Sun somewhere in the realms of the inner Oort cloud or Kuiper Belt.

Statistically significant, correlated anomalies exist in aphelia directions, perihelion distances and energies of comets. They suggest that a brown dwarf with 2-3 times the mass of Jupiter orbits at 25,000 AU.

This conclusion follows from a statistical analysis of observations, which suggests a clustering of comet orbits, or rather their aphelia along a path through the outer edge of the Solar System. The clustering indicates that an object is plowing through the Kuiper Belt, or even further out in the Oort cloud, throwing comets inward towards the Sun.

Astronomers Matese, Whitman and Whitmire stated in 1999 that their observations suggest that a major body is disturbing the Oort cloud, and sending comets into the inner Solar System in a non-random pattern. In their published abstract they state that "Approximately 25% of the 82 new class I Oort cloud comets have an anomalous distribution of orbital elements that can best be understood if there exists a bound perturber in the outer Oort cloud."

In 1984, Davis, Hut & Muller suggested the existence of a brown dwarf star called Nemesis, to account for periodic mass extinctions on Earth every 26 million years. This brown dwarf passes through a denser region of the Oort cloud roughly every 26 million years and sends millions of comets into the Solar System.

In October 1999 Dr. John Murray of the English Open University stated that he believed an undiscovered planet the size of Jupiter orbits the Sun at approximately 30,000 AU. During his studies of the Solar System's outer regions, he observed anomalies in distant comet orbits. A possible explanation in his view is that a larger object causes them.

Missing KBO

Around the planetary region of the Solar system, there is a region that contains thousands to millions of smaller rocks, many of them covered in ice. This disc is called the Edgeworth-Kuiper Belt, in short Kuiper Belt. A disc-shaped region of asteroids stretches out towards a shell of icy comet bodies that envelops the Solar system. This shell around the entire system, which contains billions of icy comets, is called the Oort cloud.

Astronomers have found a discontinuity or gap in the Kuiper Belt. This Kuiper Belt Gap or Kuiper Belt Cliff lies between 70 AU and roughly 350-400 AU from the Sun. This region has been wiped almost clean of objects. In addition, there are clusters or bands of KBO with increased density of objects.

These KBO are at fixed ratios of orbits around the Sun as described by the Titius-Bode's Law. The only planet that does not obey this law is Neptune. All others follow it to within percents, and so does the Asteroid belt between Mars and Jupiter. There is no theoretical explanation for this ordering of orbits in the Solar system; it is an empirical law.

The asteroid belt either used to form a planet, or never managed to form into a planet due to gravitational effects by Jupiter. The estimated total mass of the asteroid belt between Mars and Jupiter is approximately 4% of the mass of our Moon, which would make it a very small planet (diameter ~900-1000 km only). It seems most realistic that no planet could form there, due to Jupiter's influence.

Scientists think the asteroid belts at the outer edge of the Solar system are ordered by resonance to the orbit of Neptune. This means their orbit ratios are integer ratios to Neptune's. Observations have shown density concentrations of KBO around 2:3, around 4:7, around 1:2, around 2:5, etc., where the base (1:1) is the distance of Neptune to the Sun.

Beyond 67 AU however, the distance of 2003 UB313, or Eris/Xena, there are almost no KBO until far beyond 350 AU from the Sun. Eris, which is slightly larger than Pluto, has an eccentric orbit (eccentricity 0.44) and a strong inclination in its orbit (44 degrees.) Sedna is the next largest KBO.

Theory predicts that a larger number of KBO should have been found, however, 99% of the expected mass was not found. Something must have swept these KBO away. A distance of 350 to 500 AU corresponds with the aphelion of an elliptical orbit of 3,660 years of a heavy object orbiting the Sun. The object called Planet X.

Increasing Earthquake Strength on Earth

Thousands of times every day, earthquakes rock the crust of the Earth. The vast majority of these earthquakes never make it to any seismograph, nor does anyone notice them. They are either too remote for us to feel them or too weak to show up on any one of the many thousands of seismic instruments we use across the world.

On a more global level, there is an organization called USGS (United States Geological Survey). USGS is the predominant party that keeps track of earthquakes and studies their behavior; USGS gathers statistical information on earthquakes that occur around the world.

These numbers do not tell much of a story if they are just in a table. It is much easier to look for trends when you take the numbers from a table and put them into graphics. These graphs can then expose a possible trend across time in earthquake numbers, for example, per magnitude category; in this way they show trends that do not become immediately apparent from the table itself.

Number of Earthquakes Worldwide for 1998 – 2007 as of July 3, 2007										
Located by the US Geological Survey National Earthquake Information Center										
Magnitude	1998	1999	2000	2001	2002	2003	2004	2005	2006	2007
8.0 to 9.9	2	0	1	1	0	1	2	1	1	2
7.0 to 7.9	14	23	14	15	13	14	14	10	10	2
6.0 to 6.9	113	123	158	126	130	140	141	142	132	79
5.0 to 5.9	979	1106	1345	1243	1218	1203	1515	1694	1483	776
4.0 to 4.9	7303	7042	8045	8084	8584	8462	10888	13920	13069	5690
3.0 to 3.9	5945	5521	4784	6151	7005	7624	7932	9185	9953	4233
2.0 to 2.9	4091	4201	3758	4162	6419	7727	6316	4636	4016	1536
1.0 to 1.9	805	715	1026	944	1137	2506	1344	26	19	23
0.1 to 0.9	10	5	5	1	10	134	103	0	2	0
No Magnitude	2426	2096	3120	2938	2937	3608	2939	865	849	911
Total	21688	20832	22256	23665	27453	31419	31194	30479	29534	13252

The total number of earthquakes recorded per year has gradually increased from around 22,000 in 1998 to more than 30,000 in 2005. After 2005, the total number seems to decrease again. When we examine the numbers more closely, it looks like much of the growth is formed by an increase in the number of stronger earthquakes.

We know that the improving detection techniques do probably contribute to the increase in the statistical numbers of earthquakes we record; we are able to detect more earthquakes. Improved detection techniques, however, cannot account for the peaks we see in earthquake numbers within magnitude ranges, peaks that have occurred or are just beginning to occur.

Since 1998, peaks in numbers have shifted to higher-magnitude ranges almost every year. The development of the numbers within the magnitude ranges does not run parallel to the development of the overall number.

It is interesting to see what USGS has to say as many people from around the world have asked them the same question. Are earthquakes increasing globally? The answer USGS gives is: no, they are not.

They attribute the increase in numbers recorded mainly to improving earthquake detection techniques. Even though detection certainly does play a part, this explanation cannot cover the entire increase. It does not touch the increase in strength we see.

And it is there; if we take a look at the statistics from a different point of view, this will show why the USGS answer cannot be the full story. When we normalize statistics per year to their total numbers, we take the total number of earthquakes out of the equation. By taking the total number out of the picture, we take detection techniques out of the equation, as well.

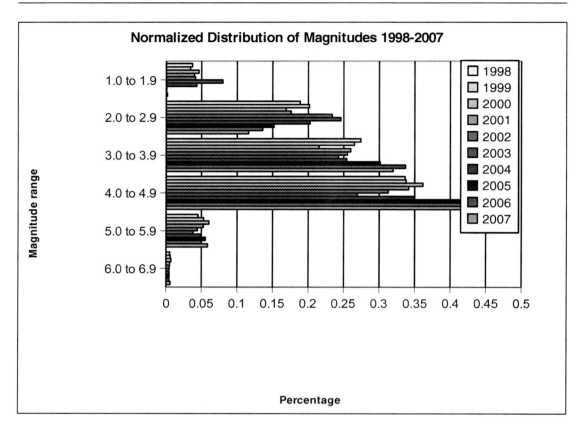

A shift towards higher average magnitude is visible. For each year and each magnitude range we multiply the number of recorded earthquakes by the average strength for that range and then divide the sum of these numbers by the total number of earthquakes for that year. A few numerical examples will explain what this means: the average between 8 and 9.9 is 9; 1 times 9 equals 9; the average between 7.0 and 7.9 is 7.5; 14 times 7.5 equals 105.

These values we sum per year for all magnitude ranges and we divide this sum by the total number of quakes for the year. We call the result of this calculation a weighted average; the bar graph shows the results per year. This weighted average shows an interesting development. It shows a strong increase after 2003 and begins to taper off again in 2007.

The following graph shows weighted average quake strength, including 'no magnitude' quakes.

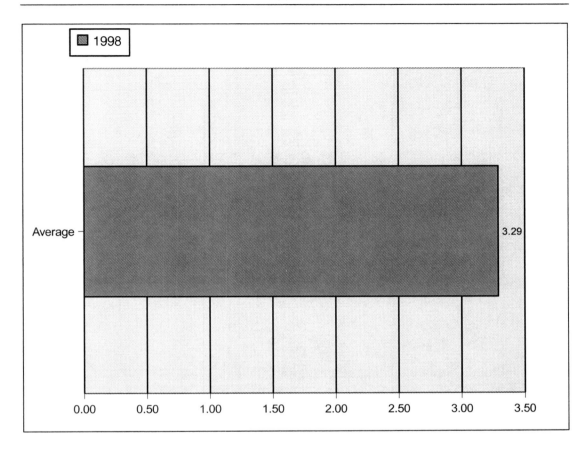

There is, however, a portion of the earthquake statistics table that manipulates the outcome of the magnitude average, it will dampen it. It is the category 'no magnitude'. Earthquakes in that category add zero to the total magnitude sum, but the sum will be divided by a bigger number of quakes, lowering the calculated average magnitude. If we leave the 'no magnitude' category out of the calculation of the weighted average, we get a different picture.

Even though the relative increase in average magnitude is not as strong, it does not taper off in 2007, instead it continues to increase! Something has been causing earthquakes to continually grow in strength since 2003.

When the weighted average quake strength from above is recalculated without the 'no magnitude' earthquakes data, a very different picture emerges.

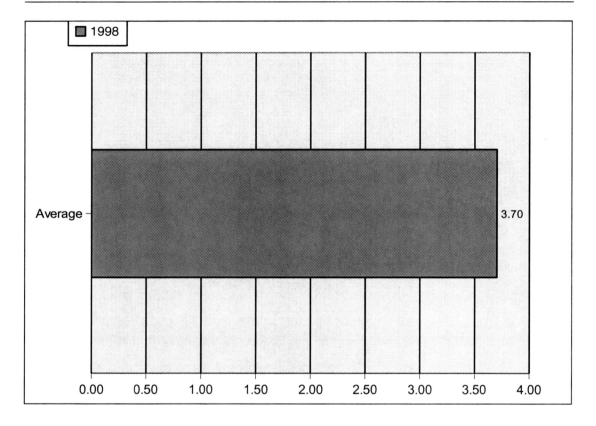

Earthquake magnitudes are measured on a logarithmic scale. A 5.0 earthquake is ten times as powerful as a 4.0 earthquake in terms of ground motion, and a 6.0 earthquake is 100 times as powerful. The energy increase with magnitude is even stronger than this. This is shown below; the table can be found on the USGS site, as well.

Earthquake Magnitude vs. Motion and Energy		
`Magnitude Change	Ground Motion Change (Displacement)	Energy Change
1.0	10.0 times	about 32 times
0.5	3.2 times	about 5.5 times
0.3	2.0 times	about 3 times
0.1	1.3 times	about 1.4 times

This table shows that relative to 2000, the average earthquake in 2007 generated up to five times as much energy as those in 2000. Something is putting this energy into the Earth. An approaching intruder disturbing the Solar system's electromagnetic field is a very good candidate for exactly that. The intruder we know as Planet X.

Print References:

- CRC Handbook of Chemistry and Physics, David R. Lide, Editor-in-chief, 82nd edition, 2001-2002, ISBN 0-8493-0482-2

- Dark Star, The Planet X Evidence, Andy Lloyd, 2005, ISBN-10: 1-892264-18-8, ISBN-13: 978-1-892264-18-3

- Bernstein G.M., Trilling D.E., Allen R.L. , Brown K.E , Holman M., Malhotra R., The size Distribution of transneptunian bodies. The Astronomical Journal, 128, 1364-1390

Appendix B — History of *The Kolbrin Bible*

The Kolbrin Bible: 21st Century Master Edition contains faithful copies of all 11 books of the historical and prophetic anthology formerly known as *The Kolbrin*. *The Kolbrin Bible* is an ancient secular academic work; it offers alternate accounts of several stories from the *Holy Bible* and other wisdom texts.

Previously named *The Kolbrin*, the work is now titled *The Kolbrin Bible* by the publisher. This is because the term *"Bible"* accurately defines the work and also has its roots in a civilization that played a critical role in its dissemination.

In the classic sense, the term *"Bible"* comes from the Greek *"Biblia,"* meaning books, which stems from *"Byblos."* Byblos was an ancient Phoenician port located in what is now the central coast of Lebanon.

In their day, Phoenician traders operated the most advanced fleets of ocean-going vessels in all the world. Before their fall to the Roman Empire, their principal trade routes stretched throughout the Mediterranean area, out along the shores of Western Europe and up as far North as Britain.

Of note to this body of work is that the Phoenicians imported papyrus from Egypt and sold it abroad along with ancient wisdom

texts. In doing so, they distributed the earliest known variant of *The Kolbrin Bible*, called *The Great Book*, to their various ports of call.

The Great Book was originally penned in Hieratic by Egyptian academicians after the Exodus of the Jews (ca 1500 BCE). Its original 21 volumes were later translated using the 22-letter Phoenician alphabet (which later spawned the Greek, Roman and English alphabets of today).

The only known copy of *The Great Book* to survive the millennia was the one exported to Britain by the Phoenicians in the 1st century BCE. Regrettably, much of it was destroyed when the Glastonbury Abbey was set ablaze in 1184 CE. The attack on the Abbey was ordered by English King Henry II, after he accused the Abbey priests of being mystical heretics.

Fearing for their lives, the Celtic priests of the Abbey fled into hiding with what remained of *The Great Book*. There, they transcribed the surviving Phoenician translations to bronze sheets and stored them in copper-clad wooden boxes. This effort became known as *The Bronzebook*.

In the 18th century CE *The Bronzebook* was merged with a Celtic wisdom text called the *Coelbook* to become *The Kolbrin Bible*.

Your Own World Books Editions of *The Kolbrin Bible*

Your Own World Books first published several print and electronic editions of *The Kolbrin Bible* in April 2005. Each edition is a faithful copy of the 20th Century Major Edition and uses the Kolbrin Citation System developed by Marshall Masters.

In May 2006, Your Own World Books published second editions of *The Kolbrin Bible*. Updated with over 1,600 typographical corrections based on the *Chicago Manual of Style*, the verbiage remains exactly the same. An index was also added.

The Kolbrin Bible	Books	Comments	Print Editions	eBooks
21st Century Master Edition	ALL 1-11	Published for scholars, this edition is available in an A4 letter-sized paperback with ample margins for notes. The typesetting is easy on old eyes with ample margins for notes.	8.268" X 11.693" Trade Paperback	Adobe Microsoft Mobipocket Palm
Egyptian Texts of the Bronzebook	1-6 Only	Recommended for those with an interest in 2012 Mayan prophecies, Planet X (Nibiru) and factual alternate accounts of Noah's Flood and Exodus.	7.44" X 9.69" Trade Paperback	
Celtic Texts of the Coelbook	7-11 Only	Recommended for those with an interest in Druid/Celtic philosophy and prophecies. Also contains newly-detailed bio- graphical accounts of Jesus Christ with several first-person quotes.	7.44" X 9.69" Trade Paperback	

Languages of *The Kolbrin Bible*

One of the most commonly asked questions is "what was the original language of *The Kolbrin Bible,* and who wrote it." The answer is in multiple parts.

The Kolbrin Bible: 21st Century Master Edition	BCE		CE		
	15th Century	1st Century	1st Century	18th Century	20th Century
	Original	Translation	Original	Translation	Translation
Book Title	Egyptian Hieratic	Phoenician Script	Old Celtic	Old English	Continental English
1. Creation	✓	✓		✓	✓
2. Gleanings	✓	✓		✓	✓
3. Scrolls	✓	✓		✓	✓
4. Sons of Fire	✓	✓		✓	✓
5. Manuscripts	✓	✓		✓	✓
6. Morals and Precepts	✓	✓		✓	✓
7. Origins			✓	✓	✓
8. The Silver Bough			✓	✓	✓
9. Lucius			✓	✓	✓
10. Wisdom			✓	✓	✓
11. Britain			✓	✓	✓

Languages Used Before the Common Era

The *Egyptian Texts of the Bronzebook* (the first six books of *The Kolbrin Bible*) were originally penned in Hieratic as *The Great Book* by Egyptian academicians, following the Exodus of the Jews (ca 1500 BCE).

One of several copies of this work was translated into Phoenician and eventually made its way to Britain. This is because Egypt and Phoenicia were both very powerful nations at the time, and their languages were widely used.

Languages Used During the Common Era

The *Celtic Texts of the Coelbook* (the last five books of *The Kolbrin Bible)* were originally penned in ancient Celtic. Work began on the earliest parts of *The Coelbook* in approximately 20 CE and finished in approximately 500 CE.

Inspired by the scope of the Egyptian texts, the Celts wrote their own historical and philosophical anthology in a similar manner, but in their own language. Viewed as a religious work by many, the Celtic texts offer a timeless insight into Druid folklore, mysticism and philosophy.

According to some historians, *The Coelbook* was also inspired in part by a visit by Jesus Christ to Britain. At the time, Jesus was either in his late teens or middle twenties and traveled via a high-speed Phoenician trading ship to Britain with his great uncle Joseph of Arimethea, who undertook the journey to inspect a tin mine he owned.

These historians further maintain that Jesus studied the Egyptian texts in Britain. This is because the Celtic texts penned following his possible visit contain a never-before published biography of Jesus.

Given the detailed and highly revealing nature of this biography, the case can be made that the biographer personally met Jesus, or interviewed someone who had. Additional corroboration comes from reliable historical accounts that indicate Joseph of Arimethea founded the Glastonbury Abbey in or about 36 CE, and that it eventually became the repository for these texts during the 1st millennium.

Stored together in the Glastonbury Abbey under the watchful eyes of Celtic priests, the texts remained safe and were actively studied until the 12th Century, when the Abbey was attacked and set ablaze by minions of King Henry II.

After the attack, the priests fled with what remained of these ancient works to a secret location in Scotland, where the Egyptian texts were transcribed to bronze sheets. At that time, the two books were still not joined, and the language of both remained as-is; Phoenician (translated from Egyptian Hieratic) and ancient Celtic, respectively.

In the 18th century, the two books were combined and translated to Old English to form the first identifiable edition of *The Kolbrin Bible*. In the 20th century, the manuscripts were transferred to London and updated to Continental English.

The latest edition of *The Kolbrin Bible* still uses the Continental English update, but has been edited according to modern rules of grammar and punctuation based on the *Chicago Manual of Style.*

The Seven Major Editions of *The Kolbrin Bible*

Born of great wisdom and love, the overall creation span of *The Kolbrin Bible* is greater than that of the *Holy Bible*.

To facilitate a historical study of the work, Your Own World Books divided the creation span of *The Kolbrin Bible* into seven "master editions" using the criteria of publication era and country.

Master Edition	Publication Era *Country*	Description
1st	15th Century BCE *Egypt*	First penned in Hieratic after the Exodus of the Jews from Egypt (ca 1500 BCE). Published as *The Great Book*, a 21-volume work. The surviving volumes are now published as the *Egyptian Texts of the Bronzebook*.
		The genesis of this secular work was a new Egyptian interest in finding the one true G-d of Abraham as a consequence of their defeat at the hands of Moses.
		The work contains many historical accounts that parallel those of the Torah (Old Testament) and warns of a massive object called the "Destroyer" that is prophesied to return in this time with catastrophic results for the Earth.
2nd	1st Century BCE *Phoenicia (Lebanon)*	The 1st Master Edition is translated into the Phoenician language. The simple 22-letter alphabet of the Phoenicians eventually becomes the root alphabet of the Greek, Roman and English alphabets.
		Before falling to the Roman Empire, they distribute the work throughout the Mediterranean area, Western Europe and Britain.
3rd	1st Century CE *Britain*	From approximately 20 CE to 500 CE, the last five books of what would eventually become *The Kolbrin Bible* are written. Now published as the *Celtic Texts of the Coelbook*, this part of the work was first penned in ancient Celtic.
		During this time, the Egyptian texts of the 2nd Major Edition were studied by Celts as well as the children of wealthy and powerful Romans. Copies of the work eventually found their way to the Glastonbury Abbey.
4th	12th Century CE *Scotland*	In 1184 English King Henry II ordered an attack on the Glastonbury Abbey, claiming its Celtic priests to be heretics. Those who survived the arson and murder fled with the surviving Egyptian texts of the 2nd Master Edition and later engraved them on bronze sheets. Stored for centuries in a secret location in Scotland, this edition is also known as *The Bronzebook*.

Master Edition	Publication Era *Country*	Description
5th	18th Century CE *Scotland*	The *Bronzebook* was merged with The *Coelbook*, and then both were translated into Old English. The new anthology was collectively titled *The Kolbrin* by its caretakers, the Hope Trust of Edinburgh, Scotland.
6th	20th Century CE *England* *New Zealand* *America*	In the years following WWI, the 5th Major Edition was relocated to London, England, where it was updated to Continental English. This master edition remained unpublished until 1992, when a senior member of the Hope Trust distributed several copies of the work. One distributed copy was printed in 1994 in New Zealand by a small religious order and another in 2005 in America by Your Own World Books. The only differences between the New Zealand (1994) and American (2005) editions appear in the front matter, and the American edition added a new citation system and was published in both print and electronic variants.
7th	21st Century CE *America*	Your Own World Books updates the 6th Major Edition with 2 significant changes. While the Continental English language and spellings remain unchanged, the text is updated to comply with the Chicago Manual of Style. Over 1,600 typographical corrections are made. Also new to this master edition is a first-ever index with over 2,700 unique entries. This master edition is also published in 2 abridged editions; the *Egyptian Texts of the Bronzebook* and the *Celtic Texts of the Coelbook*. All editions are published in print and electronic variants.

For more information about the abridged and unabridged editions of *The Kolbrin Bible: 21st Century Master Edition,* visit www.kolbrin.com.

Appendix C — Forecast Addendum

In "Chapter 2 - Planet X Forecast Through 2014," we looked at the events we can expect to occur during a flyby of Planet X through the inner Solar system.

Orbital parameters

The forecast for this coming flyby is based on an approximation for the orbit of Planet X as per the following orbital parameters:

Parameter	Value
Mean distance (a)	237.50 AU
Eccentricity	0.988
Inclination	85.00 degrees
Ascending node	200.00 degrees
Argument of pericentre	12.00 degrees
Mean anomaly	358.71 degrees
Epoch	2451545 (Julian day)

These parameters describe an elliptical orbit that measures 475 Astronomical Units (1 AU equals the distance from Earth to the Sun) from end to end.

The longest line cutting or major axis of that ellipse runs through the Sun and the closest and furthest points of the orbit. This line points to a point below the ecliptic in the direction of the constellation Cetus, which lies about 12 degrees below the ecliptic plane, in which all the signs of the Zodiac are found.

The orbit lies in a plane, but this plane does not, like Pluto's orbit, tilt just a little. This orbit does tilt;qa the far end dips below the ecliptic. But in addition to that, the orbit is rotated around this major axis by 85 degrees, like a ship that capsizes.

Planet X flies almost over the Sun's poles when it passes perihelion. The ascending node tells where it comes above the ecliptic, starting to count from a reference point in Aries. This makes the point of breaking the ecliptic somewhere in Virgo/Libra, all seen from the Sun of course.

The eccentricity tells us about the ratio between the distance from the Sun to the perihelion of Planet X and half the length of the long axis of the orbit. If that eccentricity is zero, they are the same, and the orbit is a circle. If the eccentricity equals one, the orbit breaks open and becomes a parabola.

Eccentricity = ((a) – perihelion) / (a),

...where (a) is the mean distance; see above. With these parameters the solution is an elliptical orbit of approximately 3,661 years, that breaks upward through the ecliptic on December 21, 2012 and moves through perihelion early February of 2013. This is the meaning of the mean anomaly in combination with the epoch.

The mean anomaly runs from zero to 360 and tells the angle that has been covered out of a full circle when you begin to count at zero in perihelion. The value 358.71 means that it was approaching perihelion again at the date described by the epoch number. The epoch number describes the number of days in what is called the proleptic Julian calendar, which is basically a counting of the days since January 1, 4713 BC. The value given represents January 2, 2000 in that numbering system.

Building blocks to the orbit of Planet X

How did we get to this particular estimate of the orbit? A variety of sources and a variety of clues gave input to a lengthy process of trial and error, which turned out to match even more clues found afterwards. This gave us confidence in the result of the orbital projection and forecast.

Important clues that we used to construct the orbit are as follows:

- Solar plasma was bent away towards the constellation of Cetus in 2002;

- The constructed orbit has a period of 3,661 years (the 'true number of the beast' according to Turkish researcher Dr. Burak Eldem), and an approximate fit to both 2012 and 1630-1640 BC (eruption of Thera on Santorini/Exodus from Egypt);

- The perihelion distance lies in the Asteroid Belt, where according to the Titius-Bode Law, a planet should exist but doesn't;

- The planet breaks through the ecliptic on Dec. 21, 2012;

◢ From the prophecies of Nostradamus: a second Sun will appear in the sky, and a bearded star will appear towards the North, not far from Cancer (this is where the Sun is located in the Zodiac in July);

◢ From the *Holy Bible*, book of Revelation: The beast will wait at the feet of the virgin in labor to devour the child as soon as it is born;

◢ All outer planet orbits are inclined in the same direction, their point deepest below the ecliptic lies in the direction of the constellation of Cetus when we look at it from the Sun;

◢ In a remote viewing, someone "saw" the direction of Cetus blocked from view, when hovering above the Sun. There was also a sensation of malevolence in that region of the sky.

The last clue was derived using a technique called Remote Viewing (RV).

Remote Viewing

This paranormal method dates back to the 1970s and 1980s and was extensively developed by the CIA and KGB intelligence agencies. Each investigated into the possibility of employing remote viewing to gain an edge over the other side, but neither was able to successfully weaponize the technique.

While little is known about the KGB variant, the CIA-sponsored RV research done at Stanford University in California is being studied and taught around the world. Two notable teachers are Echan Deravy of Japan and Major Ed Dames of the USA.

Deravy's remote viewing students produced notable Planet X results that placed the object inside our Solar system, with findings that correlate quite closely to those of the Major Ed Dames RV team in the U.S.

The RV members of the US research team led by Dames viewed an object passing closely by the Earth. They also viewed major Solar flares and the possible destruction of a manned mission in space as a harbinger. The findings of this group formed the basis of Dames' 2005 *Killshot* documentary.

When compared with other paranormal reports, these Japanese and American RV findings track closely with the reports of other paranormal experiences. While the authors do not use RV as a final source, it is a very sharp arrow in the quiver.

Constructing an Orbit of Planet X

If we look at the overview of clues, we see an object coming in from Cetus, on a period of 3,661 years, with its perihelion in the Asteroid Belt. The planet or planetoid that once was there has been destroyed by either gravity interaction or a direct collision with the object, Planet X on a previous flyby.

Matching this with an orbit in astronomy software led to certain restrictions for the orbit that matched some of the other clues and actually brought up the consideration of one of them.

Planet X is coming in from and located in Cetus on an elliptical orbit with the perihelion in the Asteroid Belt. It is on a 3,661 year orbit that will bring it through the ecliptic on December 21, 2012. This is an important date in many cultures, but most significant in Mayan history and astronomy. This date marks the end of the long count, their longest calendar, spanning over 5,100 years.

The location of the perihelion matching an orbit with a current position in Cetus is situated in the constellations of Virgo/Libra when passing the ecliptic plane, on 21 December of 2012. This is very near to Christmas, the celebration of the birth of the child Jesus, founder of the Christian religion.

Planet X, a brown dwarf, appearing as a reddish monster, passes at the feet of Virgo at that exact time. By this, it fulfills the passage from Revelation literally, waiting at the feet of the woman in labor, ready to devour the child when it is born. The passage of Planet X through the ecliptic will kick off the period of most violent interaction between it and the Sun.

An orbit with a current position so far beneath the ecliptic also means a very high inclination, almost perpendicular to the ecliptic plane, if it leads to Planet X (a Bearded Star) appearing towards the North (near Polaris, the North pole star).

With the orbit with this perihelion and time frame and current position in or near Cetus, Planet X will be very near to Polaris in July of 2013, which Nostradamus described as "not far from Cancer." By this time, the interaction between the two will be past the worst, but Planet X will rival the Sun in brightness during the day.

Finally, there is another clue towards an orbit with this form and inclination. This clue is the inclination of planetary orbits. All outer planetary orbits are tilted in the same direction, with their 'lowest points' near Cetus in the sky. The further out a planet is from the Sun, the more slowly it moves along its orbital path; ergo, the longer it resides in a region of the sky.

Pluto experiences a tug in one direction from a passing Planet X for a long time, much longer than Jupiter or Saturn. This explains why the outer planets are inclined the most. The outer planets only travel through a part of their orbit during a passage below of Planet X, while the inner ones complete several orbits during a Planet X flyby. This explains the stronger tilt for the outer planets.

Matching Clues

Summarizing, we see that the plasma that bent away in 2002 bent towards an approaching electrically-active intruder into our Solar system. This intruder is coming in on a highly inclined elliptical orbit with perihelion in the Asteroid Belt. This perihelion distance gives a logical explanation for the fact that no planet is there. It might have been there, but is there no more, due to the effects of several flybys.

The orbit found matches *Bible* prophesy, as well as predictions made by Nostradamus and modern time remote viewers. It also ties in with prophecies by Mother Shipton, who was a seeress and contemporary of Nostradamus, and with the predictions of Edgar Cayce.

The orbit constructed matches with the orbital inclinations of the outer planets of the Solar system; it even offers an explanation for their degree of inclination. It matches a chilling number of clues found in various sources, ranging from astronomy, via historic accounts, to prophecy and remote viewing. One clue offers resistance on first glance, however; this clue will be discussed more in-depth in "Appendix D – Kozai Mechanism and Perpendicular Orbits."

Appendix D — Kozai Mechanism and Perpendicular Orbits

In "Chapter 2 - Planet X Forecast Through 2014" (and in Appendix C - Forecast Addendum) we touched upon the Kozai mechanism (also known as the Kozai effect.) This mechanism was named after the Japanese-American astronomer Yoshihide Kozai. He discovered it while analyzing the orbits of asteroids.

The mechanism shapes the orbits of irregular satellites around planets, as well as trans-Neptunian objects (Kuiper Belt Objects) and even planets around other stars.

The Kozai resonance mechanism

The most important feature of the Kozai mechanism is that it establishes a relation between the eccentricity and the inclination of an orbit. The mechanism occurs when one body in space perturbs another.

In short, the Kozai mechanism causes oscillations between near-circular orbits with a high inclination and very eccentric orbits that have little or no inclination.

Eccentricity

We have discussed inclination before, but what exactly is eccentricity? It comes from ex-center, or out of the middle. This can be explained by drawing a simple ellipse with wood, nails and string.

First, take a flat piece of wood, two nails, a piece of string and a pencil. Drive the nails a short distance apart, and then loosely tie both ends of the string to the two nails. Then use the pencil to stretch the string so that it is taut from one nail via the pencil to the other nail.

Start moving the pencil as far away from the nails as you can by moving around them. As you do, the trace of the pencil on the wood will form an ellipse. Remember to keep the string taut and to keep the lead of the pencil pressed firmly against the wood at all times.

The sum of the distance from the pencil tip on the wood to one nail and the distance from the pencil tip to the other nail is a constant value (equal to the length of the string in our example). This works for every ellipse. Keeping this in mind, let's return to our discussion about eccentricity.

Assuming we drove both nails side-by-side along the same line, we would then get a circle as we traced the pencil around them. This is a close simulation of the orbit of Earth around the Sun.

The variation in distance of the Earth from the Sun is minimal. If the heart of the Sun coincides with one of the nails, the other nail is inside the Sun also. If the two nails coincide exactly we call it an eccentricity of zero.

The other end of the scale is an eccentricity of one. If we use our string, this will happen once the distance between the nails becomes exactly the length of the string. The string is always stretched; we can no longer draw an ellipse around the nails using our pencil, the ellipse breaks open.

The Kozai Mechanism

We now go back to the Kozai mechanism. This mechanism conserves a quantity that is, in formula, defined as:

In this formula 'e' is the eccentricity of the orbit and 'i' is the angle of inclination. What this formula states is that where the eccentricity becomes greater (the nails move further apart) the inclination of the orbit must become smaller.

$$\sqrt{(1-e^2)}\cos(i)$$

The cosine of an angle is a function that varies between zero and one, when the angle itself varies between 90 degrees and 0 degrees. The cosine will have value 1 when the orbit is perpendicular to the ecliptic, and it will be 0 when the orbit lies in the ecliptic.

The resonance formula above describes an orbit that moves back and forth between a very stretched-out orbit that lies almost in the ecliptic plane and a circular orbit that moves perpendicular to the ecliptic plane.

In most cases, this resonance will result in an orbit that becomes too elliptical to remain stable. When this happens, an asteroid, moon or planet in such a resonance situation will break away from its center of gravitation and fly away into outer space.

Or, it can crash into the Sun or the planet it is orbiting if it comes too close. Examples of this are so-called Sun-grazing comets, comets that have high-inclination, very narrow orbits. All of them so far end up crashing into the Sun.

High inclination in resonance with eccentricity

It is noteworthy to see how this mechanism influences an elliptical orbit with an almost perpendicular inclination, such as the orbit for Planet X we projected in this book. With that in mind, let's apply the formula to the orbital parameters we found for Planet X.

The first part of the formula, the term under the square root, calculates to $(1- (0.988)^2)$; this equals 0.0239. The square root of this value is 0.154. The second part of the formula, the cosine of an inclination angle of 85 degrees, equals 0.0872.

The value that will be preserved now equals the product of these two. This gives 0.0872 multiplied by 0.154, which equals 0.0135. Whatever we change about the orbit in terms of inclination or stretching out, this product value will remain the same. That is the Kozai mechanism in action.

If we make the orbit more circular, we have to let the eccentricity become smaller. Let's see what the mechanism will be if we lower the value for the eccentricity from 0.988 to 0.5.

Again we apply the formula. This gives a value of 0.75 for the term under the square root; we take the square root of that and find 0.866. This implies that the second part of the formula, the cosine, will have to be 0.0156 in order to keep the product of the two parts of the formula at the value we found before; this results in an inclination angle of 89 degrees, almost perfectly perpendicular to the ecliptic.

Now we move the other way; we make the inclination smaller and see what happens to the orbit. If the inclination angle decreases, the cosine of this angle increases. We will lower the angle of inclination to 60 degrees as an example. The cosine of 60 degrees is 0.5. This means that the second part of the product in the formula is equal to 0.5, and because of this, the first part of the formula will have to be equal to 0.027.

The square root will have the resulting value 0.027, which means that the term under the square root will be equal to 7.29e-4 (this is a simpler scientific notation for 0.000729). The value for eccentricity that corresponds to this is 0.9996, which is very nearly 1. This will be a stretched-out elliptical orbit.

The orbit development we see with this varies between a more circular and perpendicular orbit and a very elliptic and more 'flat' orbit. If the angle of inclination becomes much smaller than the 60 degrees of the example above, the result will be one of two options. Either the orbit breaks open, and Planet X flies away, or Planet X crashes into the Sun, because it came too close. Neither option is favorable to the rest of the Solar system.

There is another effect we see. The argument of perihelion, or the direction of the perihelion when we look at it from the Sun, will start to move towards, and then oscillate around, one of two values. This direction of perihelion will move towards 90 or 270 degrees from the ascending node of the orbit.

The ascending node is the place along the Zodiac where Planet X will move up through the ecliptic plane on its orbit path. In simpler terms: the extreme points of the orbit, furthest from the Sun (aphelion) and closest to the Sun (perihelion), will begin to move towards either 90 degrees above the ecliptic or 90 degrees below the ecliptic and move around these values. For Planet X, this would mean that the ends of the orbital path would gradually move to positions above the Sun's poles.

Destabilization of the system

The Kozai resonance mechanism will either throw an object out of orbit or make it crash into the parent body of the system. What is worse is that, if the orbiting object is heavy, the system as a whole will react as if the odd orbit is the rule, and all other objects will begin to adjust towards that.

In the case of the Solar system with a heavy Planet X in a high-inclination, eccentric orbit, this would mean that all other planets will begin to realign with Planet X; their orbits would tilt by 90 degrees and become very eccentric.

Therefore, we must conclude that a high-inclination, eccentric orbital path for Planet X will destabilize the whole Solar system. Most other authors reached similar conclusions when researching for their books. Yet, much of the evidence we have seen points towards this high-inclination orbit. Simulations conducted using freely available software showed a destabilization of the Solar system after only five or six flybys of Planet X.

This has serious implications for our forecast. It means that the orbit we projected cannot exist for very long. Planet X will not complete many more than a handful of orbits before seriously disrupting the order of our Solar system.

Mother Shipton Prophecy

If Planet X is indeed on such an orbit, it either had to be pushed into this orbit recently by external causes or it must be a captured object. Either way, the Solar system is in trouble, if the orbit projection for Planet X is anywhere near correct.

This puts the prophecies of Mother Shipton in a different light. Her prophecy hints towards such a scenario: *"A fiery Dragon shall cross the sky six times before this world shall die."*

According to computer software simulations, six is the number of orbits Planet X completed, before the Solar system became unstable and threw planets into outer space.

The only tenable conclusion in such a case is that Planet X has to be a recently captured rogue brown dwarf. The next flyby in 2012 will be the fifth orbit. What happens the next time after that?

Because this brown dwarf moves in a changing orbit, it will progressively destabilize the entire Solar system. Therefore, this coming flyby will be our survivable opportunity, because the sixth will certainly mean the destruction of the Earth and all life upon it.

This conclusion gives weight and perspective to the recent comment by Professor Stephen Hawking. He stated that humanity must venture out towards the stars, if we intend to survive as a species.

Appendix E — Post-2014 Medicinal Herbs and Plants

In the months and years after the flyby, natural herbs and plants will return that can be used for medicinal purposes. *The Kolbrin Bible* specifically mentions hardy and beneficial species that have endured previous cataclysms.

> **Britain Book 9:18** These are the useful herbs to be found in field, forest and wayside in the days gone by: Wolfbane (which guards against wolves and dogs), barroweed (which grows only near the dead), harwort, witchweed, tinkerbells, wayweed, skullcap, featherflowers (which cure the stone), blackberry, sundew, deadly dick, celandine (which cure the piles), windweed, moonflower (which works a spell), witchhead (called blackspear), asproot, drudbalm (which brings sleep),witchbane (which is put above the door), hawflowers, ellenberry, wimberry, dradsweet, elf eye, fairyfern, witchwhispers, quickenbush, sowerseed (which purges), bardberry (for lovers), amarinth (it never fades), windflower, goolflower, wagging, blowderbud (which heals all wounds), eventide, layganleaf, hokanmil, rillweed, boonberry, hatherswed (which women use), esislip, fullerswort, withrinweed (which makes blue dye), canweed (which quiets the heart), mayslip, kodecreeper, slanlus, sewd, (which cures men of madness), mothan (which only grows on cliffs), arkiesene, dafblowder (which cures stomach sickness), malbrig, maisbel (which heals the stomach), bormowed (which soothes burns), selerweed (which gives visions), tianwed (which heals the skin), kaincop (which makes a brew), cowslip, waybroad, satyrion (which overcomes impotency), dwail, corncockles (which men call tares), dockumdick (which gives men virility and only grows under the shivertree).

To make the list easier to use, most of the herbs and plants mentioned above are organized in alphabetical order in the table below. Compare this list with known species in your area, and particularly those known to grow naturally in the area of your safe haven. Get to know these plants now. Learn how to recognize and prepare them.

Herbs from The Britain Book in *The Kolbrin Bible*		
Some of these planets possess powerful properties. Before using them, review this list with your family physician .		
Ancient or Generic Name	**COMMON NAME** **Alternate** *Scientific* **name**	**Usage and Concerns**
Amarinth	**CELOSIA** Red Cockscomb, *Amaranthus*	"Never fades," Taken internally for diarrhea, dysentery, hemorrhage from the bowels, nosebleeds, kidney stones, and excessive menstruation. Used as a wash for skin problems.
Asproot	**SENECA** Snake root *Polygala Senega*	Evacuates the bowels, increases volume of urine to reduce body water content, causes vomiting, expectorant.
Bardberry	**SAW PALMETTO** Saw Palmetto berries *Serenoa Serrulata*	Aphrodisiac; generates greater sexual arousal and desire, as well as increased sexual potency and power.
Blackberry	**BLACKBERRY** Blackberry leaf *Rubus fructicosus*	Internal: may help ease childbirth, increases volume of urine to reduce body water content, tonic, may cure dysentery, diarrhea. External: sore throats, mouth sores, gum inflammations.
Blowderbud	**ST. JOHN'S WORT** Blowderbud *Hypericum formosum*	Heals all wounds, anti-depressant, relieves muscle spasms, astringent, expectorant, soothes nerves, brings down swelling, destroys disease-carrying microbes, stomach remedy, tonic, destroys and eliminates parasitic worms, reduces bile secretion, cures lung diseases.
Bormowed	**ALOE** Aloe Vera *Aloe barbadensis*	Soothes and moisturizes burns. The pulp can be eaten raw to treat stomach ulcers.
Canweed	**HORSETAIL** Candock *Equisetum arvense*	Quiets the heart, increases volume of urine to reduce body water content.

	Herbs from The Britain Book in *The Kolbrin Bible*	
	Some of these planets possess powerful properties. Before using them, review this list with your family physician .	
Ancient or Generic Name	**COMMON NAME** **Alternate** ***Scientific*** **name**	**Usage and Concerns**
Celandine	**CELANDINE** *Chelidonium Majus*	External, as an ointment: cure the piles (hemorrhoids); mixed with sulfur, can be used to cure jock itch. Internal, as a type of tea: liver and gallbladder cleanse.
Corncockles (tares)	**TARES** Corncockles *Agrostemma githago*	TOXIC! Reduces or stops bleeding (external use only).
Cowslip	**COWSLIP** *Primula Veris*	Relieves muscle spasms, sleep agent.
Dafblowder	**DANDELION** Dafblowder *Taraxacum officinale,*	Cures stomach sickness; naturally increases volume of urine to reduce body water content and assists in digestion. Improves function of the pancreas, spleen, stomach and kidneys. It is ground and applied as a poultice to snake bites.
Drudbalm	**BALM** Drudbalm *Melissa Officinalis*	Brings sleep, relieves muscle spasms, calms the user, stomach remedy, reduces fever.
Dwail	**DEADLY NIGHTSHADE** Belladonna *Atropa Belladonna*	TOXIC! Narcotic, sedative.
Ellenberry	**ELLENBERRY**	Made into a cider to treat something called Imbrium Fever. Second bout with Imbrium Fever was usually fatal.
Featherflowers	**CELOSIA** Featherflowers *Amaranthus*	Cure the stone (kidney stones).

| | **COMMON NAME** | |
Ancient or Generic Name	**Alternate** *Scientific* **name**	**Usage and Concerns**
Fullerswort	**WILD SWEET WILLIAM** Soapwort *Saponaria Officinalis*	Gradually restores health, produces perspiration, tonic.
Goolflower	**ROSE** Rose Hips *Rosa Canina*	Many medicinal qualities; most important for survival include: antibiotic, treats infections, destroys disease-carrying microbes, kills or slows growth of bacteria, rids the user of poison.
Hatherswed	**EVENING PRIMROSE** Primrose *Oenothera biennis*	Astringent, treats symptoms of menopause, PMS (PMDD), sedative.
Hawflowers	**HAWTHORN FLOWERS** Hawflowers *Crataegus monogyna*	Many cardiovascular and respiratory benefits.
Kaincop	**CAMELLIA (TEA) OR HOPS** *Humulus lupulus*	Makes a brew. No available modern name, so two choices here depend on the desired brew.
Maisbel	**CATNIP** Cat Mint *Nepeta Cataria*	Heals pains, spasms, prevents or relieves flatulence and strengthens the stomach.
Moonflower	**MOONFLOWER** *Botrychium lunaria*	*Magickal*, works a spell, brings love and prosperity.
Mothan (only grows on cliffs)	**PEARLWORT** Bog Violet, Butterwort *Pinguicula vulgaris*	Mostly *magickal* as a love attractant, but also reportedly effective in easing labor pains by placing a quantity against the back of the mother's right knee.

Herbs from The Britain Book in *The Kolbrin Bible*

Some of these planets possess powerful properties. Before using them, review this list with your family physician .

	Herbs from The Britain Book in *The Kolbrin Bible*	
	Some of these planets possess powerful properties. Before using them, review this list with your family physician .	
Ancient or Generic Name	**COMMON NAME** **Alternate** *Scientific* **name**	**Usage and Concerns**
Quickenbush	**ROWAN** Quickenbush *Acuparia*	Internal: The unripe fruit and bark treat diarrhea. External as an ointment or poultice: they soothe the throat and bowel.
Satyrion	**ORCHID** Satyrion Root *Orchis*	Overcomes impotency.
Selerweed	**VERVAIN** Verbena *Verbena officinalis* *V. hastata (Blue)*	Gives visions. Some medicinal treatments include treating eye ailments and sleeplessness.
Sewd	**DILL** Sewd *Anethum Graveolens*	Cures men of madness, calms the user, relieves muscle spasms.
Skullcap	**SKULLCAP** *scutellaria lateriflora*	Sleep agent, relieves muscle spasms. Used against hysteria, seizures, asthma, menstrual cramping, epilepsy, insomnia, pain, vertigo, addiction recovery.
Sowerseed	**PSYLLIUM** Flea Seed *Plantago Psyllium*	Evacuates the bowels, increases volume of urine to reduce body water content.
Sundew	**BERMANN SUNDEW** Dew Plant *Drosera rotundifolia*	Fights dry coughs, such as whooping cough and the cough that comes with measles. Good against the cough from asthma. Relieves muscle spasms, protects mucous membranes.
Tianwed	Aloe Vera	Heals the skin.
Tinkerbells	**BLUEBELLS** Wood Bells *Hyachinthus Nonscriptus*	Increases volume of urine to reduce body water content, soothes nerves, reduces or stops bleeding.

Herbs from The Britain Book in *The Kolbrin Bible* *Some of these planets possess powerful properties. Before using them, review this list with your family physician .*		
Ancient or Generic Name	**COMMON NAME** **Alternate** ***Scientific* name**	**Usage and Concerns**
Waybroad	**PLANTAIN** waybread *Plantago lanceolata*	Brings down swelling, destroys disease-carrying microbes, astringent, soothes irritated mucous membranes, increases volume of urine to reduce body water content, expectorant, reduces fever, evacuates the bowels, refrigerant, stimulant, reduces or stops bleeding, heals wounds.
Wimberry	**BLUEBERRY** Bilberry *Vaccinium Mertillus*	Astringent, eye-care, reduces or stops lactation.
Windflower	**MEADOW ANEMONE** Pasque Flower *Anemone pulsatilla*	Relieves muscle spasms, soothes nerves.
Windweed	**SQUAW GRASS** Elk Grass *Rhizoma Anemarrhenae*	Fights feverish diseases accompanied by excessive thirst, diabetes, dry cough and, with other herbs, constipation.
Witchbane	**ROWAN** Witchbane *Sorbus Aucuparia*	See Quickenbush / ROWAN above.
Witchweed	**MUGWORT** Witchweed *Artemesia Vulgaris*	Stimulant, soothes nerves, laxative.
Witchwhispers	**WITCH HAZEL** *Hamamelis virginiana*	Abrasions, cuts, bleeding, burns / sunburn, eczema, eye-care, vision, insect bites, rash, pet care, vein support.
Withrinweed	**INDIGO** *Indigofera Tinctoria*	Makes blue dye (for natural fibers)

| | **COMMON NAME** | |
Ancient or Generic Name	**Alternate** *Scientific* **name**	**Usage and Concerns**
Wolfbane	**MONK'S HOOD** Dogbane *Aconitum Napellus* *Aconitum Falconeri*	TOXIC! Kills wolves, dogs and medium-large animals (can kill humans). Coat bait and place where animal can be observed taking it or cover point of arrow or spear with juice and shoot animal. Also CAREFULLY used as a (narcotic) pain reliever, a sleep agent and an anti-diabetic (to lower blood sugar).

Herbs from The Britain Book in *The Kolbrin Bible*

Some of these planets possess powerful properties. Before using them, review this list with your family physician .

Appendix F — About the Authors

Jacco van der Worp, MSc
Author and Science Advisor

Jacco is based in the Netherlands, and he holds an MSc in applied physics. He has worked in radiation safety and currently specializes in complex systems failure analysis. He co-authored *Planet X Forecast and 2012 Survival Guide* and has contributed numerous articles to the yowusa.com web site since 1999. As a co-founder of yowusa.com, Jacco primarily focuses on space threats and alternative energy sources. He is a member of Mensa.

Marshall Masters
Principal Author

Marshall Masters is an author, publisher, media guest, Internet radio host and founder of The Sagan Continuation Project. A former CNN science features news producer and U.S. Army public information officer; he specializes in Planet X and 2012 research. His published works include *Planet X Forecast and 2012 Survival Guide, Godschild Covenant: Return of Nibiru* and *The Kolbrin Bible*. He founded the yowusa.com web site in 1999, and is a member of Mensa.

Janice Manning Contributor
Contributor and Editor

Janice co-authored *Planet X Forecast and 2012 Survival Guide* and is the editor of *The Kolbrin Bible*, a wisdom text dating back some 3600 years. Her analyses of the historical accounts regarding previous Planet X flybys in this ancient secular text were instrumental in correlating those accounts to similar accounts in the *Torah (Old Testament)*. Considered a leading authority on *The Kolbrin Bible*, she is recognized in the 2007 edition of *Who's Who of American Women* for her work. She is also a yowusa.com web site co-founder and a member of Mensa.

Alphabetical Index

CPSIA information can be obtained at www.ICGtesting.com
Printed in the USA
LVOW050959060512

280539LV00004B/95/A